BOILERPLATING AMERICA
The Hidden Newspaper

EUGENE C. HARTER

Edited by
DOROTHY HARTER

With Drawings by Ann Tucker

Lanham • New York • London

Copyright © 1991 by
University Press of America®, Inc.
4720 Boston Way
Lanham, Maryland 20706

3 Henrietta Street
London WC2E 8LU England

All rights reserved
Printed in the United States of America
British Cataloging in Publication Information Available

Library of Congress Cataloging-in-Publication Data

Harter, Eugene C.
Boilerplating America : the hidden newspaper /
by Eugene C. Harter ; edited by Dorthy Harter ;
with drawings by Ann Tucker.
p.   cm.
Includes index.
1. Journalism, Rural—United States—History.
2. Printing—United States—History.   3. American
newspapers—History.   I. Harter, Dorothy.   II. Title.
PN4888.C7H37   1991
071'.3—dc20   90–20753 CIP

ISBN 0–8191–8082–3 (alk. paper)
ISBN 0–8191–8083–1 (pbk. : alk. paper)

The paper used in this publication meets the minimum requirements of American National Standard for Information Sciences—Permanence of Paper for Printed Library Materials, ANSI Z39.48–1984.

In memory of those warm nights
and semi-pro baseball in the Middle West

Acknowledgments

Mastering this subject entailed a lot more work than I had envisioned. The back roads of history are harder to traverse.

The world is a large, sometimes fascinating, and frequently ridiculous place. Dorothy and I and our family have lived for long lengths of time in many parts of it---in Arabia, in Latin America and in the United States of America. Our home on the Rue Corniche in Beirut looked out over a city ripped apart over religious, cultural and political differences. Nearby was Iraq, where the "electorate" voted out the chief of government by dragging him to his death, with a noose around his neck.

We have also lived in Brazil, Mexico, Panama, Ecuador and in various locales in the U.S.A. But in seeking subjects for historical inquiry, the midwestern part of the United States has attracted me most. The Midwest grips America like a cultural vise, giving the country its most uniquely solid quality and a goodly amount of its strength.

Town newspapers have been that area's anthropologists and are a natural focal point. The editors of these papers have been, on the whole, preoccupied with day-to-day editions of their papers, and have little patience with the historical establishment, but their weekly and daily product is the diary of this country. I am in debt to hundreds of them. In my fourteen years in country journalism in the Midwest and upper South I was apprenticed to some excellent country editors, including Richard Wessell of the DesPlaines (Illinois) *Journal* and Roy Williams of the Garrett (Indiana) *Clipper*. Another fine instructor was Cecil Miller, the mayor of Garrett, and our printer-foreman at the *Clipper*. Cecil knew more about newspapering and its mechanical realities than anyone I had ever met.

This work also owes a debt to many others, friends in the newspaper business like Edgar Miller, Ruy Barbosa, Claudio Abramo, Jim Bade, Bob Skeets, Carper Hayes, Don Hammer, Warren Hoge, Steve Yolen, Jack Blum, Dean Howard Long and my colleagues, holders of fellowships in the 1960s and early 1970s International Conference of Weekly Newspaper Editors. Thanks also to the Smithsonian Institute, the University of Virginia, George Washington University and

American University, where I did my graduate and research studies, Washington College and Kent County Libraries in Chestertown, Maryland; Chesapeake College Library, Wye Mills, Maryland; the University of Florida Library in Gainesville, Florida; the University of Delaware Library in Newark, Delaware, Wright Robinson of the Seaford, Delaware *Leader,* and to the Kent County *News* and its editor Hurtt Deringer, a solid country newspaperman. I am indebted to the Joslyn Art Museum, Omaha, Nebraska, and the Ohio, Kentucky, Illinois and Hoosier State press associations and Beverly Nykwist of the *Publishers' Auxiliary* and the National Editorial Association; and to the International Communication Agency, an agency of the U. S. Department of State, for whom I held diplomatic posts in four countries around the world.

Finally, Dorothy and I add our thanks to our four children, now fully grown, Eugene, III, Ann, David and Melissa, for their editorial and artistic assistance.

CONTENTS

ACKNOWLEDGMENTS
v

INTRODUCTION
vi

CHAPTER ONE — ON THE TRAIL OF READY-PRINT
1

Editorial Experience Not Needed
1

One Side Was Already Printed
8

Latin Americans Would
Call it "Jeito"
9

Town Newspapers Prior to Ready-Print
10

Gutenberg, The Inventor of Handset Type
12

CHAPTER TWO — THE HIDDEN, UNACCREDITED NEWSPAPER
17

Ansel Kellogg, America's Ready-print Pioneer
17

The Ghost Editor in Chicago
22

Ready-print Exposed by Chicago Fire
30

Boilerplate
32

CHAPTER THREE — BOILERPLATING THE AMERICAN MIND
37

Newspapers, Consecrators of the American Way
37

Newspaper Fever
38

Franchising Creates A National Newspaper
39

Free Press versus Government And Private Subsidy
41

How Much Did It Cost To Produce a Newspaper?
42

Circulation Figures Rise
45

Let Us Now Praise Famous Men

Publicizing the Press Barons
47
They Don't Call Themselves Country Editor Anymore
50
Forming a National Character
With Torrents of Words
54

CHAPTER FOUR — WESTWARD THE READY-PRINT TRAIL
59
Flushing Government Out Into the Open
59
Most Americans Lived In Rural Areas, Prior to 1930
60
Instant Cities
63
Historians Have Not Known the Source
64
City and Town Journals Become Competitors
66
The Coming of the Rural Free Delivery System
70
The Newspaper Family of 100 Years Ago
73
In the Wake of the Clipper
75

CHAPTER FIVE — REVERENT HANDS,
THE OTHER READY-PRINTERS
81
British Refused to Sacrifice Individuality
81
Patterson, Who "Never Put On Airs;"
Influenced Americans for 62 Years
83
Patterson Saves Country Editors
From Embarrassment of Exposure
84
Joslyn, The Ready-print Emperor And
Patent Medicine Salesman
90
Ready-print Achieves
Respectability By Default
96
Ready-print Was
"Painstakingly Hidden"
98

CHAPTER SIX — READY-PRINT OFFERS
TABULA RASA FOR EDITORS
101
Those Who Spoke Out
107
Ready-print Tried to be Non-controversial, Profitable
114
The Joining of Two Movements:
Anti-Liquor and Religious Fundamentalism
116
The Socialist Country Editor
119

CHAPTER SEVEN — MAIL ORDER NEWS FROM CHICAGO
123
The New American
127
Survey of the W.N.U. Ready-print
129
Forms of the Western Migration
131
Generic Religion, The Building of the Bible Belt
133
Communicating With Other Isolated Americans
137
An American Language
139

CHAPTER EIGHT — EVIDENCE OF PROPAGANDA
145
Government and Private Subsidy
145
Mr. Country Editor, If You Don't Play Along
We'll Run You Out of Business
147
Charge Ready-print and Boilerplate
With Forming Sinister Monopoly to
Invade the Minds of Americans
150
A Real Case of Tainted News
156

CHAPTER NINE – THE PRINTERS SPOUTED SHAKESPEARE
AS THEY SWAYED BEFORE THE CASES
165
The Development of Writers, "Sculptors" of Words
166
Reading Upside Down and Backwards
168
The Line Casting Machine Arrives

170
Goodby to the Handsetting of News Type
174
Mark Twain's Obsession
176

CHAPTER TEN — MOVING TO TO THE CITIES, THE UN-EUROPEANS
181
Ready-print, the Trojan Horse of Town Journalism
183
A Word About Newspaper "Unions"
186
Congress and All-Home Print Fight Ready-print
188
Contrasting Views of Ready-print
192
Cutting Corners: Editors Who Aimed to Just "Get By"
193

CHAPTER ELEVEN — WHAT IS NEWS?
197
U.S. Country Editors Run Only Local News
199

CHAPTER TWELVE — GOODBY GUTENBERG!
201
On The Trail, Again
203
The Central Printing Plant
206
Democracy, No Experience Needed
209
Progress Report
210

EPILOGUE
215
Legal Versus Assumed Press Freedom
215
Cross Cultural Problems
217
Myth and Free Enterprise Economics Join Forces
218
The History of the U.S. Newspaper Syndicates
220
Newspapermen, Not the Constitution Created the Free Press
220

Introduction

Nations never develop in the same way. America has two histories: one that encompasses Colonial times---powdered wigs, slavery, machineless; and the other history describing quite a different country, the post Civil War United States—more like, and perhaps more relevant to our present day. Our study centers on this second America, an agricultural country until the 1930s.

Being agrarian in that post-war period, it should not surprise one to learn that the inland, small town newspapers were major factors in the culture. They were the most-read publications in the nation. These little journals were the "conveyors" of ready-print (the hidden newspaper) and related boilerplate; which form the basis of our study.

This study has unearthed the following:

— Ready-print and boilerplate have helped spread knowledge of the world and have shaped national attitudes and built a sense of national union in ways not realized.

-- Historians drawing on local papers for research have mis-interpreted the contents of those newspapers.

-- That American journalism was subject to homogenization much earlier than the modern chains are now credited (or blamed) for the practice.

-- Ready-print kept the large city newspapers from becoming the national voice.

— Ready-print was a prime force in Prohibition.

-- It wielded hidden monopoly power in the the late nineteenth and early twentieth century.

-- Ready-print had enormous influence on what Americans would read.

— A groundswell for democracy's free press has resulted from the large number of newspapers created by the ready-print franchising system.

In this work we take a look at the part played by these colorful town newspapers in building America. We note printing technology (or the lack of it) that led to the ready-prints of the frontier press. An outgrowth of the Industrial Age and mass production, the ready-print and boilerplate, a hidden newspaper, was a subsidy to town journals allowing them to be profitably maintained. Ready-print/boilerplate had its good side and its bad side, and we will discuss both.

Let me introduce the reader to ready-print in this fashion: If you look closely at the American newspaper trade magazines of the nineteenth century you can find an occasional reference it. Here is an example that appeared in an 1890 edition of *The Inland Printer:*

> "The March, (1890) issue of the *London Press News,* under the heading of Printing in a Wilderness, publishes what it claims to be the experience of an English printer, who, like a good many of his countrymen have done before him, left his native land to better his condition in the United States....After many vicissitudes and disappointments, he has found his elysium, and is now publishing a patent insides (ready-print) eight-page, five-column paper, in a secluded village, in the pineries of Michigan, where he 'employs no labor, pays no rent, and is not liable for taxation for twelve months,' besides reveling in the luxuries of broiled partridge and savory venison, which his soul loveth, all secured too, by the expenditure of $300."

U.S. newspapers have become cultural institutions. The death of even a small one has a telling impact. But 10,000 expired in the middle of this century. After 50 years, television and the other communication technologies have yet to come to grips with their civic function, much less achieve roles as acknowledged American institutions. In contrast to the printed page, television has yet to prove that it is a suitable medium for the communication of serious ideas. Printing on paper is unique. Its low cost portability and lasting effect on the learning process are unequaled.

Why, then, should the newspaper industry find itself in such a depressed state? Why has readership dropped? Why now in the 1990s one-newspaper communities are the norm where, in the past, three, four or more were published even in the smaller places?

Americans are now more critical of the press — "media bashing" is in vogue. Why? There has been a steady decrease in the number of newspapers, beginning in the 1920s even though the population is much larger and newspapers are easier and cheaper to start than ever.

The argument can be made that journalistic gigantism as practiced in the large cities is at most times a tepid exercise in "free press." Too many of these huge newspapers are run by efficiency experts who cut editorial labor costs at every turn, and systematically print, without question, government and business press release handouts.

These monopoly metropolitan papers with their lukewarm editorial stances, seek to discourage the establishment of competitive newspapers by molifying everybody and skirting the hard editorial issues. As a consequence they serve American democracy badly.

In the past, American newspaper editors had been held in awe, more often cast as hero than not. In the 1930s it was characteristic that the popular comic strip character "Superman" was a news reporter; that little-known small town editor Warren Harding was entrusted with the office of president and that his opponent in the 1920 election was also a midwest newspaperman; that many of the nation's most accepted writers — small town printer Mark Twain most prominent among them — routinely came from the country newspapers.

It is this exact time, the era between the Civil War and the turn of the century, the time of the country editors, the ready-print, that we center upon in this book.

The leading publishers of the hidden ready-print were a former village editor Ansel Kellogg and patent medicine salesman George A. Joslyn. A 1912 national publication reported that "America's reading was newspapers, and very little else." But what was being written in those newspapers, and by whom?

By 1916, Joslyn had taken over all of his ready-print competitors and dominated America's reading, with more than 60 percent of the U.S. population signed up (unwittingly, as it turned out) as subscribers. His hidden newspaper led the world in circulation!

Chapter One

On The Trail Of Ready-Print

> Whether patent insides (ready-print) stifled the initiative of the editor who used them, contributed to the progress of the country newspaper, or had little effect, they represented a sort of family skeleton of small town journalism. Like a common workman, they shouldered the heavy burden but entered by the back door, painstakingly hidden from the reader's cognizance.
>
> James Creighton of the St. Louis Post-Dispatch[1]

EDITORIAL EXPERIENCE NOT NEEDED!

It was 1951 and the war had been over for several years. It was a good time for beginnings. Energized, hair slicked down, newly college graduated, I set about job hunting. In a stack of publications at the library I came upon an Editor and Publisher magazine and saw rows of announcements, each with the same first line "WANTED: Editor for town newspaper, apply ....". Several said "must be able to write, sell ads, be a go-getter, must like people, willing to work long hours...."

I had no experience, and the American culture was still foreign to me, but I liked people, and I had taken one course in Journalism, taught by my college English Lit professor. Scanning the ads I decided to apply for the editorship opening nearest to home, at the Ansonia, Ohio *Times*.

Ansonia, I learned, was once the home of Lowell Thomas, famed as the writer who over-romanticized Lawrence of Arabia. Annie Oakley, the marksman, also had lived nearby in pioneer days.

Ah! the glamorous world of the print press in that unsettled time just after World War II; the movies and radio had proclaimed that newspapers were exciting places, with whirring machinery; and with reporters scurrying about on important missions, their hat brims turned up in front. I expected small town newspapers to be only slightly less hectic than those of the city; a world of wit and wisdom with contemplative editors like Mark Twain or William Allen White, who used to stand proudly before their type cases in frontier villages.

Along the way, there were fresh-painted farmhouses and "really" big red barns. The macadam tar roads had already begun their winter habit of cracking; pried apart by the ground frost. Though the countryside looked flat as a stove lid, the long road to Ansonia was bumpy.

After driving fifty miles I asked for directions, and the smiling farmer said: "Glad to he'p. Bear to the left at the bridge crossin' the cri'k. It's down the pike a piece, about four mile."

And so it was, looming up in the Siberian cold of western Ohio.

From the street the newspaper building in that low-lying prairie town seemed vacant. It did not put on airs. It had a pine wood front, unpainted. The walls were not plumb, leaning slightly from true north, away from the prevailing wind. Traces of its past history as a general store or notions emporium were still visible.

There was an unsteady sign over the door: "Ansonia *Times,* Printing, Publishing." On the window was a handwritten notice "Card Stock, All Colors, 10 cents a sheet." Through the streaked glass pane, I saw an orange glow from an electric bulb—and a man sitting at a rolltop desk which was covered with dust and pieces of paper. There was a sheep's bell on the screen door, sounding as I gripped the latch and entered.

Inside it was warmer. The man, the editor, lifted his head, stared for a second thinking perhaps that I was a reader with a complaint. He was clean shaven, neatly attired. He did not look like Mark Twain, rather more like a department store floorwalker. He stood and offered a polite handshake and we sat down facing each other.

"Mornin'," he said. After talk about the weather we got down to the business of the job interview:

"Not uh' bolshie are yuh?. The Reds are everywhere these days."

This stopped me for an instant, since one would never have suspected that the Soviets had designs on a village as small as this."

...the newspaper building in that low-lying prairie town seemed vacant.

"No, sir, go to church every Sunday, was in the Navy in the 'War', vote Republican."

"Can you sell ads? Sellin' ads in Richmond and Greenville is part of the job."

"Yes, sir. I've had several sales jobs: insurance, Stark's fruit trees, sporting goods; member of Jaycees, Kiwanis. I like people."

"Don't write poetry, do you?—poets aren't worth a hill 'a beans in this business."

"No, I haven't writ..."

Then, noting my slightly Brazilian accent, he softened: "You have a brogue, sound like one of those sugar beet farmers from South Dakota. Traveled out that way before the War, after teacher's college. Lots of Germans in this part of Ohio, too."

"Well, I...."

It was, thus, a short interview. The publisher was in a hurry, "double duty," he called it, with two newspapers to care for.

The Times' pages looked as big as a bed quilt, but the layout was like that of the metropolitan newspapers, with neat columns, taut headlines and boiled-down items of news. It had fewer pages, but looked as fresh and appealing as the cityfied daily newspaper that landed mornings at my Limestone Street home doorstep.

The issue before me was sprinkled with Hadacol and Peruna patent medicine and Royal Baking Powder ads. It had society items: weddings, births, deaths. In the middle of page three was a photo feature on the U.S. war in Korea.

"No editorial experience is needed in this job. You write in plain ol' basic English, God's own, neat enough for the linotyper to read it. We don't look f'er trouble, no writin' of opinions—not like the ol' days.

"We use boilerplate for our feature stuff, stopped usin' Ready-Print years ago.

("Ready-Print," I thought, "what was that?)

I nodded and he went on. "Typesettin' is expensive, so we keep writin' to a minimum. Forget any literature trainin' you received in college. Ramblin' editorial wind has no place in my newspaper. We keep it short, write items 'bout local events, sell ads and mind the office. The newspaper is printed at our letterpress plant thirty mile from here. You can have the job if you wan'it. Pays fifty a week, and there's an apartment you can use in the back."

Without pausing I accepted.

"Congratulations, y'er the new man." In an ordaining gesture he shook my hand. Surely I was the first Brazilian-born editor of the Ansonia Times, ever.

Thus began what my wife, Dorothy, has always called our "Norman Rockwell" era. But it was more than just a white collar job, more than a folkloric experience, I found that I had "ink in my veins," a talent and liking for the job. In time Ansonia no longer seemed isolated as the barren fields shed their snow and the field crops came into view.

Later I worked on Indiana and Illinois newspapers. I enjoyed it so much that I would have worked for nothing. So sweet was this American newspaper life that it was almost sad. I remained a town editor in mid-America for the first one-third of my working life; living on the Middle Border in towns surrounded by acres of tall, green corn. The villagers seemed to have stepped from *Saturday Evening Post* magazine covers. Town life was a parade of church choirs, earnest Presbyterian preachers, Rotary Clubs, partisan political debates, high school sports, flag-waving bands and baton twirlers, estate auctions, bake sales, lawn mowing, and ornate front porches with cane furniture. Life to us was like a charming three act play set on tree-lined streets. Our newspaper was a part of everything—recording, commenting.

It was a close-up view of the America that thrust on the world the recent presidents Harry Truman, Dwight Eisenhower, Gerald Ford, and Ronald Reagan. Richard Nixon, too, had that distinctive mark of the Midwest upon him.

It is a unique pastoral culture that has completely baffled New Englanders and intrigued foreign tourists who stumble upon it.

The country newspaper experience lasted over 14 years and brought our family to three midwest and one southern state. The towns, while each unique in character, were similar in appearance. They were laid out in efficient, repetitive patterns---at the center a courthouse, the town's Parthenon with architecture approximating the Greek, nestled in a small park. Facing were stores and lawyers' offices on all four sides. The larger shops, Masonic halls, schools, tractor dealers were located away from the square, but within walking distance.

Townspeople moved about or sat conversing, some reading copies of the local paper. From our house near the middle of town farms could be seen in the distance.

Least impressive among the town center's buildings was the newspaper. Editors had always held that it was the content of the newspaper's pages, not the façade of the building that made the town journal a success. Almost any kind of building would do, editors sought only sufficient floor space—in abandoned churches and movie theaters, masonic halls, garages, and stables.

The life-giving towns were even more important to us than the newspapers that serviced them. I once bought a town newspaper without once seeing the paper's books, offices or plant—I closed the deal after walking about the town for a couple of hours and getting a "feel" for it. I was looking, of course, at the business district and its local and national advertising potential, but the selling point was the "town spirit"—an aura that varied in intensity from town to town.

We encountered all types of people in the trade—editors who were the town moral leaders, some that were in it for the money (a surprisingly profitable business, this), some on an ego trip. A few were poseurs—disguised politicians waiting anxiously to shed the editorial mantle, to spring catlike on the voter as a candidate for mayor, Congress or the comfortable governor's chair at the state capitol.

There were personnel troubles at times at the town newspapers. Editors who could actually write, and typesetters who could read rapidly and had the nimble fingers necessary in the trade, were always in short supply. Like wild geese they would alight awhile, then fly off, always westward.

As a result, publishers sometimes took chances in hiring the help. One neighboring Indiana newspaper employed a poet whose body-alcohol level caused him to fall while inserting the type of his deathless lines into the printing form.

The somersault not only destroyed the type for the poem, but also the adjoining A&P grocery advertisement which was as difficult to construct as the works of a fine watch. This hail of hand-set type caused a 12-hour delay of that week's newspaper reaching the public.

Rather than face censure, when sobered the poet-editor left the employ of the paper. The indelicacy arising from alcohol, even though it is society's pampered drug, had no place in the tedious matter of setting type.

I would stay at these newspapers two or three years, sometimes owning them, sometimes working for another editor-publisher. Moving from job to job over a four-state area we were like Bedouins, folding our tents and looking for the better grazing land, just over the hill, westward—moving from Ansonia, Ohio to Garrett and Auburn in Indiana, then to DesPlaines and Mundelein in northern Illinois. Each job a little higher paying than the last as my family size and household expenses grew. We seemed to be moving along on what Americans call a "career," but it was more than that; we sensed that we were seeking that special, spiritual editorial home in the perfect small town.

We lived almost within hailing distance of the village in Sherwood Anderson's novel, "Winesburg, Ohio.". There was a period in Auburn and Garrett, Indiana, towns reminiscent of Oliver Goldsmith's "Sweet Auburn, loveliest village of the plain." Despite the harsh winters, we were convinced that the American Auburn was as lovely as Goldsmith's own mythical English hamlet.

I worked in a railroad town, whose publisher forbade the use of commas. He also employed a society editor who kept a meticulous calendar penciling in each wedding date, marking a date nine months later. Each week she would check the "Blessed Events" column, match it to the chart. Some weeks she would rush to the phone, and amid much tittering, reveal the results of her biological research to her friends.

We started two newspapers in well-to-do Chicago suburbs; then crossed the Mason-Dixon line and published the News-Journal in the hills of south-central Kentucky for four years. There, in our most economically successful venture, I owned and operated a semi-weekly that tripled its paid circulation during my four year tenure. It had the largest circulation of any county seat town newspaper in the state.[2]

There was discomfort at times. I can remember January mornings in the Ohio newspaper office that I shared with a State Farm insurance salesman. The kerosene stove would sputter against the sub-zero temperature outside. To protect my hands from frostbite I took to wearing gloves even when typing news stories.

There was no line between the editorial and the press room in town newspapers---we participated in all the departments, front and back. On press days we slogged elbow to elbow with sweaty tobacco-chewing printers (all of us dizzy from the effects of inhaling powdered lead in the poorly ventilated press rooms); running the line casting machine, throwing in the last piece of metal type onto a page, hammering it down with a wooden mallet and locking it up in the form---then, watching the printers, like ship builders on launching day, proudly sliding the page form across the metal table onto the Country Campbell press, an ornamented iron monster with leather belts, whirling wooden fingers and spinning rollers.[3]

What would plague the craft was not the press work, but the insertion of the tiny metal letters. Typesetting would haunt the printing and newspaper trade from the early fifteenth well into the late twentieth century. The act of placing the pieces of type onto the press was a process that resisted automation in the trade. We were not ashamed that it was fifteenth century technology proudly practiced in the twentieth century.

Typesetting had always been the most inefficient and expensive part of newspaper publishing. It remained the most costly area of the business until relieved by the introduction of ready-print, and helped again by the use of typesetting machines. The problem was "solved" in the 1960s when lithography and computerized cold-type techniques were combined to form a simpler method of getting words into print.

In the nineteenth century the need for hand-typesetters made the average newspaper printing plant a crowded place. Every print shop had its group of compositors---men, women and children, standing before neatly arrayed boxes containing little pieces of iron type. Their fingers flew as they deftly placed type together into words and sentences.

ONE SIDE WAS ALREADY PRINTED!

I first ran across ready-print in a neighboring newspaper in western Ohio in 1951, only a few weeks after I began my apprenticeship as country editor in Ansonia. I had driven my trusty Packard auto fifteen miles to neighboring Greenville to cover a patriotic parade down Main street. It was a fine affair---troops, polished and resplendent, drafted from the local National Guard.

From afar the soldiers looked alike, heavily armed matched pieces in a set. Up close they were revealed as midwest farm boys, each face quite different from the other. The parade was to honor them on their leaving to fight the Communists in Korea. Watching the procession I was reminded that I was not allowed by the publisher-owner of my paper to editorialize. I itched to argue against America's participation in yet another overseas military adventure.

On the way home in a neighboring village I turned the Packard into the driveway of that town's newspaper to borrow some lead ingots for our line casting machine. Editors, ever tight-fisted when it came to keeping large inventories, always had to beg lead from each other like neighbors borrowing eggs.

I was greeted by the editor who led me to the back shop where the lead bars were stored. Walking past their antique Country Campbell press I brushed against a pile of papers sitting on the floor. Looking down I could make out that one side of the piled paper was printed. I picked up one of the big, wide sheets, read the printed side and remarked about its high quality. It had local ads, excellent pictures, an editorial supporting our participation in Korea, all well written. "You write very well," expecting the editor to acknowledge the compliment. Instead, he answered:

"Oh! we didn't do that. That's next week's ready-print. It's similar to boilerplate, but printed on one side by the Western Newspaper Union in Chicago. We print the other side here. It saves half our effort in typesettin' and press work and it gives us the newsprint almost free since the Chicago editors sell advertisin' on their side."

My questions to him continued: "What does 'ready-print' mean?"

"The word is related to 'ready-made' or 'ready-to-wear,' an invention that saves time."

"How many companies furnish the ready-print to newspapers?"

"Only one, the W.N.U."

"How long have they been in business?

"About 80 years."

"How many newspapers use the ready-print?

"Thousands, but the number is a lot smaller than it used to be."[4]

Leaving that little newspaper with my borrowed metal, I was impelled to know more about this curious "ready-print" that saved that man 50 percent of his effort in getting out the newspaper. At the first opportunity I went to the library of the university, thumbed through the index in the well-stocked Journalism section but found almost nothing.

Could it be that all those subscribers were unknowingly receiving their news from a single source? Wouldn't this unified cultural guidance be important to social scientists and serious historians?

LATIN AMERICANS WOULD CALL IT A "JEITO"

In time, thanks greatly to the yellowed files in many small town papers and in the basement of the Library of Congress in Washington, Dorothy and I discovered that ready-print played a large part in American history, in its development of the free press system.

Ready-print began during the labor-short Civil War era when a clever fellow from the midwest introduced the process of printing one side of a newspaper in a central printing plant and selling the sheets to newspapers who then printed the other side. It was an ingenious use of the principle of mass production, resulting in professional-looking newspapers whose final printing was done by a single editor-typesetter, or at most with the aid of one or two assistants.

We discovered that the practice was hidden from most of the public from the very beginning, most journals "neglecting" to inform their readers of the origin of half of their hometown paper.

Depending on the point of view, if laid out on a scale, ready-print would lie somewhere between a swindle and a benign charade. Latin Americans would call it a "jeito,"---an act which violates principles of ethics, but is forgivable because it aids a more important cause.

Still, as with all wielders of great power, ready-print became less innocent in later years when it was taken over by a monopoly and used as an instrument of propaganda. However, its economic benefits made possible thousands of outspoken newspapers which, in turn, spawned a breed of editors now mostly forgotten, but whose number included the brave and the foolhardy who literally put their life on the line to have their say---creators of the free press.

I learned that the multiplicity of names for the process (patent insides, patent outsides, press service, co-operative publishing, pre-prints, syndicates, partly-prints, filler, auxiliary service, boilerplate or stereotyped plates) has served to confuse the researcher. Sadly for historical research, the turn-of-the-century editors who could have been interviewed 'ere long ago are now dead. Also, many of those ready-print newspapers have been lost through careless discarding and neglect by the guardians of such things.

The time of ready-print and boilerplate was a significant era of American newspapering---an era when country, not city, journals dominated the reading of Americans. It was an important time when our hearts seemed in the right place. It serves us to add it to memory if we are to know ourselves.

TOWN NEWSPAPERS PRIOR TO READY-PRINT

Typesetting by hand! What a slow, meticulous, frustrating snail's pace it was---and seemingly impossible to mechanize! There were thousands of newspaper publishers operating in America---and these thousands would fall on their knees every night praying that someone, somewhere would invent a mechanical typesetting machine that would

The earliest known photograph of Samuel Clemens (Mark Twain), proudly showing his belt buckle made of his metal printer's type

remove this handicap from their lives.

Operating town newspapers in the underdeveloped areas of America prior to the Civil War was a chancy, not always-profitable business. Typical was the example of Orion Clemens, town editor-publisher and older brother of Mark Twain. Orion stepped in and provided for the family when the father died. He operated his newspapers in the years just prior to ready-print and boilerplate and was in fact a good, hard working editor and lawyer who suffered from the frontier town newspaper system of the time.

As a youth Mark Twain, with other family members, worked long hours in the back shop of Orion's newspapers. Orion published town journals in Hannibal, Missouri; Muscatine, Iowa; and Keokuk, Iowa.

He, like his fellow publishers, suffered the consequences of the archaic typesetting methods. This part of printing was labor-intensive, slow, tedious, and technologically mindless for its age. Thus it was expensive for Orion Clemens to produce a profitable small newspaper. The use of child labor was an ingredient of getting the free press out to the people.

As the twentieth century neared it could be noted that for a hundred years the world's fabric had been produced by machine, no longer by hand on the fireside spinning wheel. Electricity had come on the scene.

Railroads, replacing horses, were transporting people at high speed across continents; deadly diseases were being conquered. In that time, printing presses had been speeded up, printing 100 times faster than before; news was being sent instantaneously by telegraph and telephone; but still the mechanical typesetter had not arrived.

It was a maddening wait for publishers. The inventor of a mechanical typesetter could look forward to a 150 million dollar market.

The mechanically-inclined from Shanghai to Baltimore were trying their hand at constructing the perfect machine that would be capable of fitting into a small press room, not too expensive, much faster than hand setting---and cheap enough to be purchased by the thousands of newspapers that were using ready-print and boilerplate. Victor Strauss wrote:

> The slowness of hand composition was particularly objectionable to the printers and publishers of newspapers. To them hand composition was a real handicap. Not only was its cost rather high, but hand composition also added to the interval of time that elapsed between the receipt of the news by a paper and the offering of this news in printed form for sale to the public. As the nineteenth century was one of highly personal journalism and of rather fierce newspaper competition, the publishers of some newspapers were among the most aggressive promoters of machine composition just as they were, generally speaking, the most persistent advocates of improvements in all other phases of printing related to the production of their papers.[5]

GUTENBERG, THE INVENTOR OF HAND-SET TYPE

Gutenberg's 1440 invention of movable individual letters, or handset type, was the marvel of its age, despite its cumbersome attributes when viewed from a modern time. It allowed the world to democratize knowledge through the mass production of printed pages, a development that was to clarify European languages—especially one of the newest of the languages, English, which then was improved and at last (almost into the 1700s) became a medium for precise prose devoid of its early "amplifications, digressions and swellings of style."[6]

Printed pages made ideas and information available to one and all in a portable and lasting form---instant access to knowledge that you could carry around with you, reading and re-reading.

One can picture the changes that occurred when persons trained through an oral culture were suddenly exposed to the marvelous pages coming from the printing press---whose product engaged the eye, the more efficient recipient of information.

One can also picture the panic that must have descended on the dominant political and clerical establishment, faced with this threat to their power.

Knowledge was set free, no longer the private preserve of the church monasteries and the copyist guilds. The invention was hailed as a miracle, a bombshell to European culture, changing established philosophies---religions, education and politics. Spawned were dozens, then hundreds, of print shops---many, quite soon thereafter, carried over the Atlantic with the explorers just beginning to settle the Americas.

The monks of medieval times, those human printing presses methodically reproducing books by hand, were much admired for their artistic product, so beautifully crafted that the pages appeared divinely inspired.

It was a rare elite wine suddenly distributed like common rum---Gutenberg's letterpress printing made knowledge available to everyone—and this brought massive social, democratic change.

On the other hand, the European Renaissance printers, the circulators of the democratic idea, carried an air of omnipotence, imitating medieval artist-monks. They were letterpress printers, "masters" of their craft. They dug in and resisted changes in the printing process well into the later nineteenth century.

The simple presses, typefaces and page designs changed little through the centuries.[7] It was as though the applying of words to paper was still part of the imperial, monastic environment of medieval times.

As in most professions, the craft adapted obscure foreign words for its processes to protect trade secrets. Putting on airs and preserving their antique processes, art and crafthood became intertwined as printers strove to convince the uninitiated that the trade was difficult to master—an art.[8]

If one could describe printing as an art, then it was a quite simple art. Like many other crafts and professions, the few improvements in the process were kept out of sight and within the guild—giving it a cloak of mystery, traces of which are still visible today.

This kind of environment did not encourage modernizing of the process. Between 1440 and the nineteenth century it seemed as though the world stood still in those dank, dimly lit print shops. Type pieces were still being handled one letter at a time.

In 1885 F.M.Lupton's encyclopedia gave this description of setting type by hand (the method is the same as used by Gutenberg in 1440 and by a few letterpress job-printers even today, 1990):

> All the types used in printing offices are sorted in cases, or shallow boxes with divisions. These are of two kinds—the upper and lower case, the latter lying nearest to the compositor. In the upper case are placed all the capitals, small capitals, accented letters, a few of the points and characters used as references. In the lower case are all the small letters, figures, the remainder of the points and spaces to place between the words. In the lower, no alphabetical arrangement is preserved. Each letter has a larger or smaller box allotted to it according as it is more or less frequently required, and all those letters most in request are placed at the nearest convenient distance to the compositor.
> Placing the copy or manuscript before him on the upper case and standing in front of the lower case, the compositor holds in his left hand a little iron tray called a composing stick. One by one he lifts and puts the letters of each word and sentence, and the appropriate points and spaces into his stick, securing each with the thumb of his left hand, and placing them side by side from left to right along the line. On reaching the end of a line he rearranges the spaces, so as to make it exactly full and secure a uniform separation of the words. When the workman has set up as many lines as his stick will hold, he lifts them out and places them upon an elongated tray called a galley, and when the galley is full an impression or proof of the types is taken, which goes to the proof-reader, whose duty it is to mark upon the margins

A printing office, in an early illustration, Lyons 1500. One of the earliest depictions of Gutenberg's printing press.

thereof such errors as may have been made by the compositor. After these have been corrected, the matter is divided into pages of the desired size, head-lines and numerals are added, the pages are secured in an iron frame or chase, and, after the matter is again carefully read and corrected, the form is ready for the pressman or electrotyper (boilerplater), as the case may be.[9]

What the description left out was the final and equally cumbersome task of re-distributing the tiny metal and wooden type back into the job cases, a letter at a time, after each little piece was washed down with gasoline to remove the old ink.[10]

NOTES

1. William H. Taft, *Missouri Newspapers* (Columbia: University of Missouri, Press 1967) p.139.
2. "Owned," in this definition, means that I held 75 percent interest. The newspaper's circulation was only to paid subscribers.
3. It was believed in most print shops of the time that the best antidote for lead poisoning among printers was to chew tobacco. There

were tobacco stains everywhere. This medical theory had no validity, but was almost universally accepted among the printing fraternity.

4. The number of newspapers in the era of ready-print were much greater than the numbers listed in the directories, as many of the country editors simply did not take the trouble to include their papers. Even today there are many that are not listed.)

5. Victor Strauss, *The Printing Industry* (New York: R.R. Bowker Co., 1967) p. 63.

6. M.M. Lewis, *Language in Society* (London, 1947), p.38.

7. The page design of today's books and newspapers owe much to the medieval monks. Page layouts were then (but not now) inescapably linked to the mechanical process.

8. There is evidence that it was the Koreans who invented movable type a few years earlier than Gutenberg, but European historians took the position that the Korean invention did not count since their methods were complicated by the combining of alphabet type and Chinese ideographs. From Douglas McMurtrie, *The Book* (New York: Oxford University Press, 1943) p. 98.

9. F. M. Lupton, *Encyclopedia* (New York: Lupton Publishing Co., 1885) p. 237.

10. For many years the town newspapers employed typesetters who were unable to speak or hear. This practice continued even late in the twentieth century when many were trained as operators of line casting machines. Their handicap was believed to be an advantage in setting type since they were less distracted by the sounds around them.

Chapter Two

The Hidden, Unaccredited Newspaper

> ...the great majority of newspapers in small towns do not, and as a matter of economy cannot, set up the type of all their reading matter.
> — *Collier's Magazine,* 1914

ANSEL KELLOGG, AMERICA'S READY-PRINT PIONEER

Milton M. Quaiffe, a newspaperman turned historian, stated in the February, 1922 issue of the newspapermen's bible, the *National Printer-Journalist:* "Ready-print worked a revolution in the rural press of America, the far reaching consequences of which defy measurement. Yet our formal histories of the press, while devoting ample space to such matters as the general idiosyncrasies of certain famous New York editors utterly ignore this development and one will search in vain for any mention of the name of the man whom above any other it is due: Ansel Nash Kellogg."[1]

The former country editor, Ansel Nash Kellogg, successfully applied ready-print to America's own special needs. A small town publisher, he was described as "a gentleman of the old school...and a journalist of high ideals" by his contemporaries.[2] Unlike some of the other ready-print suppliers who came later and were exclusively in the business for money, Kellogg envisioned a better world as a result of this cost-cutting, newspaper-creating idea.

Kellogg was born in Reading, Pa. in 1832. He and his family later moved to New York City, where he was graduated second in his class from Columbia College (later to be called Columbia University), with high honors. An intelligent, introverted man of varied talents, he searched about for a career. He first planned to become an architect; but after a year's restless study he changed his mind. In 1855 he moved to Portage, Wis., bent on becoming a newspaper editor. His move was influenced by the adventures and opportunities in the state of Wisconsin, little more than a large wilderness, being settled at a furious pace. Wisconsin, with nearby Indian troubles, was typical of the states in a transition described by historian Frederick Jackson Turner as "the meeting ground of savagery and civilization."

When asked by his urban Eastern friends why he would move to such a provincial, backwoods area still very much a frontier settlement, he replied, "To finish my education."

There were other reasons why Kellogg emigrated from the East. He was not enamored of city life, and suspected that opportunities, though yet undefined, existed in the fast-expanding western reaches of the country.

He set about to train himself in the new trade of journalism by learning the craft of printing. He became an apprentice on the Portage, Wisconsin paper.

Things developed rapidly in Wisconsin in those days. Only a year later he was in Baraboo where he started his own newspaper, the *Republic.* In 1859, in this little frontier town he met and married Annie E. Barnes.[3]

Probably no profession in the world accommodates the multi-faceted person more than country journalism since the job requires a wide assortment of talents. Kellogg fit exceptionally well, for his interests ranged from an ability to write clearly to engineering, machinery and business management.

Kellogg was also an honest man. He had an excellent reputation in his business dealings. One article about him, many years later, stated, "His is a life of unusual rectitude and purity. His character was unsullied, a constant example of sterling integrity and uprightness." He also had a happy family life.

Though he kept his restless mind busy, he could focus well enough to develop mathematical formulas, one of which was published by the *American Mathematical Monthly* and titled, "Empirical Formulae for Approximate Computation." He received a patent for an improvement on a job press in 1862. His writing was well composed, if not inspired. He also had an interest in Republican politics, but his deafness, especially later in life, kept him out of active participation.[4]

His newspaper was typical of the few frontier journals of the time, a well written, four page publication. It centered about a small Washington handpress that handled 150 sheets per hour, printed on one side at a time. While the press was slow, the typesetting was even slower. Like the other retarded aspects of printing technology, this bothered Kellogg—as it did his contemporary, Mark Twain. Kellogg felt as Twain did, that traditional printing methods must go, there must be a better way to set type and print it, if communication of ideas was to flourish.

At times Kellogg would pause in his work to watch as the type was set. It was set in exactly the same manner as Johann Gutenberg had done it 420 years earlier—with each letter placed by hand onto a little tray, hundreds, thousands of movements of the hand and arm. The composed lines were then transferred, ever so carefully, to the press, which differed only slightly from Gutenberg's original model in that it was sturdier and made of metal instead of wood. Printing, he noted, was a craft that seemingly resisted modernization.

The country newspaper usually had only one room with the machinery and editorial desks side by side. Like much of America of that egalitarian, post-Jacksonian era, inland newspapers never tolerated a class system. Everyone, supervisor and staff, dressed alike for in America it was difficult to judge a social class by what was worn. The boss never put on airs by hanging about exclusively in the front office as the proper country editor believed he should work at the side of his sweating typesetters.

There was little difference between editorial and printing. The staffs were interchangeable, with printers acting as journalists and vice versa. They all wrote. They were journalists, writing with little pieces of jagged metal type (contrast this with the environment today, with computers used to compose the news room prose). In that Victorian time they all could operate and feed the press, set type, fold papers and do the job printing. Most could also design advertising notices, write stories and even scribble a few lines of frontier poetry.

To Ansel Nash Kellogg, the life was ideal, with the exception of the crudities of the printing craft. Watching the cumbersome process of printing, it seemed to him that there must be a better way. For years this gnawed at him and he resolved to improve on the process. It took a war for him to devise a way around the dilemma.

In 1861 the southern states had seceded and President Lincoln made the decision to make a fight of it. He issued a call for volunteers for the northern army, and war ensued. The result was that Kellogg's key printer and typesetter in his little newspaper, Joseph I. Weirick, joined the northern (newly named "Union") forces.[5]

Newspapers were hard hit by the armies' need for volunteers.[6] Kellogg found himself short of manpower, especially good, fast typesetters. The loss of Weirick was the last straw, making it impossible to put out the regular four page issue.[7]

Kellogg, moving fast, took a trip to the nearest large newspaper printing plant, located at the daily in Madison, Wisconsin. He contracted with them to print one side of his newspaper on the big, faster presses available there. He then took the half-printed sheets back to Baraboo, where he edited and printed the other half. Since the Madison newspaper was also at the wilderness end-of-the-line of the press telegraph, Kellogg's readers, located in the northern woodlands of Wisconsin, were given the advantage of fresher dispatches from the war front and news of the world.

This event, the birth of American ready-print, took place on July 10, 1861, and shortly thereafter other Wisconsin publishers, who were faced with the same shortage of printers, asked to join in, and by the war's end the Madison daily paper was serving over 50 newspapers with partly printed sheets. Kellogg sensed a business opportunity. In 1865 he sold his paper to his returning printer, Weirick, and went to Chicago. There he set up a company devoted exclusively to the producing of pre-printed newspapers.

Prior to ready-print, America's country newspapers had a variety of appearances. Columns varied in length and width. Types and page layouts were different. The only standard was the size of the sheet, which had to fit the presses then in use.

To create a volume market for his product Kellogg set about to standardize newspaper appearance as well. This was done so that the sheets coming off his Chicago plant's press would not only fit the town editor's Washington and Ramage handpresses, but the print would also match the Chicago side of the sheet. Columns, type faces, page design had to look the same to be a single newspaper, not two different papers, back to back. The standard "look" of American newspapers was thus born.[8]

Kellogg's writers made his country editor-customers look more skilled than they were. He offered the towns cut sheets, blank on one side, with the other side skillfully designed, masterfully written and tightly

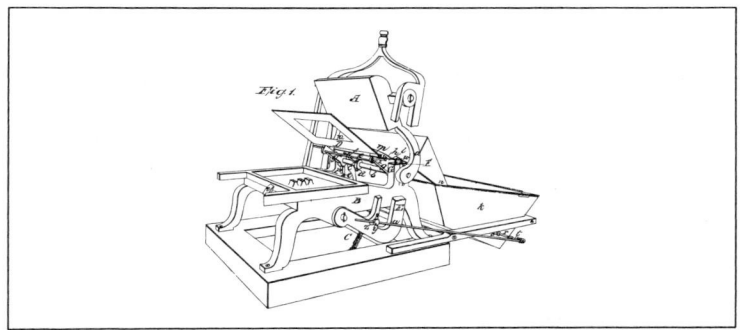

Ansel Kellogg invented this press in 1863.

edited. Many a reader must have been puzzled by some of the beautifully-crafted prose that suddenly seemed to flow from their town editor's previously uninspired pen.

A system of trade-in was worked out so that the rural editor could turn in his old typefaces and borders in exchange for new matching designs.

Kellogg's method of doing business was to stay within the codes of newspaperdom's craft. Since he, himself, came out of the business, he understood his editor-customers, knew their foibles, their missionary spirit, their insecurities and their ambitions. He spoke their "language."

At times the Chicago side of the sheet appeared on the front of the town paper, and at other times it was on the inside. The inside was preferred by most town publishers for the ready-print. No date or accreditation line was used, so there was no way of knowing that the Chicago side of the sheet was Kellogg news. In fact, in the communities in which it was distributed, the local editor took credit for the entire newspaper by running his name at the top of the page, followed by the title: "Editor and Publisher." Kellogg, in a very real sense, also the editor and publisher, was never identified by the local paper.

The country editor had half his work done for him, and the Kellogg newspaper was able to sell advertising on his side by offering advertisers the second-highest circulation of any newspaper in the world. By 1871 the Kellogg ready-print national newspaper had been in existence six years, and had accumulated a circulation of over 140,000 throughout the Midwest. At this early date in ready-print's history, only *Le Petit Journal* of Paris exceeded it in circulation.

In 1875, Kellogg introduced "boilerplate," pre-etched printing plates. He offered the plates, laden with news features and columns, at two and one-half cents an inch. Many other town papers that had held out against the use of ready-print gave in and ordered the boilerplate.

Four major partly-printed newspapers had sprung up by the time of Kellogg's death in 1886. In addition there were many sub-offices located in most major cities in the U.S. East coast newspapers joined the bandwagon and the New York Newspaper Union had 1,200 franchised customers; Western Newspaper Union had 1,250; the Chicago Newspaper Union had 1,000 and Kellogg held the lead with 1,500. Even the most detached observer of the time must have noted that the town newspapers in several areas had begun to look mysteriously alike.[9]

In all, one third of American weeklies were partly prints by 1886, and most of the rest were users of boilerplate.

Kellogg became a wealthy man, and applied his time to world travel and further inventions. He returned to the East, living comfortably in New York City where he invented improvements for printing presses and dabbled with more mathematical formulas.

In the mid 1880s he suffered a stroke and in an effort to recover he and his wife traveled leisurely through Europe. He returned home, but his health never improved. On March 23, 1886, he died while at his vacation home in Tompkinsville, Georgia.

THE GHOST EDITOR IN CHICAGO

Besides Kellogg, many other country editors were forced into improvisation by the bloody, national war which threatened the continuity of their papers. In the North, early in the war, it was unthinkable to shut down the local journal, especially with the need for war news, with invaders, the "Reb's," ranging about, heaven knows where. Southern armies came out of their camps in the South and were invading places close enough to be familiar to all the North, like the suburbs of Washington, D.C., central Pennsylvania, western Maryland, along the Ohio river and Missouri.

Even the uppermost reaches of the North felt the need for news, to be warned in advance of trouble, or invasion. Besides, every town, even those consisting of three or four hundred people, had to have its newspaper if it were to be considered a town at all. Shopping, government and newspaper, that's what a town was.

In the South, though the need for newspapers prevailed, ready-print was not used until after the war.

The cost of ready-print was small. It was delivered for a fee of five dollars or less per week. The ready-print supplier could do this because of the revenue generated by the advertising appearing on the Chicago side. The Chicago-printed, ready-print side was a newspaper in its own right. The addition of the other side at the local publisher's plant made it into an amalgam of varied and interesting impact on the reader of the time.

At first, ready-print was published by four companies, three in Chicago and one, smaller, in New York. Later, as a consequence of competition, after the turn of the century, the number of ready-print suppliers was reduced to only one, Chicago's Western Newspaper Union.

In all town newspapers it was treated as a hidden publication, not as an insert. It was buried inside and disguised to look exactly like the newspaper onto which it was grafted. It was written, edited, illustrated, headlined and printed in far-off Chicago by a ghost central editor and publisher, though portions of the ready-print were prepared in regional satellite printing plants. The identity of the ready-print supplier was never revealed to the reader, and, because of his massive circulation this supplier exercised enormous influence on what Americans from coast to coast would be reading.

There was in America a free-wheeling, frequently deceptive, business climate in that era of the robber barons. Ready-print fit into its time with its questionable practice of bald-faced planting of false clues on the printed page, imitating the local paper's page style and type-faces. It also listed the local newspaper owner as the editor of the entire issue.

To keep ready-print hidden, both the local and the Chicago publishers exhaustively devised intricate ruses and camouflage. To make both sides of the sheet look more alike, local publishers were advised to send their long-running advertising notices to Chicago to be imprinted with matching type faces permanently on the ready-print side. Thus "institutional" advertising from funeral homes, lawyers and medical doctors found their ads mixed among the Chicago side's cocaine headache remedies, while the groceries and department stores with weekly price and item changes had to be placed in the locally-produced pages—sometimes on the front page.

At times this practice worked to the detriment of the local publisher when an advertiser took offense at editorial content and rushed in to cancel his ad. If the notice had been appearing on the Chicago side it took months to get it removed since there was no way it could be erased. Meanwhile the publisher received a weekly scolding from the offended advertiser, baffled by the inability to make the change.

In that Victorian time, traveling salesmen, nibbling donuts and sipping coffee at the town restaurant would glance over the local paper and note how similar these newspapers were in the towns along their routes. Like the latter-day historians they mistakenly assumed that the busy local editor spent much time scanning other newspapers, copying articles that suited him.

In time, about the turn-of-the-century, the ready-print companies solved the "look-alike" problem. The Kellogg Company, later to be absorbed by the Western Newspaper Union, created a system whereby the stories never appeared in neighboring newspapers on the same date and were mixed throughout the issue in a thousand different ways.

Because of the mechanical difficulty this meant cutting down on telegraphic news and the increased use of timeless, encyclopedic, "evergreen" articles—stories that could run anytime, this year or next.

The Western Newspaper Union in its news sheet the *Publisher's Auxiliary,* regularly advised ready-print publishers how to handle tricky public relations aspects such as the paper's need to hide the ready-print from readers. There were various degrees and methods of hiding the ready-print.

Most papers slipped it into their back pages without notice. Others, believing that their readers would detect the change, offered vague, veiled references to the service.

As an example of this technique: in the February, 1912 issue of *Publisher's Auxiliary* local publishers were offered an example of an announcement designed for a newspaper just entering into the ready-print field. It should be pointed out that the announcement bragged about the ready-print without ever mentioning where it came from, who wrote it, or what it was.

Note also the absence of the word "ready-print" and the unwillingness "to take up the readers' time" to explain it. Also the newspaper notice disingenuously claimed that the "news service" would be devoted "almost exclusively" to the second, third, sixth and seventh pages, implying that they could change those pages if they so desired. Of course these cited pages were indelibly Chicago-printed backs of the sheet and the local paper could not change them. The notice read:

> ...A newspaper in Kentucky... has begun the use of the Western Newspaper Union newspaper service. The paper is a six-column quarto and one of the live newspapers in southwestern Kentucky. In the first issue containing this service appeared the following editorial under the caption "A Better Paper:"
> "With the aim always to improve the *Enquirer* from not only a financial viewpoint, but from the view of the readers, we have just completed arrangements for the most up-to-date 'news' and 'feature' service ever instituted on any county paper. We will not take up the time of our readers' trying to prepare them for this departure, but we leave it up to your own judgement, dear readers, as to the extent of the improvement. ...this new service will be devoted almost exclusively to the second, third, sixth and seventh pages. Feeling sure that the public will appreciate this venture and stamp it with their approval, we leave it with you. The service begins this week."

The charade was practiced by most of America's newspaper editors and publishers. They found ready-print profitable, thanks to its effect on reducing operating overhead. As mentioned before, it cut press and typesetting time in half and the ready-print pages sent by railroad express cost only a few dollars a week, about the same as blank paper.

But the disadvantage to the editors was the loss of editorial control over half, or more, of their pages. Historical researcher James H. Creighton called it a "conspiracy of silence" among the town editors, in his study of town newspapers in Missouri. Creighton cited the case of the Huntsville, Missouri, *Herald* which dropped its ready-print and became a "home-print" newspaper in 1897 and was complimented by his neighboring editors. Unlike four years earlier, when the *Herald* was expanded to eight pages by adding four of ready-print, the editors had "carefully avoided" mentioning that the ready-print had been added.[10]

The use of ready-print and boilerplate, however, persisted as the country expanded westward and new towns depended on the establishment of community-bonding facilities like the newspapers, clubs, churches, schools and business services to attract millions of immigrants from the east coast. Ready-print and its cousin boilerplate, because they were unidentified, were unlike any press service, either in the nineteenth or twentieth century. The readers did not know that it was an out-of-town editorial product they were reading---unlike the magazine inserts and wire stories clearly labeled in today's U.S. newspapers. It is not easy to determine with exactness why ready-print in the late nineteenth and first half of the twentieth century sought so diligently to hide its out-of-town source. The practice continued until the 1920s—when, grudgingly, accreditation tags finally appeared in many articles and columns, but in typeface so small as to be almost invisible.[11]

Why was ready-print hidden? Was it simply a tradition that began without reason long ago and became imbedded in the culture? Or was it that discovery would have exposed the local newspaper editors' lack of experience and writing talent. There were papers from time to time that were so poorly edited on the "home" side of the sheet, that the readers were puzzled at the contrast with the "Chicago" side.

The town editor was encouraged to keep quiet about the "foreign" source of his news. More likely it was money, rather than editorial ego or pride of authorship that was involved in the decision to continue hiding. To the Chicago ready-printers it may have been paid propaganda---hidden advertising---that caused them to camouflage themselves since news stories were more readily believed if the reader saw them as locally written.

Who sees what? From what source? To what effect? In the light of extensive research, modern social scientists know that communications credited to unknown, or low credibility, media are thought by the reader to be biased and unfair. An opinion of a friend (or of the respected local town newspaper) carries more impact than that of a stranger.[12]

Morris Ernst, in his book *The First Freedom* pointed out a study made by Chilton Bush of Stanford university that indicated that both news and advertising are read more closely in small newspapers than in large ones, with a ratio of about three to one.

Ernst, who has written extensively on the subject of monopoly, also stated that: "...an intimate relationship exists between the reader and the run-of-the-mill events of his community. Above all it must be noted that weeklies and small dailies have been usually locally owned and managed. The editor lives with the problems of his readers. He has a concern for the community---the essence of democracy. He is quite a different species from the itinerant, temporary editor, operating for an absentee owner.[13] The local owner-publisher of a weekly is an

In Chicago, the hand setting of the ready-print and boilerplate pages required the services of a large group of skilled type compositors.

indigenous creature bearing slight resemblance to the publisher tycoon of Detroit or Chicago who by remote control from such metropolises runs a paper...."

Another reason for hiding ready-print was that, in that time, America discovered that it did not have enough writers and editors. Thousands of newly-formed towns in the pioneer wilderness needed to prove their existence by having a newspaper. Town editors were important men in their communities, but rarely talented writers.

One typical example, of this type, of the author's acquaintance was an editor who had been a banjo player in a traveling circus that had disbanded in a Kentucky town in 1910. Looking around for a way to make a living, he thought first of starting a saloon. But with so much talk of "prohibition" in the air, he settled on opening a newspaper (he had, over the years, hung around newspaper offices, talking to the printers, and placing advertisements for the circus). Not deterred by his lack of formal education and business experience, he launched the paper with his last eighty dollars. Not a writer or poet, the circus performer depended heavily on ready-print news matter shipped from Chicago.

His town journal began as a four page sheet, growing, prospering financially and developing a loyal readership, until it dominated that part of Central Kentucky. When interviewed by the author over 50 years later, the publisher, then in his eighties, was still at his job on the paper and had the largest house in town.

"I never again had to play the banjo for a living," he boasted.

Though normally open and forthright, when I asked him about his use of ready-print, he preferred to change the subject, saying that the reason for the success of the paper was its efficient coverage of local news and society items. The editor abhorred investigative stories, saying: "Editorials and muckraking just get you in trouble." To him the free press meant the opportunity given him to publish profitably, pleasing as many local people as possible, especially the advertisers and some of the publisher's political friends who supported the paper with donations and advertising at election time.

But America had all kinds of town editors. In contrast to this publisher, the author has also encountered better-read, more-outspoken editors who threw themselves into editorial causes and whose newspapers filled their "home" sides with their personal views and comments. This expression of the free press grew from the opportunity presented by the blank side of the Chicago sheets.

The story of ready-print was a bitter-sweet one. Ready-print made it possible to start many newspapers in its time: because to survive and participate in the free press system the newspapers had to make a profit.

The town press was half slave (to Chicago) and half free. There existed a free press on one side of the sheet, enslaved to a "foreign" press on the other.

Politicians (even Presidents), preachers and patent medicine advertisers flocked to ready-print's pages, eager to influence the millions of loyal readers. As early as the 1870s its circulation was many times larger than the fabled newspapers of today and yesterday: many times more than today's New York *Times,* the Washington *Post,* the London *Times, U.S.A Today,* and Russia's *Iszvestia.*

Like being fed canned soup while told that it was Mom's home-cooking, Americans were served up, from a central source, a well-written, highly readable mix of ideas, moral beliefs, recipes, news and editorials that helped form their personal values. It was a philosophical stew and news mix unique in the world. This was done, all the while, with the lulling (to the subscriber), mistaken belief that the editorial product they were reading came from, or was under the control of, the town's civic leader and booster, the respected editor.

Despite the occasional complaint by a non-ready-print competing newspaper or a press association, most readers were taken in.

"Our ready-prints haint come!"

READY-PRINT EXPOSED BY CHICAGO FIRE

America was an underdeveloped country in 1871, the year of the great fire that almost wiped Chicago off the map. Four people lived in the rural areas for every one living in the smallish cities (most were merely overgrown small towns) of the time. The covered wagons were still rolling westward. General Custer had not yet entered the Black Hills to meet his fate at the hands of the Indian chief Sitting Bull.

America's hidden newspaper, on one occasion, was exposed for a short time to readers in a dramatic way: the truth about ready-print might have remained a secret to most readers had the Chicago fire of 1871 not burned the heart of that city to the ground. As a result, for several weeks following the disaster many town papers suspended publication and nearly 200 weekly newspapers hundreds of miles away, throughout Wisconsin, Iowa, Illinois and Minnesota were received by their subscribers with blank inside pages.

Prior to the Chicago disaster the 200 local editions of the Kellogg paper had looked almost exactly alike on half of the pages, except at the top of the front page the paper was given a different name for each of the towns, such as the *STEVEN'S POINT PINERY, THE RED WING ARGUS, MATAMORA SENTINEL,* and the *PAXTON RECORD,* newspapers from the smaller towns in the states around Chicago.

Some of the affected papers carried a notice which informed readers that their "hometown paper" was in part a local edition of a newspaper, published by the A. N. Kellogg Co. located at 110-112 West Madison Street in Chicago—and whose plant had been in the path of the flames and destroyed.

The inside story of the mysterious partly-printed newspapers was revealed in the pages of the *Scientific American* magazine, November 11, 1871 issue; luckily for the ready-printers, the magazine was read by few of the small town subscribers.

Scientific American magazine offered few details, writing: "One of the leading printers of Chicago did a large business in printing these 'outsides' (or 'insides') in duplicate and sending them to different places, where the local publishers printed the news on the other side. The farmers who depended upon these sheets for their weekly news must have been puzzled to know how the Chicago fire could have deprived them of their village newspaper while the (town) home office remained intact."[14]

But the memory of the odd half-blank sheets faded away in the routine of village life. The Kellogg Company quickly rebuilt its plant, replaced the melted presses and type and soon resumed regular shipments of half-printed sheets to the local newspapers. Kellogg realized that the brief surfacing of the ready-print secret would cause only a momentary stir among readers, unacquainted with the mechanics of printing.

There were also routine delays in publishing the town papers. The delays were usually for a variety of reasons. Most frequently it was because the publisher, who had been taking in eggs and vegetables all week in payment for subscriptions, found that he did not have enough money to pay off the hard-nosed freight agent at the train depot who was holding onto the sheets of ready-print.

Despite the excellent service offered by the ready-print firms, there were occasional times when the railroads would lose the paper, or would deliver them late, causing much consternation. In 1904 one editor chose to express his sentiments in typical town newspaper "American-style" poetry, printed in the in-house, newspapermen's magazine *The Journalist*. The poet reports that the entire staff, from the Old Man (publisher) down to the boy-helper (devil), threatened to close down and return to their family farms because the Chicago supplier was late in sending along the week's ready-print sheets. The poem, otherwise quite truthful on the whole, claimed that the tardiness of the ready-prints was revealed to impatient readers:

THOSE TARDY READY-PRINTS

> The hour of pressing had arrived,
> The forms were on the press.
> The foreman and the office force
> Were harassed by the stress;
> Old man and devil both were sore
> Of thoughts of coming toil.
> Each stoutly swore he wished he were
> A tiller of the soil.
> But suddenly amidst the din
> Of busy hands and feet,
> Rang down the sanctum's grimy walls,
> The printer's ears to greet.
> A bit of news not fit to print,
> That disappointed some—

> The angry boss proclaimed the scoop:
> "The ready-prints hain't come!"
> The foreman's face took on a look
> That jibed well with his oath,
> And now to wholly "cut it out"
> The print-shop's force was loath;
> The boss and devil both declared
> That they were printers born—
> Much rather'd get the paper out
> Than cultivate mere corn.
> They stoutly cursed the railroad's crew
> And vowed its beating up,
> Likewise the ready-printing firm
> Got its due jacking-up.
> And all who passed the shop and asked,
> "Why don't the presses hum?"
> Received the same forlorn reply:
> "Our ready-prints haint come!"[15]

The Chicago fire was not the only time that ready-print was brought to the attention of the public. Everett Dick, in the *Sod House Frontier*, described other newspapers of the middle west and how they handled the problem when the ready-print failed to arrive at the railway express office: "In pioneer days not over half the paper was printed at home. The rest of it known as the patent 'outsides' or 'insides,' was printed in Chicago, or at times at the company's satellite presses in St. Paul, Sioux City, or elsewhere, and shipped to the town newspaper office. Usually there were four eight-column pages.

"When severe storms tied up transportation facilities and the patent insides failed to arrive, a small edition was sometimes printed on the job press. During the great Dakota storm of 1881 there was no train service for weeks and the papers 'came out' with their diminutive editions on brown store wrapping paper or wallpaper. These legalized the land office notices and other legal advertising."

BOILERPLATE

The word "boilerplate" is now better known than "ready-print" and has come into usage in a pejorative sense, meaning repetitious dissemination. It is an alternate word to the early eighteenth century

The pouring of melted lead over a cast created the boilerplate (stereotypes). It was a hot, uncomfortable job.

"stereotype" (as in "stereotyped opinions," also of printing origin).

The expression "boilerplate" found its way into the English language from the uses of the thick metal printing sheets similar to those used to construct boilers. The plates were etched (moulded) on top and were placed, whole or cut into pieces, onto the press, face-up---ready for printing.

Before the invention of boilerplate, the type for a story, editorial or advertisement had to be set by hand over and over again in each of the thousands of newspapers. Boilerplate was created by squeezing a sheet of damp cardboard over the type, which was then dried, lifted, turned over and molten metal was poured onto the cardboard (papier-mache), making a cast. By this method, thousands of molten castings were produced at relatively low cost and sent, one to each subscribing newspaper.

Boilerplate metal castings were introduced by Kellogg to the town newspapers as an additional news service in 1875, a supplement or substitution for the printed ready-print pages. Boilerplate was more expensive to use than ready-print because it required the use of a press run. But to a slight degree it loosened the chains on the country editors, allowing them to move the location of the stories on the page. Many country editors grasped onto this bit of freedom, though it meant more work and expense for them. Stressing the system's convenience, Kellogg promoted the idea with announcements such as this one:

> The A. N. Kellogg Newspaper Co., 72 Jackson St., Chicago are now prepared to furnish almost everything in the shape of reading

matter from the latest telegraphic news for daily papers, to interesting miscellaneous articles for weeklies, includes serial stories, tales, illustrated and otherwise, travelling sketches, poetry, religious reading, scientific articles, and semi-news matter of particular interest. Their illustrated plates, though but recently introduced, have already become immensely popular and the demand for them is daily increasing. The economy and convenience resulting from the use of stereoplates have made them a necessary part of the outfit of the country office, while the services now rendered by them are so varied and their forms and style and make-up such that every publisher desiring their services can be suited. This firm is now furnishing eleven different sized columns, full length, ranging from 13 and one-half inches to 25 and three-quarter inches, thus saving all cutting and adjustment.[17]

Thus the time had come that newspapers were free to choose either the ready-print or the boilerplate. Some of the papers bought both services, in effect "pre-printing" both sides.

The cost of boilerplate was higher than ready-print, but still reasonable for the local publisher. In 1871 Kellogg offered the first continued story in his ready-print, and in 1872 the first illustrated articles. The expansion brought added services. In 1874 it opened branch offices in Cincinnati, St. Paul and Cleveland. By 1880 his five offices were serving more than 800 papers.

The Kellogg Company in 1893 offered a wide variety of material at attractive rates and publishers across the country snapped it up. The company advertised the articles as "incomparable in their freshness, in sparkling English:"

"Humorous Page - $3.00
Illustrated Page - $2.00
Exciting Events Page (Semi-Sensational) - $2.00
Weekly Novelettes (by well-known writers) - $1.50
Woman's and Household Page - $1.20
Young People's Page - $1.20
Building and Science Page - $2.00
Soldiers' Department - "Devoted to the Great War"- $2.00

The boilerplate was made ready on Saturday and shipped by the following Wednesday of each week. Payment was Cash on Delivery, paid at the freight office.

With boilerplate, utilizing a saw and a lot of patience, local editors could reposition their stories or tediously rout out (by drilling into the metal plate) to obscure offending sentences or short articles before going to press. Moving stories to the top of the page gave the article more prominence, and one could leave the story out completely, if it suited the editor's preference. A Democratic editor in Ohio used another, rather crude, method, hammering dents on any Republican-biased story leaving an unreadable smudge (few editors, however partisan, would go to these extremes and damage the appearance of their paper).

Importantly, by using only boilerplate instead of ready-print, town news editors could now claim their papers as "home printed." This came in handy if they wished to demean an opposition paper that used the ready-print process. Most papers, however, stayed with the more economical and money making ready-print method of publishing their newspapers---in addition, supplementing the other side with boilerplate.

In sum, the instituting of boilerplate could deprive readers of locally written stories and editorials as country publishers, more and more, chose to take the easy route and insert the pre-typeset boilerplate into the "home" side of the sheet.

Ironically, though seldom the case, it became possible to put out a newspaper even if the local editor were almost functionally illiterate.

NOTES

1. Milton M. Quaife, "How A. N. Kellogg Revolutionized America's Country Press," *The National Printer-Journalist,* Feb. 1922, p. 21.

2. Elmo Watson, op cit, p. 24. On March 25, 1886, the Wisconsin State Journal of Madison headed the story of Kellogg's death: "Inventor of Patent Insides Dies." The term "patent insides" evolved into an unflatering connotation by 1900, with many people complaining about the noxious and poisonous patent medicines so freely run on the ready-print pages. W. N. U. switched to the word "ready-print" in 1900, then to "auxiliary service" in 1920.

3. Watson, ibid, p. 5.

4. Records, U.S. Patent Office, patent no. 37,293.

5. Note, town newspaperman Mark Twain also left the trade to join the opposing ("Confederate") army of his state, Missouri.

6. *History of Hennepin County, Minn.* (Minneapolis: North Star Publishers 1881). This and other county histories form a good source of reference material on the impact on newspapers by mass enlistment. Ex. "Amos Jordan, printer's apprentice, with four other compositors of *The Atlas,* owned by W. S. King, enlisted in the First Minnesota Infantry...so they closed the office."

7. "When Mr. Kellogg's Printer Joined the Army," *Publishers' Auxiliary,* Oct. 7, 1922, p. 1.

8. Unlike magazines which flourish in an endless variety of shapes and appearances.

9. *R. L. Watkins Advertiser's Gazette of 1888,* p. 107.

10. James Creighton, "Patent Insides and the Missouri Editor," unpublished monograph, University of Missouri, p. 20.

11. Columns in author's collection.

12. Carl I. Hovland, in his *American Psychologist* paper (pp. 8-17, issue 14, 1959 stated that the reader's perception of the source tends to influence its interpretation and acceptance of the content.

13. On the other hand, some perceptive chain publishers have appointed respected local newsmen as permanent editors.

14. *Scientific American,* Nov. 11, 1871.

15. *The National Printer-Journalist,* 1904, p. 753.

16. Everett Dick, *The Sod-House Frontier,* (New York: D. Appleton-Century Co. 1938) p. 422.

17. "Improved Stereoplates," *The Inland Printer,* 1885, p. 69.

Chapter Three

Boilerplating the American Mind

> Look who's comin' through that door. It seems we've met somewhere before....
> —Garrison Keillor[1]

> Boilerplate. It aids in the standardization of thought and custom. It provides a better breeding place for propaganda of one sort or another.
> —Lynn Montrose[2]

NEWSPAPERS, CONSECRATORS OF THE AMERICAN WAY

It has been written that the nation's soul lies in the inland countryside and small towns--regions of wheat and corn and dairies and little groves. There was created the remarkably uniform American Way, far away from the media and book publishing centers that hugged the eastern coastline.

It is from a relatively recent agricultural past that Americans formed their view of things. In 1870 fully three quarters of all Americans lived on farms or in small towns. As recently as a few years before World War II fewer Americans resided in the cities than in the countryside and villages. Therefore it should not surprise anyone that even in this Atomic Age, in the latter Twentieth Century, most Americans take comfort from reminders of the Western Migration. Inland values still live. Rustic manners, insular conservatism and flag-waving continue to serve as the national politician's most efficient route to election.

The inland parts are acknowledged as the most distinctively American sectors because, as Lord Bryce pointed out, this is the area in which the country as a whole differs from Europe--where the polyglot of cultures truly melted together.

How did this building and spread of an intensively uniform language and culture come about in so short a time? How did the vast heartland with its unofficial capital city of Chicago develop its tribal similarity among its isolated people who seldom, if ever, met each other? Farms were large spreads, and towns were "island communities" largely unconnected in a country three thousand miles wide.

Social scientists, in analyzing the American system, would profit from studying the newspapers of those days; for papers played a large role in the formation of the society. Especially in the inland area, north and south, away from the early-settled strip along the Atlantic seaboard. In that inner domain the country papers were the dominant teachers and consecrators of social ideas, political movements, religions and custom. This wilderness America, sparsely settled, read the country editor's journal with a special intensity. Frequently, an expression like: "I saw in the papers that..." would dot conversations and give credence to a debatable or unsettling fact or idea.

Inland cultural values and their methods of dissemination did not escape the notice of national politicians. William Jennings Bryan, thrice candidate for president in the latter nineteenth century took on the trappings of country editor early in his political career. Like many American political figures, he founded a boilerplate-laden weekly newspaper, *The Commoner*, to give airing to his populist ideas.

NEWSPAPER FEVER

According to 1890 Census figures, newspaper publishers outnumbered paperhangers. At its most fevered moment, the rush to start newspapers in the U.S. approximated a stampede. Between 1870 and 1900, over 25,000 were founded--more than twice as many as existed in the entire rest of the world at the time.

Printers and English teachers rushed to become publishers. Supporting services built up around the boom. The development and building of sturdy, transportable, presses became a major industry. Type foundries, ink factories, and advertising agencies sprouted. Paper mills began to spring up in the piney woods of the South and

Northwest. A cheaper form of newsprint was developed to serve the need.

Newspapers came and went with such frequency that even state press associations couldn't record them fast enough. A specialist, called a "newspaper developer" appeared on the scene. This individual would go into a town, start up a newspaper, operate it for several months then sell it at a substantial profit. These restless "Johnny Appleseeds" of journalism, added to the infectious spread of newspapers.

Perhaps the most frenetic of these was John Harper who started and operated twenty six different newspapers, most of which he sold. Harper created one in each of the twenty-six years he was in the business. There are "John Harpers" today still in the town newspaper business.[3]

The Wayne, Nebraska *Herald* was typical of the new journals springing up across the country. It was an eight page newspaper, half ready-print. To aid the editor-publisher it employed in 1912 only two people: a lady who set type for $7 a week, and a man who set advertisements and the job work who received $15.[4]

The ease of entry into the publishing business resulted also in the creation of short-life, political, religious and special interest journals that lasted only as long as the proprietor's enthusiasm and funds held out. Newspapers were started to promote diverse causes, mostly political. Among the most popular were the Democratic, Republican, Greenbacker, Free Soil, Granger, Gold and Silver Standard, Populist and Socialist parties.

Most religions were well-represented, including the Methodists, Mormons, Catholics, Lutherans, Baptists and a hundred others.

FRANCHISING CREATES
A NATIONAL NEWSPAPER

Typical of franchises today are multiple automobile dealerships, and restaurants like Kentucky Fried Chicken, McDonald Hamburgers and Pizza Hut. Daniel J. Boorstin, in his writings on the history of late twentieth century retail franchises, gave us some insights into the effects of the franchise system which has standardized retail operations, creating repetitive facades that mark the nation with areas of sameness. He stated: "The Franchise offered an opportunity to own and yet not to own, to risk and yet be cautious. It democratized business enterprise by offering a man with small capital and no experience the benefits of large capital, large-scale experiment, national advertising and established reputations."[5]

Nineteenth century ready-print was a franchise in every respect. When the ready-print company applied the franchise idea to newspapers it gave an economic boost to the trade but also applied a level of sameness to the product. In his contract the new editor received training in running a newspaper, the opportunity to get into the business with a small investment, instant national advertising on the ready-print side of the sheet (which almost paid entirely for his newsprint paper and half of his editorial, typesetting and printing costs).

However, from this seemingly humble business idea resulted a national newspaper, subscribed to by most of the American population. Americans, whether they knew it or not, were reading two newspapers, "pasted" back to back. One one side of the sheet was the national newspaper, the ready-print product of the Chicago editor, and on the other the country editors' newspapers, thousands of them---the country's dominant free press.

Ready-print began at a time when the battle-scarred Second America was obliged to start over---it's family quarrel finally settled by the bayonet. The four-year war brought about changes that had taken most of Europe a century and a half to undergo. This vast new America was an improvement as a nation, though the South had become an economic stepchild.

The country to the north and west was "going places." The financial and human waste of the war between the states had ended and the industrial revolution was joined with enthusiasm. The nation's quarrelsome population was enlarged and calmed by new immigrants, who moved west in unprecedented numbers. Everything was in motion.

In a land not known for reading books, the task of communicating intellectual substance to the population west of the Alleghenies fell to the town newspapers.[6] School libraries were quite small. *McGuffey Readers* and a few other books of considerable variety made up the average school's supply at that time. At the center of this migrating effort were born town and city newspaper-publishing establishments by the thousands, a tenfold growth dramatically higher than the increase in population would have warranted. The number of newspapers grew not only in the new towns but in the established communities as well.[7]

Only $200 or $300 was needed to start. Guided by the regional

An example of turn-of-the-century ready-print

ready-print office, the new editor would obtain a handpress, an assortment of type—and some advice on how to run a successful village newspaper from the regional manager who usually was an experienced ex-country editor. The franchise agreement was for the new editor to purchase a specified number of pre-printed newspapers, with payment in cash on delivery at his town's railway express office.

FREE PRESS VERSUS GOVERNMENT AND PRIVATE SUBSIDY

Some significant local, state and national government assistance to newspapers does exist and has existed since even before the Civil War. Most government financial assistance to newspapers has been doled out quietly and in relatively small amounts in the form of cheap postal rates, job printing and legal advertising. To the country editor this revenue sometimes amounted to the difference between life and death for the newspaper and the revenue has been avidly pursued.

Historically, town and city newspapers receive legal advertising ("legals,") frequently awarded at the discretion of town or county political administrators. This subsidy usually favors the intrenched, older newspaper in the community, but on occasion the subsidy has been used to finance the starting of a new town newspaper, friendlier to those in power.

"Legals" are government notices of various types, such as lists of delinquent tax payers, invitations to bid, register of voting precincts, etc. Some communities and states require them, others do not.[8]

Incentive to newspaper operation has been the below-cost postal rates. In controlling these rates the Federal Government (and its quasi-independent postal service) holds a measure of control over the press. Unlike their city counterparts, town publishers depended heavily on the mails for the distribution of their papers, and with the co-operation of friendly presidents and congressmen in Washington their postal rates were kept low.

With the addition of the legal advertising income to his ready-print "subsidy" the frontier journalist of the late 19th and early 20th centuries usually got off to a very good start in business. All he had to do to guarantee success was to go into partnership not only with the ready-print office, but with Uncle Sam: The profit came from permits to cut timber which were run at $10 each; notice of land ownership cost $10; contesting a claim cost $5; and mining claims were charged in proportion to the area of the land to be staked. It was a surefire money-maker for the paper located in areas where miners or homesteaders were settling.

Not even a village was necessary to start up in. A large shady elm tree in a meadow would do just fine. One frontier publisher confessed that it made going into business a cinch. An example was the Mountain Journal, published at Red Bird, Arkansas, located in Montgomery County on the edge of a large forest reserve about to be partitioned out to homesteaders. The town and printing plant were located 35 miles from the nearest railroad point, and stood alone in the midst of a two-acre clearing consisting of a single cabin. The net profits from government notices alone were over $80 a week from the very beginning of the venture—all from an initial investment of $250.[9]

HOW MUCH DID IT COST TO PRODUCE A NEWSPAPER?

Let's take a look at the income of typical country editors in the 1890s: the typical inland weekly charged from fifty cents to a dollar a year for a subscription—though subscribers were usually slow in paying their bill the newspapers would "carry" their subscription on the roles,

A large shady elm tree in a meadow would do just fine.

hoping that they would come in and pay up—and they usually did. The other source of revenue, advertising, averaged about eight cents per column inch in the nineties, rising to about 25 cents by 1940 and $2.50 today. Special rates for longevity or volume were worked out, as well.

In 1891 F. S. Greenleaf of the Savanna, Illinois *Journal* presented a paper on average newspaper costs before his state's press association convention. He entitled it, "How Much Ought It To Cost Per Year To Produce An Average Newspaper of 1,000 Circulation." By "average newspaper" he stated that he meant a ready-print newspaper, "because they were cheap." He used the labor of three persons.

The annual expense items were: Wages-$1,650, Paper (Ready-Print)-$360, Rent-$150. Power-$50. Ink and Rollers-$12, Postage-$18, Correspondents-$50, Fuel and Oil-$40, Taxes and Insurance-$35, Incidentals-$15, Wear and Tear-$50; adding up to an annual total cost of $2,430. Sixty seven percent of his cost was for typesetting, even though it was a ready-print newspaper.

Machinery was readily available at a reasonable price, on credit. A small operation used a Washington or Ramage hand press. Larger circulation town weeklies or small dailies would operate with a more costly hand-cranked cylinder press, some type, tables, heavy stones as a resting place for the type while it was composed (tombstones worked very well for this) and the ready-print houses would furnish the half-blank sheets on a weekly basis.

Some of the publishers were proud enough of their success in the business to write the ready-print companies, giving hearty endorsements to the process. J. B. Burwell, publisher of the Staunton, Virginia Argus was one of the many boosters of the ready-print process. He wrote, in a letter: "...In 1887 when I entered the field there were three weekly home-print papers here, the subscription price of each was Two Dollars per year. I charged One Dollar per year using your (ready-print) service, and within three years had a larger edition than that of either competitor. By using the Ready-Print Service I saved one press run per issue, and have always been able by helping some with the mechanical part, to get along with one printer, whereas, if I had printed all-at-home, another printer would have been indispensable, and the cost of the blank paper would have been about the same as that furnished half printed.

"I started with a Washington hand press and within three years bought a power press that I am still using. My outfit at the start cost about Two Hundred Dollars, and that was about all I had available, and paying Two Dollars and Fifty Cents per month for a third story room, in which I had my office, seemed a burden. Now, after nearly twenty-three years of work and the use of your Ready-Print Service, I have a three story brick office building (built in 1893) costing Twenty-five Hundred Dollars, with a house and lot; a brick residence that cost with the lot Four Thousand Dollars (my home); a cottage I let out that cost with the lot, One Thousand Dollars, eight years ago; about Twelve Hundred at interest, and do not owe anything I cannot pay off at an hour's notice. My success has been due to the use of the Baltimore (WNU) Ready-Print Service, my work as a practical printer with some knowledge of the newspaper business, and practicing economy."[10]

CIRCULATION FIGURES RISE

The author's fourteen years in editing and publishing town newspapers have taught him to be suspicious of a newspaper's circulation claims. Advertisers demand readership from the newspapers and until the founding of the national Audit Bureau of Circulation many newspapers claimed large circulations that were mostly phantom. However, Elmo Watson stated that in those Victorian times legitimate circulation was on the rise:

> The decade from 1880 to 1890 was marked by the greatest increase in the number of newspapers American journalism has ever known. They multiplied at the rate of two new publications every day. But more significant were the soaring circulation figures during this decade and the next. From 1880 to 1890 more than 37 million Americans became newspaper subscribers, as compared to 11 million during the previous decade. And from 1890 to 1900 another 37 million were added.[11]

Watson credits the syndicated news service (ready-print and boilerplate being the most dominant) for the gains he cites. The most dramatic increase occurred in the 1880-1890 decade when the number of country newspapers increased by 7,000, almost doubling the previous total.[12]

With these massive circulation gains, the ready-print had begun to feel its strength. It had become more than just an "auxiliary" to the press. It had grown to become a national phenomena and a cultural influence of massive proportions.[13] The rapid growth spread ready-print to every section of American life, from California to Maine.

In 1894 in an attempt to sum up its history, the *National Printer-Journalist,* the magazine distributed within the trade, ran the following story that laid claim to major achievements for the process, and its impact on American society.

The article was a public relations "puff" for the Western Newspaper Union, but it demonstrates the confidence that the observer had in claiming an immense impact on the development of the United States, especially in its Midwestern and Western area. W.N.U. had the problem of maintaining the hidden quality of ready-print, yet still advertising its services to prospective country editor clients. The first lines are a little perplexing since country editors of that time were, on the whole, quite cognizant of the large number of town newspapers in the United States, and the extent of ready-print's influence.

> Few readers of the *National-Printer Journalist* have any ideas of the proportions to which the ready-print business of this country has grown. Just after the close of the Civil War the first ready-print house was established. The idea met with but meagre success. Country newspaper owners were not then ready for co-operation. To canvass the publishers of established papers was a most disagreeable task. To some of them the suggestion that they could, with profit, adopt ready-prints was almost intolerable. Had the growth of the business depended upon the acquisition of papers already established it would have died early. The campaign had to be fought along new lines. The Western country had just begun to develop, and with the springing up of new cities and villages came the necessity for new papers. To the enterprising journalist with limited capital the ready-print business proved a most welcome boon.
>
> Without going to the expense of purchasing a costly outfit and employing printers to come from the large cities (an impossibility at that time) he could set the "home side" (consisting of local news, personals, ads, etc.) himself, and depend on the ready-print establishment to furnish the other side containing the telegraph news of the world, serial story, miscellany, etc. In this way hundreds of weeklies that are now considered the "best in their locality" were started. Soon every village of any size had its local paper and the news of the world up to date. Papers became

cheaper and became more generally read. The pressure to supply the demand became enormous, and to meet the same, auxiliary houses were established at convenient supply points east and west of the Mississippi river. The spread of intelligence had its effect in more ways than one. The civilizing influences of the country paper penetrated even into the rude hut of the back woods, planting new hopes and aspirations in the hearts of the people. Churches and schools became more numerous. It is only justice to say that the rapid development of the West is due more to the country press than to any other agency. And if to the country press, why not to the ready-print business which made the country press possible?

There are at present half a dozen ready-print concerns in the United States. The number of papers printed by each ranges from 500 to 3,000. To the Western Newspaper Union, "the old reliable," belongs honor of printing the largest number of papers of them all. The main office of the Western is located in Chicago. It has branches in Detroit, St. Louis, Omaha, Kansas City, Denver, DesMoines, Lincoln, Wichita, Houston and Dallas. The average number of papers printed in each office is 300. It requires the entire product of one of the largest paper mills in this country. In some towns it supplies as high as three or four customers without duplicating reading matter. The wonderful success of the Western is due to the large variety of its literary features. Fifty pages a week is the average output of reading matter. This includes current history, correspondence, fashions, science, humor, religious, boys and girls, theatrical, sporting, sensation, camp fire, short stories, serial stories and numerous other departments. Several pages of political reading also are issued weekly. Republican, Democratic, Populist, Free Silver and Prohibition papers are supplied with appropriate matter.... [14]

LET US NOW PRAISE FAMOUS MEN:
PUBLICIZING THE PRESS BARONS

When the reader strolls among the shelves of public, private or university libraries he discovers little or nothing about country editors, frontier press or even the press of inland cities (even in the archival and manuscript sources). Instead one sees huge numbers of books about New York newspaper publishers: William Randolph Hearst, James

Gordon Bennett, Charles A. Dana, Adolph Ochs, Joseph Pulitzer, and Horace Greeley. Without adequate explanation, one is baffled by the deluge that seems culturally ingrained.

And such banner publicity has had its effect in stifling the small-newspaper voices. New York-style newspaper gigantism is encouraged across the country and these single voices seem louder than they should be. Bigness is equated with success, and newspapers strive for large circulations by employing the philosophy and accounting practices of monopolists and the merchandising methods of P.T.Barnum.

Publishers of New York newspapers with large circulations seem to have become famous for being famous. In no other business have entrepreneurs such as these received so much blazing notoriety from historians. Pulitzer's eye problems and ostentatious yacht; Hearst's castle and art collection; Bennett's news-gathering passion; Ochs' enlightened moderation; Greeley who "had made his Tribune a tremendous engine of democracy;" Charles Dana's apolitical editorial philosophy; — all have become steady grist for newspaper histories and library book shelves.

Publicity was good for the big city press, but not for the secretive, clandestine ready-print "newspaper" comfortably hidden in the revered small town journals. In the nineteenth and early twentieth century the metropolitan newspapers prospered, but only in and around their cities.

In the countryside their circulations ranged from moderate to non-existent -- in comparison to the town newspapers, with their ready-print and boilerplate.

An invasion of the provinces by the large-city press never took place in America in the early 20th century. On the other hand a large number of town papers found their way into the big cities that were teeming with recent arrivals from the rural wilderness. In 1920, writing about a news stand in downtown New York that carried 350 different newspapers from towns all over the country, Bruce Barton noted this comment from the proprietor:

> There are some New Yorkers who have spent a lifetime here without ever giving their hearts to New York. They're just pilgrims in a foreign land; Attica, or Holbrook, or Valley Falls is their home. If you will step around to my stand some day at five minutes after eleven, I will show you a man who has come every morning at exactly that hour and bought the St. Joseph *Press* for

A New York City newstand at the turn of the century.

fourteen years. He is successful, as New Yorkers go: he has his own business, his home, and his car; but all the wiles of New York have left his affections unscathed. He makes his living here, but he really lives in St. Joe."[15]

There were many reasons for the fragmented influence of the metropolitan press in that era in the heartland of America. Not the least reason was the diffusion of "national capitals" in the United States.

Unlike European countries dominated by their capitals such as London, Paris and Berlin---each with its national newspaper, America had many "capitals"--some cultural, or business and others governmental. They were widely scattered, with Boston, New York, Philadelphia, Chicago and Washington sharing the titles. With no national newspaper dotting the land, the country press held sway. Burton Allbee, writing in 1892, voiced these frequently-heard opinions of the time:

> ... it would be impossible for any city-bred newspaperman to understand fully the wonderful influence and power which is wielded so conscientiously by the country press as it exists throughout the United States today. In no other nation is it so powerful. Among no other nation is it so well supported. With no

other people has grown up such an institution with the growth of the country from the very foundation of its government, and it is so safe to say that no other nationality under the skies would so well appreciate and support a country press. There are many causes that have tended to develop the country press. Some of them are rooted deep in the institutions of the nation, others are the outcome of peculiar environments; and still others are the result of a different national organization from that possessed by any other people on earth.[16]

The country press, the direct line to the people, was especially indispensable during wartime, but being half-edited from Chicago sometimes posed problems. Writer Hal Borland in his autobiography *Country Editor's Boy* wrote that just prior to America's participation in World War I, in his home town well outside of Denver, Colorado, there was only mild interest in the war, and the only noticeable effect was that the price of wheat went up.

In his book Borland reports that his father's paper, *The News,* carried only a column of war news each week, a syndicated summary, part of the ready-print of the paper.

The ready-print, with its wishy-washy "please every subscriber" style of writing, had a large anti-war readership among the German immigrants in the north central states and thus did not take a pro-war stand. Borland's father, apparently noting this, took matters in hand when the United States entered the conflict and editorialized in support of the war (on his side of the sheet). This caused a change in the town's attitude from indifference to active patriotic enthusiasm—producing a surge in the number of enlistments in his own town.[17]

THEY DON'T CALL THEMSELVES "COUNTRY EDITOR" ANY MORE!

The newspaper structure in America is traditionally composed of two importantly different groupings: the newspapers that appear every day (or sometimes only five or six times a week) that call themselves "dailies." Newspapers that appear less than five days a week are known as "weeklies." But, obviously, the words "weekly" and "daily" do not describe the variations that exist within the two categories for they have distanced themselves from each other in many ways. Subscribers

Newspapers in the United States from 1810 until 1935

Year	Weeklies	Dailies
1810	302	22
1820	422	31
1830	650	50
1840	1,141	83
1850	1,902	157
1860	3,173	190
1870	4,517	574
1875	6,144	718
1880	8,005	909
1885	10,430	1,207
1890	13,795	1,662
1895	16,627	2,056
1900	16,387	2,190
1905	16,776	2,326
1910	16,899	2,343
1915	16,711	2,447
1920	14,405	2,324
1925	13,672	2,283
1930	13,079	2,219
1935	12,390	2,199

From the N. W. Ayer and G. P. Rowell & Co. Directories

of dailies live in a one-day world; and the rural readers of weeklies adjust to a one-week world.

In 1988 there were about 1,800 daily newspapers in America. Of these about 1,450 are in the small cities and towns (as small as 3,000 or less) and 350 newspapers are in metropolitan areas.

There are 10,000 weeklies in America and they range in size from two person "man-and-wife" operations, to those with hundreds of employees. With a few exceptions, as towns get larger their weeklies tend to convert to dailies. Most dailies in this country were published once a week at one time in their early life. Most American newspapers, daily or weekly, in their early period, were ready-print and boilerplate publications.

The dailies (especially middle-to-larger size ones) run a vast amount of news written by an outside, accredited central source, distributed to them by mail, railroad express or telegraph wire.

Noted earlier, weeklies were more widely read than dailies when America was an agricultural country in the first three-quarters of our history (especially the nation's third quarter from the 1870s to the 1920s). One researcher has noted: "The limitations of the metropolitan press became evident in the essentially local character of its circulation...."[18]

Weeklies have encountered a dramatic decrease in national importance as they shifted away from editorial commentary and national and international news. However, in general, the town weeklies and small dailies still dominate within their own immediate areas. Foreign (outside of town) newspapers--no matter how high-blown their reputations still do not compete well with the town press, even in some suburban towns very near to cities.

The current American town editor's (they do not refer to themselves as "country editor" any more) newspaper's mind-numbing content belies its past influence in American society. Historically, in the time of ready-print, its impact was strongly felt because the newspaper carried more of the information load about local, national and international events. At the turn of the twentieth century only one in three hundred rural Americans west of the Alleghenies subscribed to a big city daily newspaper. The town paper was dominant.

Typical was Muncie, Indiana, which was made a focus of a town study in the Lynds' classic *Middletown*. Muncie was very much an average community along the Western frontier. In 1885 it was a quiet county seat town of 6,000, but grew to 20,000 by 1900 after a gas

> All ORIGINAL, FRESH and INTERESTING COPYRIGHT Matter,
> Especially Designed for Literary Editions of the Large Dailies
> and Weeklies having a Sunday circulation.
>
> ### ☞ LOOK AT THE NAMES OF THE CONTRIBUTORS! ☜
> And be convinced of their HIGH CHARACTER as Newspaper Writers.
>
> AMONG THEM ARE:
>
> | Blakely Hall, | Howard Fielding, | Eliza P. Hoaton, |
> |---|---|---|
> | Amos J. Cummings, | Smith D. Fry, | "Pecos Jim," |
> | John Swinton, | Horace Townsend, | Mellville Phillips, |
> | Moses P. Hanly, | Will C. Ferril, | Frances Stevens, |
> | David Wechsler, | Ellen Osborne, | George R. Cromwell, |
> | W. E. S. Fales | Agnes Merle, | Alice Strictland. |
>
> This matter is used by a number of prominent daily papers in the different large cities. We have made arrangements by which we offer it to you so that you can produce it CONTEMPORANEOUSLY WITH YOUR METROPOLITAN COMPETITORS. It will prove an attractive feature in your paper, and be a valuable franchise. We produce three pages weekly, two of them finely illustrated. We can offer you this franchise on exceptionally favorable terms: no such high class of matter has ever before been within the reach of any except some of the very largest dailies. Write us for further details.
>
> ### A. N. KELLOGG NEWSPAPER CO.,

In this 1889 advertisement Kellogg offered the country papers the same features that appeared in their competitors, the big city dailies.

deposit was uncovered nearby, turning it into a small industrial city in short order. However, the reading habits of its citizens differed only slightly from those of neighboring small towns—despite the addition of industrial wealth and a glossing of "sophistication" to the city. Muncie's newspapers used ready-print and/or boilerplate even into the twenties when the population had grown to over 35,000. Loyalty to the local papers, in contrast to outsider journals, was overwhelming as reported by the Lynds:

"The local morning newspaper distributes 8,851 copies to the 9,200 homes of the city, and the afternoon paper 6,715, plus at least half of the additional 785 sold on street and news stand. The out-of-town papers include an average of 800 copies of one paper from the state capital (Indianapolis) and 125 from another, eight copies of the New York *Times* (39 on Sunday), 170 copies of the Chicago *Tribune* (800 on Sunday), 63 Chicago *American*, 42 *Christian Science Monitor*, 60 Cincinnati *Enquirer* (240 on Sunday), one New York *World*, fourteen Detroit *Free Press* (61 on Sunday), four Cleveland *News-Leader* (21 on Sunday)."[19]

If you would total up the figures gathered by the Lynds, the local paper wins the circulation battle 16,351 to something less than 1,500 for the big city press. The count was taken in 1924.[20]

Actually there never was much of a void for the metropolitan press to move into since even the smallest town newspapers in their patent insides pages offered the same basic general interest features of big city journalism: national and international affairs, fashions, literature and the arts.

FORMING A NATIONAL CHARACTER
WITH TORRENTS OF WORDS

Widespread was the use of ready-print and its cousin boilerplate (the "national newspaper"). It was reported that George Joslyn, owner of the Western Newspaper Union, the monopoly ready-print supply house, made $175 million (in 1988 dollars) by the time of his death in 1916.[21] It was quite a brisk business for his company, a "semi-cooperative" of participating small town newspapers. Ninety five percent of the town newspapers used one or both of the services. This amount of ready-print business translates into considerable influence--financially, politically and culturally, and it also says something about the cultural homogenizing that existed in America.

Culturally, there are many examples of the prevalence of America's tendency to display sameness, even today: An example would be the national political parties—there are consistently only two of importance, the Republican and the Democrat. These two are dominated by centrists who think, act and look alike and work closely together behind the scenes.

Writer Walter J. Ong, wrote: "No one who knows only American culture knows very much about American culture." For this reason research on the American character owes much to foreign observers like the Irish James Bryce, France's Alexis de Tocqueville, the Swedish Gunnar Myrdal, the English Alastair Cooke, Scotland's Dennis Brogan and the Brazilian Vianna Moog. These analysts have noted that Americans are surprisingly alike in values and appearance, notwithstanding the great size of the country and the existence of its many farflung, remote areas.

Unlike China, the Soviet Union, Nigeria, Britain, France and many other countries, internal cultural differences in the U.S. are at a minimum—with the exception, depending on your definition of cultural limits, of southerners. But North or South, East or West what one notes in the United States is a sameness that quickly and efficiently changes immigrants to its ways, usually within two generations.

The American stands out in sharp contrast in a group, believed Carlos Oliveira, the author's chauffeur in southern Brazil in the 1970s. He could always point out the American, even in the huge São Paulo airport packed with similarly-dressed, affluent travelers. Carlos had been able to perform this trick all of his long life in his job with the United States consulate in that South American country. Americans at the consulate were occasionally embarrassed by letting an arriving U.S. notable, assigned to them for the duration of their visit, slip by them in the airport crowd. Like the proverbial searchers in a haystack, Carlos had the assignment to find the American ("North" American, he called them) lost in that crowd—and he always did.[22]

Novelists and social scientists sometimes capture the essence of the conformity of Americans. We have evidence that Americans in an earlier time objected to the straightjacket of sameness. Novelist Louis Bromfield, in *The Farm* wrote of the change in American culture which he indicated occurred in the latter part of the 19th century and early twentieth century. The change caught up with many people who had lived in the earlier time, and were "passing from the day when people were encouraged to be individuals into a day when eccentricity of character and even independence of opinion aroused distrust and resentment."[23]

Conformity extended also into matters of dress, manners, writing and speech. When faced with the anxiety and guilt-ridden post-Civil War political climate, ready-print newspapers and, to a much lesser degree, magazines and books, distributed the national guidance and reassurance needed by a United States of America forcibly united by military action. Many journalists came from the training ground offered by country newspapers. They played their part in forming this new post-War country as they moved from their heartland surroundings to the big cities.

American historians have generally downplayed the journalist's role in the creation of their country. However, an exception was Page Smith who wrote about the flood of trained, country journalists arriving in the big eastern cities and joining the staffs of magazines and newspapers.

Smith stated: "It has been observed that the first generation of young exposé journalists and editors was, almost without exception from the Midwest and Far West, although the meaning of this has been less generally commented on....they signified the displacement of the New England literary establishment by a wholly new and fundamentally more 'American' type....They stood outside what we would call today the old-boy network....As outsiders they saw everything freshly."

In another passage in his book *The Rise of the Industrial America,* he attempted to nail down the reason for America's uniqueness:

"In traditional societies the information that its members need is conveyed by a complex network of cultural artifacts--by institutions, ceremonies, myths, folktales, and religious forms. American society was too diverse, unformed, chaotic, and above all, *new,* to have developed such agencies--other than the Constitution itself (a document, estimable as it was, that left untouched large areas of American life). The nation had, therefore, to develop or adapt and vastly alter agencies and methods for disseminating essential information at all levels of the society. Newspapers had performed this function from colonial days to a degree unprecedented in other societies. They had, to be sure, performed it on the whole badly, commonly in the spirit of partisan rancor that so disgusted Charles Dickens and other foreign visitors. But in a remarkable demonstration of the adaptation of popular institutions to democratic needs, they performed it superbly in the last decades of the old (nineteenth) century and the first decade of the new. Indeed, they did it so well that they created what was, in effect, a new form of expression (and protest)....

So one feels that the nation, ready at any instance to fly apart or simply to disintegrate into its disparate and warring elements, was held together, not by politics but by words, torrents and rivers and oceans of words, describing, explaining, and, in the last analysis, reconciling Americans to each other and to the United States of America."[24]

Social scientist Michael Schudson, on this same subject, wrote: "...the daily persuasions of journalists reflect and become our own."[25]

This was the era of the hidden newspaper. The ready-print and its partner boilerplate acted like cookie-cutters standardizing to an unknown degree much of the nation's character through the gatekeeper function, doling out selected news products to areas of America that had little else to read. As a cost-cutting device it proved its worth. It aided the establishment of America's free press system; for despite giving over to the Chicago publishers half of the available space in the local papers, there was still plenty of room on the other side to allow America's editors to experiment and to develop new methods of editorial writing, investigative reporting and government watch-dog journalism.

There were a limited number of ready-print companies (in 1912 the Western Newspaper Union published almost all of the nation's ready-print and the American Press Association produced most of the boilerplate--by 1917 W.N.U. took over both the boilerplate and ready-print). The impact of this national newspaper's immense circulation, by far the largest in the world, undoubtedly affected much of our national thinking and helped shape American values. Its consequences are worthy of study, consequences perhaps beyond estimate given the limited human science resources available to historical researchers.

Notes

1. As quoted in *Discovery Magazine,* Spring issue, 1988, p. 8.
2. The *New Republic,* April 11, 1923, p. 190.
3. New York *Tribune,* June 9, 1895, p. 26. Harper would start up the newspaper with the use of ready-print then after a year would sell it, making a tidy profit. Harper was one of those editors who could fit quickly into a new community, building a solid circulation, accrue good will and a good advertiser following, giving the paper a solid value.
4. "Building a Newspaper Par Excellence," *National Printer Journalist,* November, 1922, pp. 22-25.
5. Daniel Boorstin, *The Democratic Experience,* (New York: Random House, 1973) pp. 428-29.
6. In speaking of this Victorian era and not of today: one should not mistake this American habit of avoiding books in favor of newspapers as a sign of illiteracy. As Paulo Freire and Michael Schudson have pointed out, the apparently high literacy rate of Americans was linked to the freedoms they were seeking. This search for extensive civil rights may have contributed to America's reputation for having a higher literacy rate than the European nations.
7. Note chart giving number of newspapers in America (page 51).

8. Another form of income to newspapers has been the practice of charging a higher "political" advertising rate to candidates standing for election.

9. George Sherman, "The Frontier Weekly A Good Investment," *Inland Printer*, 1910, p. 755.

10. From copy of letter, dated October 26, 1910. In the author's collection.

11. Elmo Scott Watson, *A History of Newspaper Syndicates*, (Chicago: self published, 1936) p. 83.

12. Figures from N. W. Ayer.

13. See chart of number of newspapers.

14. The *National Printer-Journalist*, 1895, pp. 481-82.

15. In clipping of New York newspaper, undated (author's collection).

16. Burton Albee, The Influence of Country Newspapers, *Inland Printer*, August 1892, p. 595.

17. Hal Borland, *Country Editor's Boy* (New York: Lippincott, 1970) p. 227.

18. Harold A. Innis, *The Bias of Communication* (Toronto, University of Toronto Press, 1951) p.171.

19. Lynds' *Middletown* (New York: Harcourt, Brace & Co., 1929) p. 471ff.

20. From 1962 to 1966 the author edited and published (I owned three-fourth's of the stock)a newspaper in Taylor County, Kentucky with a paid circulation of 7,800, largest of any county seat weekly in the state. We had 12 employees. The two largest nearby cities to our county, Louisville and Lexington, Kentucky, had sales of less than one thousand in our county.

21. Paul A. Samuelson, *Economics -- Tenth Edition* (New York: McGraw-Hill Company, 1976) p. 271.

22. Carlos was the author's friend and chauffeur while the author was consul in Brazil from 1971 to 1973.

23. Louis Bromfield, *The Farm* (New York: Harper & Bros. 1946) p. 301.

24. Page Smith, *The Rise of Industrial America* (New York: McGraw-Hill Company, 1984) p. 403.

25. Michael Schudson, *Discovering the News* (New York: Basic Books, Inc. 1978) p.194.

Chapter Four
Westward the Ready-print Trail

> In the landrush West, two especial outfits can always be found near the head of the procession---one a wagon loaded with whiskey bottles and glasses, the other a similar vehicle freighted with a handpress, cases of type and the necessary paraphernalia for publishing a small newspaper.
>
> — The *Journalist Magazine,* 1887

FLUSHING GOVERNMENT OUT INTO THE OPEN

The American free press system has been an accident linked more to the economic system than to the Constitution. Profit margins for small newspapers went up dramatically with the institution of the pre-printed sheet, and the number of newspapers grew as well.

The American Free Press System lives a day at a time---fighting off the powerseekers trying to control or manipulate it. The value of the free press is not always understood, or sufficiently valued, by the American electorate that gains so much from it.

Press freedom in America was brought into being by the weight of numbers---the momentum of thousands of newly-created small town news publications---separate and independent voices, grass roots newspapers. With the power of the word, masses of editors flushed political office holders and office seekers out into the open.[1]

Because of their enormous numbers in that Victorian era, newspapers and other forms of the media in America operated generally unmolested; despite sedition and criminal libel laws that have lurked menacingly. Turn of the century America had as many newspapers as the rest of the world combined. Government allowed the press to move about quite freely, avoiding stirring up the beast. Politicians gave grudging respect, influenced by the sight of those thousands of individually owned journals.

Historian Daniel J. Boorstin did not discover the reason for their vast number, but understood its significance. He wrote:

> "Diffusion of the press was a deep-rooted institution of the new world.... The local variety and wide dispersion of the American newspaper press made it extraordinarily difficult for any government to control or restrain it. While the history of the press in England and on the continent is a chronicle of stamp taxes, censorship, government control, and only partial and gradual liberation from them—and there the laws of libel have long inhibited free expression in print—the American newspaper press has had a degree of freedom bordering on anarchy. Elsewhere too, in countries with fewer and more centralized newspapers, circulation of newspapers outside the capitals was far more dependent on the rise of a postal system; hence papers were more easily controlled by the government's control of the post office. But who could muzzle a newspaper press that was diffused into every corner of a vast continent?"[2]

MOST AMERICANS LIVED
IN RURAL AREAS PRIOR TO 1930

It is the nature of cities to draw an inordinate amount of noisy electric attention to themselves. In this period of history the few big cities in America were no exception. The metropolitan areas of that time housed the smaller part of the nation's population.

America had long been an agricultural country, populated by farmers and those who supplied their needs. Not until the 1930s did urban dwellers begin to outnumber their country and town cousins.[3] Back in 1787 Benjamin Franklin stated: "The business of the continent is agriculture. For one artizan, or merchant, I suppose we have at least a hundred farmers.[4]

James Bryce, in studying the organs of American public opinion in the 1880s, wrote that the cities of America had less influence than the countryside in that period, in contrast with Europe. He noted how scattered and agricultural was the American populace, in contrast to his own Britain, for example. He wrote: "In England and Wales over half

AMERICA - MAINLY SMALL TOWNS AND FARMS UNTIL 1930
Population from Census Data

Year	* Urban	Rural
1850	2,897,586	20,294,290
1860	5,072,256	26,371,065
1870	8,071,875	30,486,496
1880	11,790,085	38,790,000
1890	18,244,239	44,703,475
1900	25,976,240	50,900,000
1910	35,570,334	56,401,932
1920	46,307,640	59,402,980
1930	60,333,452	62,441,594

*Population in cities of 8,000 or more inhabitants

of the population was in 1911 in 60 cities each with a population exceeding 50,000. In France opinion is mainly produced in, and policy, except upon a few of the broadest issues dictated, by the urban population, though its number falls much below that of the rural. In America the cities with a population exceeding 50,000 inhabitants were in 1910 one hundred and nine with an aggregate population of about 24,500,000, little more than 25 percent of the total population. The number of persons to the square mile was in 1911 618 in England and Wales, and was in the continental United States (1910), 30.9."[5]

In the three decades or so after the U.S. Civil War more land was settled than ever before in the history of the continent. It gave people a propertied stake in society. Thousands of communities sprang up to serve these farmers and ranchers, who headed west and each town, along with church, school and other institutions, granted itself at least one newspaper, and more likely two or three.

Though there was no central planning, across the country the pattern was similar. The small town was America's norm, with groups of tiny communities clustered among the farms --- satellites about a larger (1,000-population, more or less) business center "to which they looked for markets and supplies, credit and news", wrote Robert Weibe.[6]

The influence of the agricultural West and midwest continued even as the people moved to the cities. The farms mechanized at a rapid rate creating more industry in the manufacturing East. The farmers of Iowa, alone, in 1920, had a larger investment in machinery than the farmers of New England and the Middle Atlantic states added together.[7]

The Civil War was over. The grass roots newspapers sprouted willy-nilly; as America righted itself. Politics and change were in the air. There was "reconstruction" in the South, pioneering in the west, industrializing in the north and immigrants arriving from the east—and everybody wanted to read about it.

Town newspaper influence rose as their fact-filled pages informed, challenged and entertained the readers. In the average home in the rural sections, books were considered a luxury; out of reach. A visitor in the tiny parlor would probably find only a leather-bound Bible, a medical self-help manual, an English novel and a scrapbook; and not until more efficient postal routes were developed early in the twentieth century were magazines to become numerous in American households. Not books, magazines, or city journals, but village newspapers monopolized the reading habits of most Americans. By 1915, over 22,000 journals had been founded—dailies, semi-weekly, tri-weekly and weeklies. They displayed in their ready-print and boilerplate a literate and varied output.

Aside from conforming to a few Post Office regulations, the legal requirements for becoming a publisher have been minimal in the USA. Freed from the need for federal or state licensing, the would-be editor merely carted his equipment and paper into a chosen community, sometimes at the invitation of its leaders, but more frequently on his own initiative.

Newspapers were eagerly sought by pioneering villages. Solicitations were made and qualified prospects interviewed. The New York *Tribune* ran an article about newspaper-building in the West which contained a letter by a man from a manufacturing village. The letter stated: "We have a store, a church, a hotel and a schoolhouse. The store has a big stock of goods, from garden seed to silk dresses; the hotel is a good one, with everything to attract the drummer or the tourist; the school is the best for miles around and our church is the pride of the place. What we want now is a newspaper."

The paper reported that the call was answered by a young man who had learned the printer's trade and who impressed his friends with so much confidence that they aided him in fitting up a printing shop in the little place, from which *The Weekly News* was to be formed...with visions of steam presses, typesetting machines, a large circulation and a journalistic reputation, the village paper was launched. [8]

INSTANT CITIES

Many of the the midwest states aggressively undertook to increase their populations in the era following the Civil War. Wisconsin, for example, described itself as healthy, wooded, watered and progressive. It promised a living and a voice in government to all who would migrate there and join in the experience of frontier living.

Railroad companies joined in the nation-building effort. One railroad operating in North Dakota, Montana and Minnesota offered free town lots to newspaper publishers, blacksmiths and others who would agree to go into business in the new towns.[9]

Competition demanded the compression of time. Towns and cities had to appear quickly to draw the immigrant and the restless masses in the East. Promoters utilized ready-print to drum up customers for their land. Deception and shady deals abounded. In the developing West where towns and cities seemed to spring up overnight, the "false-front" was almost a way of life. Residents, recently arrived and still strangers to one another, made much of surface appearance. Business buildings often used the device of stage set designers, erecting thin false front walls, making the structure look much larger than it really was. From the outside at ground level one could not detect the deception.

The "false front" newspaper, too, prevailed---using ready-made ready-print to fatten up a newspaper that covered news in communities that barely existed. Ready-print also disguised financially shaky publishing enterprises. It added heft to political party organs, whose management had little interest in looking for news, but were intent on staking out a political position of power.

Two perceptive historians, George Bird and Frederick Merwin, took note of the role of ready-print in this deceptive ambience in their 1942 work *The Newspaper and Society*. This example tells about the "cities" that were mirages, springing up overnight, mostly composed of tents and a ready-print newspaper:

> ... 'Boom towns' built along the route of proposed railroads, on land owned by these companies, dotted the map. Local pride in these communities demanded that they have newspapers to cater to the optimistic belief of their citizens that their mushroom

village would grow into a metropolis. So, one of its first business establishments was invariably a newspaper office. Sometimes this office was only a tent pitched along the main street which wandered crookedly through the collection of 'soddies', log huts, or one-story frame 'false-fronts.'

In this canvas shelter the adventuring editor, equipped with an old Army or a George Washington press and the traditional 'shirt-tail full of type' began operations as an exponent of frontier journalism. If the final railroad surveys revealed the fact that this future metropolis would not be on its route, 'ye ed' like the other businessmen, loaded his equipment in a wagon and drove away to the new town site along the railroad right-of-way.

To such pioneering and peripatetic journalism, the ready-print was an invaluable aid, and it was a life saver to many publishers, struggling under the handicap of inadequate equipment and an uncertain future. If the publisher had had to depend upon local news and advertisements to fill his paper it would have been little more than a two-page handbill. But with two, four, six and eight-page ready-prints available, he could get out a newspaper whose size suggested that it was published in a flourishing little city.[10]

Speculators jumped in to sell land in many of these make-believe communities, made to appear real by the presence of an imposing ready-print newspaper. Travelers across the United States sometimes stumble upon the evidence of these shadow cities. Many of them simply disappeared off the map, and now consist merely of a dusty general store with a gas pump out front. Others are now mere names for empty fields.

Lord Bryce in the 1880s wrote about the frantic promotion of American towns and would-be towns in this way: "Many a place has lived upon its 'boom' until it found something more solid to live on; and to a stranger who asks in a far western town how such a city could keep up four newspapers, it was well answered that it took four newspapers to keep up such a city."[11]

HISTORIANS HAVE NOT KNOWN THE SOURCE

Historians, broad brush generalists in the main, now use newspapers as an important research source. But those lacking knowlege of printing mechanics, or editing of the grass roots press, operate at a disadvantage. They frequently cannot tell the difference between local and national-source news copy. This could skew the findings of any serious survey of the Western Migration, in tracing the character and knowledge of the pioneer subjects of the survey. Not knowing the real source of the articles they were reading, they usually assumed that the material they saw was written, or at least edited, by the local paper.

As an example, historian Michael Lesy, in his book *Wisconsin Death Trip* analyzed the content of town newspapers and noted the flow of news dispatches from distant places like Cuba and St. Petersburg. Lesy incorrectly identified the source of the news as coming from state and national wire services. The wire services were available but seldom used by the town press which had its own ready-print and boilerplate; the actual suppliers of the foreign news.[12]

In his book *Whoop-Up Country,* historian Paul Sharp, (Univ. of Minn. Press), writing of Minnesota newspapers in the 1870-80 era, states that "newspapers played an important part in the transfer of culture to the frontier. The catholicity of interests and universality of coverage provided for readers a fund of information...brought stories from the far corners of the earth to frontier America. Essays on moral philosophy, aboriginal life in South America, or court life in Europe were paramount, though they were sometimes pirated from eastern journals without credit...Benton, Minnesota's newspapers were a vital link to the outside world and were cherished the more for Benton's relative isolation from the national scene."[13]

The editors of Benton's papers were not in a position to research news "pirated from eastern journals without credit," as this historian states. The editors merely placed an order for ready-print, with its pages printed on one side, to impress local readers and inform them on the happenings in far-away places. Because the typeface was similar, local readers (and modern historians) were fooled into thinking that the stories and advertisements were set locally.

Lewis Atherton of the University of Missouri stated in his book *Main Street on the Middle Border,* (in writing about the 1870s) that small town storekeepers used "heavy advertising twice a year with advertisements remaining unchanged for long periods." Atherton based some of his historical assumptions on this, but was not aware that changes in the advertising frequently had to be made in far-off Chicago, not in the town paper's own back shop. It was impossible to change copy quickly from one week to another since a re-setting of the type had to be made and the town and Chicago were far apart. As a consequence most storekeepers advertised only on the "home-print" side, which was set locally.

"Not putting on airs", is a frequently heard phrase indicative of the remarkably characteristic and consistent American cultural value that influences many mainstream sectors of national life from politics to ways of dress. In seeking a cultural link to the American character, historian Daniel Boorstin cited Mathew Arnold's statement in 1888: "Everything is against distinction in America," and the small, one column advertising that prevailed in the Victorian era seemed to rise out of this innate subconscious shyness—in Boorstin's interpretation.

This seemed an important finding about the American character. But Boorstin was the victim of technical misinformation in the mechanics of printing. In his study of the development of American advertising he links the newspapers' use of column rules (those thin horizontal lines that separate the columns) and small advertisements of the time to the American's cultural habit of avoiding the limelight (not putting on airs).[14] But this was incorrect. Americans were not instinctively shy about their accomplishments for the reason he gives. The smallness of the advertisements was due to the design of the printing presses. Well into the 1880s newspapers printed directly onto the loose type that was squeezed and locked together into "forms," and placed on the press.

The column rules (long metal thin pieces that stretched from the top to the bottom of the type page) held the tiny loose type together. Later, when one-piece, stereotype (same printing method as boilerplate) metal printing plates were employed, larger ads without the supporting column rules were able to be used.

Historian-educator Frank Luther Mott was technically trained in the country press. He explained this in his basic Journalism textbook; noting that the breaking of column rules for double-column cuts and advertisements was made possible by the introduction of stereotype forms. He pointed out that the older Hoe type-revolving presses required the full-length column rules to hold the type pieces to the curved surface of the cylinder—the metal cast system did not.[15]

CITY AND TOWN JOURNALS BECOME COMPETITORS

Country editors have always been pleased by Ralph Waldo Emerson's saying: "The near facts are the great ones." The big-city press was taught this lesson in its circulation combat with the country press until early in the twentieth century, trapped in their cities by the lack of the Rural Free Delivery system, the metropolitan dailies could only sit back and watch the little country papers (with their ready-print and boilerplate sections) pick up all of the rural subscribers; limiting the giant papers to circulations extending only a few miles from the city limits.

One writer reported: "As for news, one newspaperman who knew rural America in the 1880's and 1890's very well, estimated that not one farmer in 300 took a daily newspaper in the 1890's, and he could not have been far wrong." Only farmers who lived close enough to a post office to get their mail every day could take full advantage of a daily.

Otherwise, daily papers came a "sackful at a time," as one pioneer Nebraska woman once remarked, and under the circumstances it was more sensible to take a county weekly than a daily that arrived weekly.[16]

The big dailies saw the ready-print in the town press as a minor hindrance to their own plans to sell their papers in the outlands. But almost overnight the city dailies found themselves surrounded by little newspapers in the suburban and nearby villages that featured up-to-date news from the state, nation and world. These smaller papers, most of them weeklies, became less picturesque, less folkloric, and more sophisticated—carrying features that even the big dailies did not have---like segments of famous novels and pictorial displays of news events.[17]

This news mix was just fine with small towners and farmers. The big city press, knowing that the bulk of America seemed to nest just out of their reach, always had ambitions to annex the readership in the countryside, and tried to publish weekly editions designed for that purpose. But most attempts met with little success. With the exception of the towns lying directly on the railroad right-of-ways, speedy delivery of the dailies to the farms was impossible prior to 1900.

The special city weekly editions, much balihooed by the city press, was designed for the towns and farms sometimes as much as 75 miles away. But they failed to reach the farmers prior to R.F.D.'s beginnings in the early twentieth century.

Geared for battle, the ready-print increased local coverage in the country newspapers to beat off the challenge from the city press. Soon thereafter, a survey by the trade press entitled "Effect of Metropolitan Dailies and Weeklies on the Circulation of Interior Dailies and Weeklies" showed that at the turn of the century, the big city press had been kept out of the countryside. Ninety percent of the towns surveyed indicated that the big papers were not selling well in rural areas. One of the surveyed town editors (Patchogue, N.Y. *Advance*) included this comment with his survey form: "A small percent of a rather ignorant class of people will read the cheap evening daily and ignore the local weekly...." Another (Ovid, N.Y. *Independent*) stated, "My paper is not affected at all as I can see, although several large dailies circulate here. I try to give a local flavor to every item...."[18]

There was one occasion when the low-lying, concealed-from-view, ready-print was discussed openly on the pages of northern Ohio's newspapers. The subject of ready-print was forced into the open by the competition between city and town newspapers. The arrival of ready-print and boilerplate had not gone unnoticed by the metropolitan newspapers; and the Western Newspaper Union, always one to see a commercial advantage, fanned the flames of the conflict, running ads telling the weeklies that their ready-print service "makes possible a 'real' publication that will command the interest of all readers in the community, and stop the inroads that papers from the larger cities are making in every local field."

One of the first big papers to note in public the competition of the well read ready-print country press was the Cleveland *Herald*. It bothered the *Herald* that ready-print newspapers disturbed the political status quo.

Looking down its nose at the small weekly papers, it declared that rural journalism was deteriorating and blamed the ready-print. The self serving editorial added:

> The patent insides and patent outsides have damaged (the rural press) seriously by coaxing into feeble life a host of little rivals published in the smaller towns. Formerly in counties like Lake, Geauga, Portage, Summit and Trumbull there were but two papers—one of each party and sometimes a minority party failed to sustain an organ. Now, the small cost of issuing a paper on a "patent inside" or "outside" has encouraged the starting of new sheets at almost every petty village. Of course, they divide the total business of the county and draw away a part of the support of the older and larger journals...They are a tax to the communities where they are published, but they gratify local pride...They cut down expenses, discharge local editors, get discouraged and relax that eternal vigilance which is the price of a good newspaper."[19]

The attack by the Cleveland *Herald* caused the local weeklies (those hamlets close enough to the big Cleveland dailies to be competing with them) to be drawn into an open, public discussion of the traditionally hushed-up ready-print. Several of the country editors responded. A town weekly, the Ravenna (Ohio) *Republican Democrat,* defended ready-print, saying: "...but for the co-operative (ready-print) plan of publishing, the city weeklies would nearly, if not quite, root out the country weeklies."[20]

Another weekly, the Geauga (Ohio) *Republican* also responded with an editorial: "...The time has gone by when...people would support the country paper merely for a sense of duty. It must be made self-sustaining by meeting the popular demand or it will languish...What the country weeklies need is a plan whereby, while maintaining its own special features, it can combine with these enough of the essentials of a general newspaper to enable it most successfully to bear the competition of the city press. And this end is answered in the 'patent insides and outsides, now so common.'"

The little weekly went on to attack the dailies for also looking alike: "If it be objected that it is alike in all co-operative papers, as much may be said of the same departments of the *Herald* and *Leader* and all other city papers that keep up with the times."

The counter-charge that the big dailies also were looking alike had validity, as the practice of putting syndicated, wire service and the same boilerplate news throughout their issues, took hold in the big city press. W.N.U., Kellogg and other syndicaters offered boilerplated news to both dailies and weeklies, but the bulk of their trade (and their bias) was with the rural press.

Well to the west of Ohio the countryside was less populated and the town and city did not compete. In 1900 in Yampa, Colorado the publisher of the *Leader* strove to fill his paper with fresh news. Basking in the glow of having run the entire State of the Union address of President Taft only three days after the speech was delivered, he philosophized in print about the ready-print services he was using: "The country newspaper which does not use this auxiliary service must either entirely ignore the news of the outside world, or it must be content with an inadequate reference to it, and in exact proportion with the amount of space given to matters outside of its own community must the home news be neglected. The *Leader* has always believed that its duty to its readers demanded the use of the auxiliary pages, as it is thus able to give those of its subscribers who do not have a city daily a complete summary of the news of the state and the nation, and the energies of the (local paper) office forces are left free to cover the happenings of Yampa and vicinity and of Routt county as they deserve."

THE COMING OF THE RURAL FREE DELIVERY SYSTEM

Prior to the turn-of-the-Century the bad roads, long distances and limited postal service isolated the big metropolitan newspapers from potential country subscribers. In a speech to the New York Press Association in 1873, Henry Ward Beecher stated that he noticed that the country papers were growing in power, in spite of city journalism.[21]

The Rural Free Delivery, in place by 1910, was widely hailed at the time as the factor that would kill off the small town press. It meant that mail would be directly delivered to the farm, rather than only to the town post office. R.F.D. was a boon to the big city press, but despite the flood of outside reading matter that began to arrive directly to the farm homes, the weeklies held their own. They countered by rejecting yellow, sensationalist journalism and emphasizing local news, and, thus, kept the majority of the town and country readership.

The grass roots journals, well established, were held almost in reverence in most towns for they had the kindly, local news about friends, relatives and neighbors. Circulations held steady and even grew. Local vital statistics: births, deaths, weddings and community events increased in volume on its pages.

Newspapers have always been more than just bearers of news. Their psychological component is an adjunct to some form of human clock. Somehow, gripping in one's hand a newspaper brought psychic rewards of knowing that life existed on a vaster scale than immediately apparent; of belonging to a "community." Rural America in those Victorian days looked forward to Thursdays, going to the town post office to pick up their papers that still smelled of ink. A glance at the pages reassured them that the world was still in working order. They could face another week knowing that in their lives, and that of their neighbors, all was well; and most disasters seemed to occurr far away. Ready-print always reported distant disasters like ship sinkings and earthquakes in great detail.

The enemy of the farmer was isolation. Malcolm Willey stated that the Rural Free Delivery was an important step in a series of innovations which were to result within a few decades in the breakdown of the rural isolation which had persisted from the colonial period.[22]

The isolation was overwhelming. Harlan Douglas described the agriculturist in this fashion: "The farmer breakfasts with no evidence of neighbors but the distant crowing of cocks and baying of dogs. His family separates silently to its tasks, themselves often remote from one another. Possibly two men and teams may be working in the same field, but commonly beyond the range of conversation. For other human society there is just a chance that the neighboring farmer will be plowing or cultivating across the fence, or that one will reach the end of the corn row at the highway while a team is passing. But day may come and go—and many days do—without essential break in the family isolation of the farm home and its laboring group."[23]

Supporters of the Rural Free Delivery system believed that the more efficient method of delivering the mail would end the emigration of farmers into the city. They hailed the system, believing that it would end the isolation of farm life.

Instead, R.F.D. meant exposure to the lure of city lights as many a farmer became deluged with the propaganda from the labor-seeking industrial cities. The cities seemed to offer a more secure financial future, away from crop failures and unstable crop prices.

Rural Free Delivery
(From Annual Reports of the Postmaster General)

Year	Number of Routes	Mileage of the Routes
1900	1,214	29,000
1905	32,055	721,000
1910	41,079	993,000
1915	43,877	1,076,000
1920	43,445	1,152,000
1925	45,189	1,223,000
1930	43,278	1,335,000

As the chart shows, the R.F.D. system was eagerly adopted across the country, allowing city newspapers and magazines easier access to farmers. In essence, the Rural Free Delivery System was the direct delivery of mail to the farms, instead of the prior system of having the farmer come to town for his mail, he could now pick it up at his mail box on the road in front of his farm. The change for the farmer was dramatic, and the Post Office department was deluged with letters thanking them for this new development.[24]

Even happier were the magazine publishers and big city press, long frustrated in their attempts to reach out beyond city limits. Cyrus H.K. Curtis bought the nearly defunct magazine the *Saturday Evening Post* with its circulation of 2,000 readers for only $1,000 in 1897. Aided by the services of the R.F.D. the publication rose in circulation to one million in ten years, eventually rising to three million.

As America became more centralized into their cities and the amount of mail from the big-city presses began to be delivered directly into farmer's homes, a change in attitudes and buying habits occurred (Sears and Roebuck's mail order company substantially increased its business of catalog selling with the advent of R.F.D).

Farmers had long pleaded for free delivery directly to the farm, and it began in earnest in 1898, after a slow start. Some have called the coming of the R.F.D. as the most influential communications development in the country's history.

It might be concluded that the heyday of the rural press and ready-print came to an end with this new mail service as the R.F.D. began its slow incursion into rural newspaper readership.

Ready-print responded to the challenge and upgraded its service. The quality of ready-print output was equal in most respects to the big city press, and farmers were not easily convinced that a "foreign" city paper carrying the same news (though in a more nervous, splashier form) would benefit their lives. From 1898 until approximately 1925, with the birth of radio, rural readers continued to shun the metropolitan press.

R.F.D. brought on the closing of thousands of the smaller post offices around the country. It caused the failure of many town businesses such as the general stores because postal business was usually conducted at that establishment. This downturn of business in the smaller villages (usually those of populations of 400 or less) caused many newspapers to go under, or to consolidate with a competitor.

Isolation offered quiet times for reading. Wilderness America was populated by readers---but to read you first had to learn to spell. Edward Eggleston in his novel *The Hoosier Schoolmaster* tells about the community "spelling matches," a part of every heartland town. "Spelling is the national game in Hoopole County. Baseball and

croquet matches are as unknown as olympian chariot-races. Spelling and (corn) shucking are the only public competitions."
Eggleston also told about the emphasis on spelling in school, as well. He said "It seemed that the chief end of man was to learn to spell."[25]

THE NEWSPAPER FAMILY OF 100 YEARS AGO

Here in America in the late twentieth century—the era of the selfish "me" generation and foggy Freudian theorizing—the family structure has undergone a severe battering. Surviving families are now viewed almost like museum pieces. The family social group is debated in church, academia and, grotesquely, in the bitter cold wars between the U.S. political right and left. However, in the U. S. town and farm environment of fifty-to-100 years ago things were quite different. Families were large and babies and children were more warmly welcomed and better cared for, even though they appeared at unscheduled times as though heaven sent.

One of the charming, nostalgic, cultural aspects of American town journalism has been the existence of the family newspapers—still called "man-and-wife" operations in the trade. Like the homesteading family farm, the family newspaper was something of value---with little experience required.

Family newspapers became part of the structure of grassroots journalism, giving continuity to these journals as they were passed from parents to children, then on to the grandchildren. Hundreds of them existed then, and a few still do, even after the death of ready-print. Looking through the record of old trade newspapers, the researcher can see many want ads headed: "FOR SALE: 'Man-Wife' Weekly Newspaper," "man-wife operation," "just right for family couple," etc.

In these operations the husband and wife, a team, shared the writing, advertisement-selling and printing production load. Family members alone (with the possible exception of a "hired hand" or two) manned the paper. If the couple had children, they would be brought in on Thursday press day to augment the staff, stuffing and addressing newspapers as fast as they arrived off the press and delivering to the homes and post office. It was hard work, but the adventure and shared experience bonded many families tightly together. Dorothy and I and our children gained much from this life in the 1950-60s.

Frank Luther Mott was a Pulitzer prize winner for American History in 1939 and one time the editor of the prominent literary magazine

Midland. He authored the basic textbook used in almost all of the journalism schools in America. He wrote about his own family's newspaper at the end of the nineteenth century. The equipment and techniques he describes are the same as the author used in most of my own newspapers, even though Mott's newspaper existed in the 1890s and mine in the 1950s and 1960s. He wrote:

> The newspaper press most commonly used was a flat-bed machine with a big tympan-bearing cylinder known as the Campbell....We printed only the front and back pages, buying the sheets already printed on the second and third pages from the Western Newspaper Union in DesMoines. These 'patent insides' were filled with miscellany suited to the small-town and rural audience, including farm and garden hints, a serial story, the Sunday school lesson, and a lot of advertising....The duties of my brother and I ranged from sweeping the floor and burning trash in the back yard to setting type and learning to feed the small jobber (press)....My Uncle Artie worked in Father's printing office for several years....My own mother, when her family was small, used to help fold papers on press-day. Some editors' wives worked so much in the office that they became practical printers, and occasionally one of these plants was operated entirely by the editor's family. But on any paper, the tensions of press-day were bound to affect all the editor's family, and everyone helped as he or she could---with the news, the mechanical work, the folding, wrapping, and mailing, and the final carting of the papers to the post office.[26]

These family operations were numerous and no doubt the family structure influenced the editorial content of town newspapers. Typically, mother, after finishing the supper dishes, sent out the bills or wrote the happy social columns detailing intimately the Belgian lace inserts in the bodice of that week's wedding gowns. But quite often, mother also led the editorial fight for Prohibition and Women's Suffrage, writing stinging editorials.

Father handled the crime, political news and the other local editorials that so frequently incensed the pols down at the courthouse. Sometimes these roles were reversed.

The Country Printer's Publication Day
(From the 1890 *Inland Printer* magazine)

IN THE WAKE OF *THE CLIPPER*

Nestled one thousand miles from the sea, in inland Indiana's corn-growing DeKalb county, is the Garrett *Clipper*. The paper took its name from the fast sailing ships that brought news to America from around the world. The name "Clipper" was more appropriate in 1885, the date of its founding, but with the death of ready-print, only local news was now carried in its columns.

Despite the long time span it was remarkable how much *The Clipper* and Mott's 1890 country paper were alike. The floor layout of American country journalism had been ritualized. The *Clipper's* floor design was almost exactly the same as thousands of other country newspapers at that time. Looking like a giant spider with its front feet in the air, the same Country Campbell press dominated the room. It rested on the rough, tobacco juice and ink-stained pine floor. The type job cases, paper cutter and printing stones, the job-printing presses---even the office safe---were grouped in 1890 fashion.

It was, in a way, a family-operated newspaper during the 1953-1956 years that I apprenticed there. The publisher's wife, father-in-law, and children would on occasion help out with the proof reading, folding and other tasks around the premises.

The publisher-editor, the advertising manager-assistant editor (this author) and the society news writer sat up front in the office portion. Everyone worked in the plant on press day, ink smudged along with the printers---folding papers, putting type into the page forms, stamping the addresses on the mailing copies and correcting trays of metal type.

The 90 year old Country Campbell press (bought used) would turn balky at times, throwing inked sheets of paper all about, especially during winter days when static electricity hung like a ghost in the air. The printers would solve the problem by pouring buckets of water over the floor (and our feet) to moisten the air. It was cold, it was dirty, it was wet---but it was wonderful, for we were the free press, the newspaper of our town!

In 1955, our owner-editor-publisher bought a window air conditioner (replacing the cake of ice and electric fan arrangement used to cool the plant in summer). He redecorated the front office walls with brown squares of plastic, in the latest fashion. New, modern, departmentalized metal desks, with drawers that slid easily, replaced the old ones. However, nothing changed in the plant; and the two line casting machines continued to clank on, giving off large amounts of smoke and heat, more than matching the air conditioner.

That year the paper also celebrated its 70th anniversary, putting on airs by issuing a special edition. In it, *The Clipper*, told its readers that it was the "mirror of community life," and had "not missed a single edition since it was founded in 1885."

The paper also reminded the readers of its motto: "READ BY MORE GARRETT PEOPLE THAN ANY PUBLICATION IN THE WORLD," the motto had been used for many years, even when four of the paper's eight pages were furnished by the Western Newspaper Union, out of

Chicago, through its Fort Wayne branch.

Long known as one of the best little papers in Indiana, it was minutely and skillfully proofread by the staff before issuance. With justifiable pride the 1955 article recounted the life of the newspaper and the community. It told about the conversion from a ready-print newspaper to an "all home-print" publication. The "all home-print" title was a misnomer, however, since the paper still used W.N.U. boilerplate. In addition, much of the rest of the type was from elsewhere as *The Clipper* also bought (at five cents an inch) much pre-set county news left over from the press run of the nearby county seat daily paper in Auburn.

The town of Garrett was founded in 1875 and had a population of about 4,500, remaining about that size through the years. It was serviced by several papers, but all failed in head-to-head competition with the solid, line casting machine-equipped, *Clipper.* The others, a passing parade, were also ready-print newspapers and were called *The News, The Herald, The Headlight, The Public Press,* and *The Daily Press.* The demise of the last competitor *(The Daily Press)* in 1911, coincided with the arrival of the *Clipper's* Linotype machine and the giaving up of hand composition.

According to the article in the 70th Anniversary issue, no serious competition was experienced after that time by the newspaper.[27]

Notes

1. For an account of the history of the free press read Leonard W. Levy, *Emergence of a Free Press* (New York: Oxford University Press 1985).
2. Daniel J. Boorstin, *The Americans,* the National Experience (New York: Random House, 1973) pp. 133-34.
3. U. S. Census Bureau figures.
4. "Comfort for America..." by B. Franklin, *American Museum,* Vol.1, (January, 1787), p. 6.
5. James Bryce, *The American Commonwealth,* (New York: 1891), Vol. II, p. 283
6. Robert H. Wiebe, *The Search for Order* 1877-1920 (New York: 1967) p.2.

7. Commager, Nevins, *Short History of the United States* (New York: Knopf, 1966) p. 361.
8. "The Work of the Genuine Newspaper," *National Printer-Journalist,* Jan. 1897, pp. 22-24.
9. Lewis Atherton, *Main Street on the Middle Border* (Bloomington: Indiana Univ. Press, 1954) p. 7.
10. Geo. Bird and Frederick Merwin, *The Newspaper and Society,* (New York: Prentice Hall, 1942) pp. 185-86.
11. Bryce, op. cit., p.703
12. Michael Lesy, *Wisconsin Death Trip.* From the years 1890-1910 Charles Van Schaick, the photographer featured in this book took over 30,000 photographs of pioneer life and the citizens of that area---a marvelous source of material for researchers.
13. Paul Sharp, *Whoop Up Country* (Minneapolis: Univ. of Minn. Press, 1964).
14. Daniel J. Boorstin, *The Democratic Experience* (New York: Random House, 1973) p.137.
15. Mott, *American Journalism,* 3rd Ed. (New York, MacMillan, 1962)p.401.
16. Wayne E. Fuller, *RFD, The Changing Face of Rural America* (Bloomington: Indiana Univ. Press, 1966) p. 291.
17. Elmo S. Watson, *History of Newspaper Syndicates,* (Chicago: self-published, 1936) p. 81.
18. *National Printer-Journalist* 1898, p.537.
19. Elmo S. Watson, op.sit., p. 81.
20. Ibid, p. 82.
21. From the proceedings of the New York Press Association *Fifty Year History,* F. A. Owen Pub. Co., Dansville, N.Y. 1873, author's collection.
22. Malcolm M. Willey, *The Country Newspaper* (Chapel Hill: Univ. of No. Carolina Press, 1926), p.108
23. Harlan Douglas, *The Little Town.*
24. "Rural Free Delivery", *National Printer-Journalist,* p. 214, author's collection.
25. Edward Eggleston, *The Hoosier School Master* (New York: Grosset & Dunlap, 1913) pp.54-55.
26. Frank Luther Mott, *Time Enough* (Chapel Hill: Univ. of No. Carolina Press 1963) pp. 56-61.
27. The Garrett (Ind.) *Clipper* newspaper, October 3, 1955, pp. 2-3.

The enemy of the farmer was isolation.

Chapter Five

Reverent Hands, the Other Ready-printers

> The small town newspaper's message is the sweet intimate story of life... If you could take the clay from your eyes and read the paper as it is written, you would find all of God's sorrowing, struggling, aspiring world in it, and what you saw would make you touch the little paper with reverent hands.
> — William Allen White

THE BRITISH REFUSED TO SACRIFICE INDIVIDUALITY

In a story datelined November 18, 1871 an American, London-based correspondent for the Chicago *Evening Journal* took offense at British comments about the American ready-print when the practice was revealed by the Chicago Fire: "Some of the London papers are making merry over the discovery that a large number of local newspapers were formerly furnished with their "outsides" by certain enterprising printers in Chicago, and describe in humorous language the dismay that must have ensued throughout Illinois, Iowa, Wisconsin and Minnesota when the Great Fire deprived them of this resource. I happen to know that the same thing has been, and is, still done in this country (England), only here it is the "insides" and not the "outsides" which the London contractors furnish to the country press.

"These "insides" are made up of the current general news of the day, cribbed editorials, tales, essays, poetry, etc., while the "outsides" are reserved for home advertisements, local news, etc. There is no harm in the system. On the contrary, the country people get a much better local newspaper than they could obtain in any other way.

The British were early users of ready-print and boilerplate, and were probably the inventors of the process. But they were not able to apply it successfully despite their efficient transportation system of established railroads, a necessity for getting the service quickly to the provincial papers.

One of the earliest attempts at selling the partly printed scheme to newspapers of limited capital and printing capacity took place in London in 1832. Alaric Watts applied it in an attempt to revive an unprofitable string of conservative newspapers which were under his management. He allowed word of his plan to become known, and earned criticism from contemporaries. One stated: "Watts is the head nurse in a hospital of rickety newspaperlings which breathe but to die."[1]

While it was used there 30 years before the Americans, the preprint idea never took root in the British Isles. There, distances were short between villages and the commercial and cultural center of London; and the Londoners had their national newspapers with its vast and loyal readership in the villages.

The British ready-prints sprang, historically, directly from the London dailies. With a large number of weeklies in the suburbs and in the provinces, many of the local papers supplemented their small local news output with news summaries and feature stories furnished on preprinted sheets and later in reproducible mat, boilerplate form furnished by agencies in London.

As Alexander Andrews wrote in *The History of British Journalism:* "A service was the one offered by Charles Knight's *Weekly Newspaper* (in 1851) which by the removal of the outer sheet and the substitution of another could be transformed from a London to a country paper. The internal sheets were to contain all the general news, so arranged that the country printer need only add a sheet outside with his local title, news and advertisements, to produce a first-class paper." Others in the British Isles to adapt Knight's idea successfully were John Cassell, Edward Spended, William Saunders and William Eglington. The *British Quarterly Review* of October 1880 credited Eglington with the invention of the process.

But the ready-print did not take hold. One British writer stated: "The idea did not secure general acceptance, most provincial newspapers deciding that the economy and convenience would not compensate for the sacrifice of individuality, and eventually the scheme faded out."[2]

Like their American cousins the British also favored hiding the source of the ready-print, preferring to give the impression that the news was written and edited by the local village editor.

So small the country, and so close was London to the provincial villages that several London journalists edited the village newspapers from their city offices. In his autobiography, William Jerdan, editor of London's *Literary Gazette* revealed that he edited several country journals, providing the non-local editorial features: probably the earliest recorded example of what is now known as syndication.

England has habitually kept a weather eye on its ex-colony, America. Harold Herd, noting the success of ready-print in the U.S. commented on Britain's inability to apply the process to their press system. He wrote: "The (British) experiment proved a failure; it was probably too early."

PATTERSON, WHO "NEVER PUT ON AIRS;" INFLUENCED AMERICANS FOR 62 YEARS

Shortly after the turn of the century the four major ready-print publications, together with their boilerplate business, were reduced through mergers to only one, the Western Newspaper Union. The entire editorial product was the responsibility of a single person Wright A. "Pat" Patterson.

Folksy, galluses-snapping "Pat" Patterson, was editor and columnist until ready-print went out of business in 1953. He died in 1954.

Patterson, "Mr. Country Editor", though somewhat humorless in his later years had the appearance of a Mark Twain. He was with the two companies for 62 years, influencing Americans with his unaccredited editing, articles and columns from the terms of Presidents Grover Cleveland until Dwight D. Eisenhower.[3]

He spanned the time from post-Civil War reconstruction until the era of the global Cold War, helping to form American perceptions and values, his words regularly read in their local papers by the majority of the population.

He was intelligent, though possessed of little formal education. Patterson was a product of the Western Migration, that national preoccupation. He exuded the character of the frontier villager, provincial to a fault---at the time when towns were still amid Indian problems and were composed of tents, sod huts, log buildings, and mud streets. Born in Kirksville, Missouri in 1870, son of a circuit riding Methodist minister, he was educated through the eighth grade. At sixteen, he dropped out of school to go to work.

He looked about for employment requiring little experience, and happened onto the country weekly field---then in the throes of tremendous expansion across the inland parts of America. He began as a printer at a weekly in Ainsworth, Iowa and after a short apprenticeship as typesetter and news writer he moved to two small dailies in Madison and Keokuk.

Patterson then became editor of a town paper at Farmington, Iowa; later moving to Montrose in the same capacity. In 1890, on a trip to Chicago to visit an aunt he dropped into the offices of the A.N. Kellogg Co., where his newspapers had been buying ready-prints. There he applied for a job and was hired on the editorial staff at a salary of $10 a week. Chicago was growing tremendously following the fire that gutted the city. Employment opportunities were high and he was also able to supplement his income with a part-time job on the *Inter-Ocean* daily newspaper. He worked his way up the ladder at Kellogg's. In 1904 at age 34, was named editor-in-chief.

PATTERSON SAVES COUNTRY EDITORS
FROM EMBARRASSMENT OF EXPOSURE

Early in his job Patterson came to the attention of the bosses by devising a fool-proof system to hide the ready-print more efficiently. The idea was to obscure the ready-print's identity and avoid occasions when papers in nearby villages would run the same pages on the same day.

The importance of hiding the ready-print was obviously on the minds of Patterson and the Chicago ready-printer as later, during an interview with *American* magazine, he boasted of this scheme as though it were one of his proudest achievements. The procedure called for news stories to be distributed and positioned on their ready-print pages in such a way that no two papers looked the same. After printing each paper's supply, the stories on the W.N.U. press were re-positioned for the next press run --- and the process was repeated on all following press runs. They were mostly the same stories, just in different areas on the pages. It was something like the parlor game "musical chairs" with the same stories mixed about so that they alighted on different portions of the page, with an occasional new story added to the mix. Patterson proudly describing it: "the service is so organized that papers in the same town, or nearby towns, never are embarrassed by both getting the same material."

Privately, in their in-house newspaper distributed to the country

An example of ready-print

editors, W.N.U. made much of their "system" of mixing the news pages so that area papers did not look much alike and they credited this improvement in their service for their ability to beat their few surviving competitors.[4]

As editor, Patterson was the news gatekeeper. He chose, edited and wrote much of what appeared, while WNU owner George Joslyn handled the business and financial side. Patterson handled the day-to-day operations. His name became a household word among country editors, though never with the general public. Pious, with a benign, honest countenance, he was invited into the inner circles of the country editor's journalist fraternity. He attended many state press associaton meetings and was elected president of the prestigious Chicago Press Club, which was founded by Mark Twain.

Joslyn, on the other hand, limited his membership to Chambers of Commerce and other business organizations.

The editor's *Publishers' Auxiliary* wrote about Patterson's influence in the country, saying: "He was the friend and confidant of many notables...his advice was heeded by officials in Washington, including Presidents Theodore Roosevelt, Woodrow Wilson, Calvin Coolidge and Herbert Hoover."

Patterson was a Mason and a Republican. He served in the Army Reserves, in the First Illinois Cavalry. He was a First Lieutenant in the Spanish-American War. In 1915 he wrote a book entitled *Ideas in Newspaper Making* (unfortunately, copies have not been found by the author). He relinquished the position as editor-in-chief in 1940, and moved to Orange, California from where he wrote his WNU newspaper column appropriately entitled "Grassroots" throughout the balance of his life. His death at his California home in 1954, like his ready-print, went largely unnoticed in the metropolitan press. A small obituary, hidden on the back pages, appeared in the New York *Times.*

Patterson, though a friend of kings and presidents, was not a man for "puttin' on airs"—for that would be bad for business. He became a big city Chicagoan, but town and country editors were his trade.

Though after he was 21 he never again lived in a small town, he maintained a provincial appearance, for he was the "front man" of ready-print, known to all country editors.

He was described in a magazine article as a man who "acquired that intimate friendly knowledge of human nature essential to the country newspaper. ... Upon him for years has rested the burden of deciding what shall be offered to the vast audience of readers which the W.N.U.

commands."

In the interview Patterson bared some of his soul, giving us a peek at the man's assurance, cultural values and homespun middle border philosophy. The magazine told of Patterson's position in the national power structure. It described hims as tall, lean, and mild-mannered, "with unsuspected reserves of reminiscence, humor, and human understanding." It told of his acquaintance with Presidentsm prime ministers, a kings, generals, senators, etc. In 1918 he was one of the twelve newspaper men to go as guests of the British and French governments to visit European battle fronts.

Additional knowledge of Patterson is gained from analyzing his remarks in the interview. Here is a sampling:

> People are as many sided as a falling cat. There are folks who will read any side of any question with open minds; and there are others who cannot read anything on certain subjects without becoming angry." He stressed variety in news subject matter, never too much on a particular subject. He bragged about the novels that were run in segments in ready-print's pages. Our readers average a high degree of intelligence: witness when we were running cross word puzzles, the complaints were that, they were too easy, when the same puzzles brought the opposite complaints from big-city readers!

He said that American readers had a large amount of curiosity about all sorts of subjects. His rural readers, he described, lacked the "nervous strain" found in cities; and they did not like the sensational stories featured in the metropolitan press. "It is a little surprising how much fiction the American farmer and his family will read...The story that depends chiefly on salacious incidents, or sex interest doesn't go at all. The mushy love story wins little or no interest. The 'misery' story, showing unhappy people with sufferings long drawn out, and ending gloomily, isn't wanted; nor except in rare cases, is the story with a foreign setting."

"The stories that go best usually have swinging action, much of it out of doors, with interesting American settings. They represent clean-living, clean-thinking, successful people, worth emulating. The love interest is manly and womanly, and never too obtrusive."

Patterson stated that *Main Street* would not do for his ready-print. "It caricatured small town people." Historical novels of American life were popular, he gave as examples some of his ready-print regulars:

Booth Tarkington, Mary Roberts Rinehart, E. Phillips Oppenheim, Conan Doyle, Edgar Rice Burroughs. He stated that he would "go far to avoid saying anything reflecting on religious belief, specially in jokes." (One expression frequently heard in American society, especially in the inland areas, is "I never criticize a person's religion").

He spoke about Prohibition (then in force)—a subject that ready-print had kept before the readers for over 30 years: "Nine tenths of present day humor seems to be built around bootleggers and illicit liquor...Any joke on the subject offends a good many people for the simple reason that they do not feel that good citizenship is promoted by ridiculing the law of the land."

Besides ready-print, most American newspapers, either daily or weekly, have practiced a form of time-saving deception called "advance pieces." The advance piece is a story written by the reporter in advance of the event, such as obituaries of well known people - still very much alive, or political speeches to be delivered too close to press time to be included in the day's editions. This practice down through time has helped close the gap between inefficient typesetting and press technology and the need to get the news out to the readers. Patterson told about one ready-print advance piece that went wrong: "Once we prepared such a piece about President Taft's inauguration as it was expected to happen. The piece would have been highly accurate, but on that day Washington, D.C. had the worst snowstorm in its history! Consequently all precedents were upset. There was no inaugural parade. Taft did not speak from the Capitol rostrum, but took the oath of office and delivered his address in the Supreme Court chambers. Our piece, nevertheless, appeared in something like a thousand papers before we could stop it. Curiously, we never received a single complaint from any reader or editor."

Patterson's life was similar to many Midwesterners of his time. His values were those of the prairie states. We know too little about him, this man who influenced millions of Americans for so many years. Like the proverbial "which was first, the chicken or the egg" story he believed he was giving the readers what they wanted—in giving it he became a part of the cultural process, spreading out his choice of information, giving it validity, interpreting it. In so doing, he perpetuated America's values and beliefs, as he saw them.

In interviews he would attempt to describe his editorial philosophy and the type of stories he chose for his national newspaper read by more than sixty million Americans.

Observe one of his statements:
"Controversial subjects must be handled as if we didn't have a single opinion of our own."
What power this editor had in doling out such information made to look like it was dispensed by an unseen, god-like hand. Such selective and minimalizing circumstances also played their cultural part. He also described more of ready-print's philosophy:

"We have to appeal to the native-born, and the foreign-born, Protestants and Catholics, Republicans and Democrats, young and old, the well-educated and poorly-educated. Western Fiction is in greater demand than any other single class, stories of this sort that make the greatest appeal deal with characters and situations strictly American. Probably one reason for the demand lies in the fact that a large part of the romance in the building of the United States lies in the country's expansion westward."

Ever the good 'ol boy, he repeated, "A man's religion is one of the things he is touchiest about (Beirut, the author remembers has 27 private armies, many of them religions)...Prohibition, too, is one thing we do not joke about....But I'm no prude, I like beer, I smoke. I enjoy a good story as well as the next man.

He could change his stance from one moment to another. Patterson, the editor, news gatekeeper, the employer of religious writers, did not see the hypocrisy when he stated immediately thereafter: "My father was a minister of the gospel, I learned a decent respect for the cloth by early training, and absorbed the idea that there are certain things which no minister can do and retain his self-respect. I, for one, will buy no sermons from a man who drinks, smokes, and tells smutty stories in private, and publicly advises his readers not to do those things...I have prejudices...this organization, great as it is, could be ruined in a few weeks if we took sides in the effort to foster private projects, or attempt to do anything else than tell the straight, honest news in as straight and honest a way as possible, etc."[5]

The political advisers to national politicians were among the first to realize the importance of editor Patterson's national ready-print newspaper, and they made sure each of the candidates and office holders eventually were informed of this direct pipeline to America's people. President Theodore Roosevelt apparently learned about it after he became president (according to a story in the October, 1927 issue of American Magazine entitled "Patterson helps to edit 12,000 Papers"). Patterson complained that the city press was getting news leaks and

special interviews that were denied to the ready-print newspaper:
"Theodore Roosevelt stood by his desk in the White House.
'You are known for giving every man a square deal,' said his caller, a tall, rangy man in the late thirties.
'That is all I am asking: a square deal for the country newspaper. Why shouldn't readers in small towns and on the farms have first-hand news of the Administration, such as city readers have?'
The President bared his famous teeth. 'You win right there!' he said.
At that moment a door opened. Edward B. Clark, veteran newspaper man, stepped into the executive office. He spoke to both men.
'Mr. President,' he said, 'I wonder if you know exactly who this is you are talking to?'
'Yes,' said Roosevelt emphatically, 'Mr. Patterson, of the Western Newspaper Union. He wants White House courtesies for his staff representative. I have just told him they are his.'
'But,' went on Mr. Clark enthusiastically, 'do you realize that Patterson helps to edit twelve thousand newspapers; that the biggest paper in the country has nowhere near so many readers as he has!'[6]
The look in the president's eye, merely courteous before, deepened to interest.
'How long are you staying in Washington, Mr. Patterson?' he asked.
'When can you tell me all about it?'"

JOSLYN, THE READY-PRINT KING AND PATENT MEDICINE SALESMAN

While country editors were aided economically by the ready-print, they apparently did not benefit nearly as much as George A. Joslyn.

Two of the newspaper publishers who worked and lived in entirely different fashion and operated within the free press system of America were H.N. Jennings and George A. Joslyn.

In the 1890s typical country editor Jennings, and his hardworking daughter Elizabeth, on an average Wednesday would be laboring until two a.m. at their small Fenton (Michigan) *Independent* country newspaper.

Contrast that with the life of George A. Joslyn, the publisher of half of Jennings' newspaper, who would be relaxing, basking in celebration of his wealth on the grounds of his Nebraska estate.

Jennings long days and nights setting type and tending the smoky

Editor H. N. Jennings and his family published the weekly Felton (Michigan) Independent. He operated a bicycle shop in the same room.

Olds gasoline-burning steam engine that powered his press, would have been more comfortable had Joslyn shared more of the ready-print revenue with him. With the profits from the advertising on the Chicago side of the sheet, Jennings could have bought time-saving equipment or hired extra help.

"The business of America is business," was the saying in that time. The thousands of country editors who used ready-print, were not disposed to criticize their rich "partner's" lifestyle, and his other commercial ventures in questionable patent medicines. Always, there were expressions of praise for Joslyn's ability to acquire wealth.

Jennings, like others, probably felt obligated, crediting Joslyn's ready-print (the time-saver) for keeping him in business and his costs down.

Still, there were some doubts about the ready-print publisher who headquartered in Chicago but lived in Omaha. Many town editors wondered about the large profit gained by Joslyn for the "public relations" income and advertisements on the Chicago side of the ready-print. Not one cent was ever passed on directly to the town papers who, after all, distributed locally and finished the other half of the publication in their own plants.

Joslyn, with gold flashing in his teeth lived like a corn-pone Arab sheik. It was decadence even by world standards. In an article in the Omaha World Herald in 1973 about families that had been prominent in Omaha's history, writer Frank Santiago offered this description of the Joslyn lifestyle: "It was a living style never seen before in Nebraska and likely never to be seen again. While the snow gently settled on the grounds, the 32-room mansion was ablaze with poinsettias, grown in the house's conservatory. There were legions of guests for teas and warm conversations by the fireplaces.

"There were concerts on the pipe organ played by a man imported from New York for the occasion. When the weather warmed, the grounds swarmed again. Sarah Joslyn had a brass cannon hauled from storage to be fired on July 4 to the delight of the neighborhood children.

There were massive trees shading the stone house, riding horses grazing in the grass, a gardener probing a garden that yielded strawberries big as a child's fist and melons sweet as sugar. It was the way millionaire George Joslyn and his wife, Sarah, lived at 3902 Davenport Street, a five-acre spread dominated by the 'Joslyn Castle'."

He was ready-print's corporate baron and a patent medicine salesman as well (the same type of nostrums so liberally advertised in the pages of his "patent insides."). To him, the ready-print newspaper "service" was strictly a business --- to be run unhampered by subtle editorial codes, philosophical and constitutional restrictions, or other such barriers to free commerce. A national patent medicine company or a national newspaper were truly one and the same to him.

He was a short, stocky man with a level gaze that invited confidence. Joslyn was not originally from a midwest town, but was a product of New England. He was born in Lowell, Mass. in 1848. His family moved later to Waitsfield, Vermont. During the Civil War, at age 17, Joslyn moved to Montreal, Canada. In 1874 he married his first cousin, Sarah L. Selleck of Montpelier, Vermont and they returned to the United States in 1876.

Joslyn, who owned almost all of the W.N.U., believed himself the living embodiment of the Horatio Alger stories that ready-print promoted so consistently. He was not an educated man, and rose from relatively meager surroundings to take over the American ready-print industry. He reigned as America's news emperor for many years—and from 1906 until his death in 1916 his rule was complete.

Joslyn moved to DesMoines, Iowa in 1878, where he managed several hotels. Later he took a job, at $18 a week, as shipping clerk with his uncle's Iowa Printing Co., a ready-print supplier. Shortly thereafter, the company changed its name to the Western Newspaper Union and Joslyn took over the Omaha branch.

He rose rapidly in the corporation, assisted by his family connection and his natural sales ability. He soon headed the two main branches of the company at Kansas City and DesMoines. He became general manager, then company president in 1890.

The sudden rise of Joslyn in the ranks of W.N.U. is believed by Omaha residents, even to this day, to be linked to his part time job as a patent medicine manufacturer and peddler. On the side, while selling ready-print to newspapers in his Nebraska sales territory, he also bottled and sold nationally an elixir called *Big G* (named after the five foot, six inch "big" George Joslyn, himself). In his sales pitch he claimed *Big G* was a cure for syphilis, and most other diseases. By investing real estate and *Big G* profits in W.N.U. shares, he became the principal stockholder. The history of *Big G* ended in 1910 when the Federal Pure Food and Drug Administration ordered him to stop selling the *Big G* product for it contained drugs and poisons not fit for human consumption.[8]

The Joslyn castle was the most imposing residence in Omaha, pointed out to visitors with pride. It was built in Scottish baronial style, all high turrets and decorative battlements — designed to conform with the rich man's tradition of conspicuous consumption. The house served as a billboard proclaiming his fortune, estimated in 1988 dollars at $175 million.[9]

There has always been in Omaha an aura of mystery about the man, and the source of his immense wealth. It seemed to those around his home town that a medium-size patent medicine business and a supply house for weekly newspapers could hardly have garnered the millions that Joslyn had obviously acquired and there was much talk.

Remarkably quiescent in the face of all this luxury were the country editors still using his ready-print. Only occasionally was heard a demand for more of a share of the income from the advertising that appeared on the Chicago side of the ready-print. Joslyn kept up the style, building the Joslyn castle in 1903. It had bowling alleys, greenhouses, stables and marble drinking fountains for his dogs. His partners, the town publishers did not even complain about the displaying of his horses in Madison Square Garden, and his summering at Saratoga Springs, New York.

One of his wife's pet causes was Prohibition, and she saw to it that Joslyn's editor in Chicago, Wright Patterson, knew about it. It was reported that the Joslyns gave food to the poor who appeared at their back door, attracted by the baronial surroundings. But they would not give them money because Mrs. Joslyn feared that it "might be improperly used." By having them sit on a special chair in the yard to eat, she felt that they would be less likely to waste the food.

Not surprisingly Joslyn hated taxes, especially those imposed on himself. At one time when he felt he was being overtaxed on his business by the state legislature, he, very publicly, moved to Saratoga, New York, letting sheep graze over his lawns. He did not return until the legislature capitulated and ruled in his favor.

He loved parties and was a member of the Omaha Country Club, and a member of the Republican party -- "...but took no part in politics beyond voting," reported his hometown paper (without knowing, one presumes, of the political editorials that appeared constantly in his ready-print). He was also director of the Merchants National Bank and the Commercial Club.

The Joslyns made known their philanthropy, giving to the Women's Christian Temperance Union, nurseries, a school in Mississippi, old people's homes, the University of Omaha, the Art Institute and the community playhouse. Practical jokes, music, parties and gambling were Joslyn's favorite forms of relaxation. It was rumored that he would sneak friends through the back of the greenhouse, into the heating tunnels, and through a closet to play cards and gamble (Mrs. Joslyn disapproved of gambling).

In the midst of all this type of living, Joslyn tried to inject a bit of the "simple life" into his image by always appending to his tie a 25 cent stickpin that advertised chewing tobacco. In the midwest frontier city of Omaha it was prudent to strike a democratic pose and not to "put on airs."

The stickpin was an attempt, successful it might be added, to divert view of the ostentation, the 25-person household staff, and to be accepted in Omaha as one of the good ol' boys. His daughter was quoted as saying: "The Joslyns struggled (early in their lives) to earn their bread, and believed in a simple practical approach to life."

This democratic image in social life is part of the midwesterners cultural value system and ready-print helped pass it onto the rest of America. "Anyone who dressed better than his neighbors, who put on airs, who flaunted domestic help, was looked upon with suspicion," stated Nevins and Commager in their *A Short History of the United States*.[10]

His death on October 4, 1916 came as the result of a stroke, after his long confrontation with the Federal Government. In his obituary in the Omaha *World-Herald* Joslyn was quoted on his business practices: "Work for and consider your customer's interest first; allow no how the pretty spoonholder got broken, ich he, Uncle James, got Santa Claus to ng mamma last Christmas."

Before long Freddie had so far recovered his erest in life and worldly affairs as to be able play a little, and to mamma's kind inquiry to how the heart felt now, he replied: 'Oh, it's all better; Jesus knows all 'bout it d will forgive Freddie, and I made it all up th cook—nice 'cooky'—and mamma has forven me, and"—with a regretful sigh—"well, guess Uncle James will forgive me too when knows how misble it made Freddie's poor, tle heart."—Faith Irving, in The Watchman.

BOYS AND THEIR MOTHERS.

I am sure you would have liked the two ings that Royal Lowrie did next—things at he was accustomed to do every morning t his life.

First, he went to the bureau and took up a icture that stood upon an easel-frame—the ortrait of his mother.

"Good morning, my dear mother," he said, ayly, and kissed the picture tenderly and everently, just as a few years later he might o that of some other woman whom he hoped o make his wife. Indeed, Royal Lowrie was very much in love with that beautiful mother, so that no woman was fairer or dearer, or more worthy of knightly service than she.

Oh, my dear boys—for it is you especially for whom I am writing this story—no matter how large you get or how busy you become, or how manly you fancy you are growing, don't ever get too big or too busy or too manly to be in love with your mother—she who loves you as no other woman ever can; she who would gladly die a thousand deaths for you. Oh, never so long as you live turn her out of the first place in your heart. Never, so long as you live, let there be a time when, in the slightest attention even—the quick offer of an arm or the stooping to save a step—you will prefer another to her.

I don't mean to moralize to you, or preach to you very much in this story, but I can't help saying this. For I know too well how surely will come a time when you will thank me for it. You do not think very much about it now, as you go about the house singing, with feet that keep time to the home music. And when the day comes for you to go out from the home-life, you will run lightly down the steps and ride away, scarcely looking for the last look at the loving mother who stands there in the door-way with eyes that fill so fast they can scarcely follow you as you go. And when you come back at Christmas, or Easter, or midsummer, though you may notice, perhaps, that some little change has taken place in your absence; the dear mother face has grown thinner, the step slower, or maybe the gray hairs have become more frequent, yet still you will laugh and turn away and forget; until sometime, late, I trust, but surely sooner or later, there will come a change which you will not laugh away or forget. Sometime when you

IMPORTED KID GLOVES AND LACE TIES.

IMMENSE REDUCTION IN PRICES.

We have just purchased one thousand dozen ladies' and misses' kid gloves at less than one half the cost of importation. Our stock embraces a full line of sizes from 5¾ to 8, also a complete assortment of colors and shades, including white and black, cream and light shades, usually styled opera. Our lady friends should not fail to avail themselves of this rare opportunity to secure fine imported gloves at about one-half the usual retail prices. In ordering state size and color desired, whether light or dark. Price per pair, **60 cents**, or 90 three-cent postage stamps; 3 pairs for **$1.50**; 6 pair, **$2.75**; 1 dozen 1 pair, assorted sizes and colors, if desired, **$5.00**; by mail, postpaid. Dealers can readily retail these gloves at from 75 cents to $1.00 per pair.

NOTTINGHAM LACE TIES.

We have just secured (at a great sacrifice to the manufacturers) an entire consignment, consisting of two thousand dozen ladies' and misses' cream lace ties, which we now offer at astonishingly low prices. Our illustration is a photo-engraving of one of the ties, and is therefore an exact representation of these beautiful imported goods. They are very fashionable for spring and summer wear, and we know of nothing else in ladies' wearing apparel so attractive and pretty as such a trifling cost. Length of ladies' tie from 18 inches, width 8 inches. Length of misses' ties 10 inches, width 4 inches. Price of ladies' tie, 25 cents; 6 for 60 cents; 1 dozen, $2.00. Misses' tie, 12 cents; 3 for 30 cents; 1 dozen, $1.00 by mail, postpaid. Postage stamps accepted the same as cash. For 10 cents extra, we will send goods by registered mail. Address all orders to

EUREKA TRICK AND NOVELTY CO.,
87 Warren Street, New York.

THE NEW NICKLE CALL WHISTLE.

A puzzle for any body to blow on until shown how his done. Rolls, thrills, or makes an ear-piercing note that can be heard for miles. Blow it and hand to a friend, and he can't get a sound out of it. Lots of fun in it. Useful for many purposes—to stop a horsecar, omnibus, or stage, call a dog, make signals in the night, call help from a distance, in field or workshop. Is small, and can be carried in the vest pocket, or hung on the watch-chain. Sells wherever shown. Agents wanted. Price by mail, 15 cts.; 2 for 25 cts.; 1 doz, 75 cts. Address A. D. PORTER & CO., Mfrs., 79 Milk St., Boston, Mass.

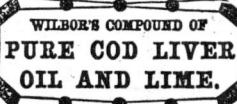

GOLD MEDAL, PARIS, 1878.

BAKER'S Breakfast Cocoa.

Warranted *absolutely pure* Cocoa, from which the excess of oil has been removed. It is a delicious drink, nourishing and strengthening; easily digested; admirably adapted for invalids as well as persons in health.

Sold by Grocers everywhere.

W. BAKER & CO.,
Dorchester, Mass.

CHILLED PLOWS.
FURST & BRADLEY MFG CO. CHICAGO, ILL.
Deep chilled and splendidly shaped for light draft.
SEND FOR PAMPHLET.

WILBOR'S COMPOUND OF PURE COD LIVER OIL AND LIME.

To One and All.—Are you suffering from a Cough, Cold, Asthma, Bronchitis, or any of the various pulmonary troubles that so often end in Consumption? If so, use *Wilbor's Pure Cod-Liver Oil and Lime,* a safe and sure remedy. This is no quack preparation, but is regularly prescribed by the medical faculty. Manufactured only by A. B. WILBOR, Chemist, Boston. Sold by all druggists.

I CURE FITS!

When I say cure I do not mean merely to stop them for a time and then have them return again, I mean a radical cure. I have made the disease of Fits, Epilepsy or Falling Sickness a life-long study. I warrant my remedy to cure the worst cases. Because others have failed is no reason for not now receiving a cure. Send at once for a treatise and a Free Bottle of my infallible remedy. Give Express and Post-office. It costs you nothing for a trial, and I will cure you. Address DR. H. G. ROOT, 183 Pearl St., New York.

CONSUMPTION.

I have a positive remedy for the above disease; by its use thousands of cases of the worst kind and of long standing have been cured. Indeed, so strong is my faith in its efficacy, that I will send TWO BOTTLES FREE, together with a VALUABLE TREATISE on this disease to any sufferer. Give Express and P. O. address. Dr. T. A. SLOCUM, 181 Pearl St., New York.

THIS NEW ELASTIC TRUSS

Has a Pad differing from all others, is cup-shape, with Self-Adjusting Ball in center, adapts itself to all positions of the body, while the BALL in the cup PRESSES BACK the INTESTINES as a PERSON WOULD WITH THE FINGER. With light pressure the Hernia is held securely day and night, and a radical cure certain. It is easy, durable and cheap. Sent by mail. Circulars free. **Eggleston Truss Co., Chicago, Ill.**

GOLD MEDAL AWARDED the author. A new and great medical work, warranted the best and cheapest, indispensable to every man, entitled, "The Science of Life, or Self-Preservation;" bound in finest French muslin, embossed, full gilt, 300 pp., contains beautiful steel engravings, 125 prescriptions. Price only $1.25. Sent by mail; illustrated sample 6 cents. Send now. Address Peabody Medical Institute, or DR. W. H. PARKER, No. 4 Bulfinch St., Boston, Mass. **KNOW THYSELF**

To any suffering with Catarrh or Bronchitis who earnestly desire relief, I can furnish a means of Permanent and Positive Cure, A Home Treatment. No charge for consultation by mail. Valuable Treatise Free. "His remedies are the outgrowth of his own experience; they are not experiments, but are the result of years of study and practice."

An example of ready-print

competitor to better serve patrons than you serve them; if there be a legitimate doubt, give your customer the benefit of that doubt; never run up the white flag; when financial disturbances darken the sky, reef your sails; watch little things, for many little things made big things; whenever possible, make a friend of an enemy."

The obituary listed his W.N.U. (and his holding company, Central West Printing Co.) business associates: H.H. Fish, vice president and general manager; John F. Cramer, vice president; and C. L. Farnsworth, secretary and treasurer. "All men of marked business ability and executive force," the paper reported.

His widow became known as Nebraska's leading philanthropist. Sarah honored his memory by donating $50 million dollars (again, in 1988 terms) for the building of the Joslyn Museum, which is known today as one of America's most respected art institutions. Twenty five thousand people showed up on the day of its opening. Its structure, planned in 1922 and finished in 1932, is of subdued Art Deco design, and believed to be the finest building of its kind in the United States—with 38 different kinds of marble from eleven countries. It has an excellent national reputation, especially in its showings of Western artists. Artists in this country usually refer to it familiarly as "the Joslyn."

READY-PRINT ACHIEVES RESPECTABILITY BY DEFAULT

The ready-print and boilerplate scheme after being subject to derision from many within the trade for thirty years, finally achieved respectability by default. This came about because there were no critics left within the trade because almost all the editors joined up—then became silent.

In 1893 a respected name appeared among the ready-printers. Walter Williams, editor of the Columbia, Missouri *Herald* and ex-president of the National Editorial Association and long a foe of "patent-insides" made a turn-about and went into the ready-print business for himself. His stated aim was to offer an alternative to the monopolizing W.N.U. and Kellogg company products and to share the profits more equitably among the country editors.

The entrance of Williams into the 1890s world of ready-print must have surprised a lot of his fellow country editors for he had been a long-time foe of the ready-print, or "patent-insides," as he

The heavy Country Campbell press was used by the country press until the 1960s. Most were built in the nineteenth century.

was a vocal, moral force in the newspaper business in America. A man of discipline and industry, Williams was more than just an average newspaper editor, he was a figure who caught the eye of the national media. No ordinary entrepreneur, he was a world traveler and later, though he lacked a college degree, served as one of the founders and dean of the Missouri University School of Journalism, the first journalism school in the world. Widely quoted, later he became president of the university.

Typical of his sayings were: "I would rather be editor of a good country journal than to hold any other place in journalism; it is the most independent and self-satisfying of all newspaper positions...the country editor molds the thought of his constituency and enjoys as much of their confidence and respect as though he swayed the destiny of states." In his lectures at the university he advised his students to shy away from the "political newspapers," advising his students not to enter journalism in the search for power. He stated that service should be the highest aim of journalism.[11]

Printed off the type forms (leftover type from the daily run) of the *Herald,* Williams sent his ready-print sheets to over 100 area newspapers. He offered the new ready-print service at half of the price charged by W.N.U. and the Kellogg company (the "monopolists" or "trusts", as they were called by their critics). In announcing his ready-print company in 1893, Williams and his partner, E. W. Stephens stated in full-page ads that his service was "...Something entirely new, original and unique, and furnished at half the cost of the old ready-prints...a model in its news, literary and typographical features....

The idea of disguising the paper and making the ready-print side look like the home print side was obviously an attractive feature to newspapers as a line on Williams' ad offering the service stated, "the only ready-print which looks like home print." You couldn't tell them apart.[12]

"Something entirely new" meant that William's ready-print contained no advertising (a policy that he abandoned later on). One hundred Missouri country editors signed up in short order, but the endeavor failed to show the kind of profit that Joslyn's W.N.U produced. Lasting only seven years, Williams' ready-print went out of business in 1900.

READY-PRINT WAS "PAINSTAKINGLY HIDDEN"

William H. Taft, in his book *Missouri Newspapers,* described the creation of the Missouri ready-print project. He included research material by journalist James Creighton. Creighton, who studied the effect of ready-print while at the University of Missouri is now the feature editor of the St. Louis Post Dispatch.[13]

In Creighton's academic paper he described the dilemma of the journalists: "Whether patent insides stifled the initiative of the editor who used them, contributed to the progress of the country newspaper, or had little effect, they represented a sort of family skeleton of small town journalism. Like a common workman, they shouldered the heavy burden but entered by the back door, painstakingly hidden from the reader's cognizance."[14]

Creighton studied Missouri town newspapers and Williams' ready-print. He wrote: "Missouri's country editors seemed almost to be maintaining a conspiracy of silence, aimed at keeping their subscribers ignorant of ready-print's existence. As the *Herald* patent insides reached near saturation distribution in central Missouri, readers must have become aware that their newspaper was remarkably like that published in the neighboring village, prompting editors to switch to a less common patent (insides). The Columbia *Herald* itself refrained from mentioning the auxiliary in its editorial columns...."[15]

The competition, WNU, offered patent insides pages that did not all look the same—and this proved more attractive to the town publishers. Creighton offers the suggestion that the comparatively drab content and format of Williams' ready-print also may have contributed to the decline. He added, "The country editor's long-standing uneasiness toward ready-print, whether state or national, may have been even more responsible. The comments of Missouri's weekly editors indicated that they used ready-print, not because of any intrinsic faith in its value, but because it was necessary if they wished to publish a 'respectable-sized' newspaper."

It was evidence that newspapers had found a route to success by increasing the size of their papers with ready-print. Though operating in a avowedly classless society, it was an allowable form of "putting on airs" for the reason of higher profits.[16]

After aborting his ready-print project, Williams, often described as a handsome man of force and charm, moved on to other careers. He was a leader in education, one observer stated: "When he was on the platform, his oratory had a golden quality in which his personal philosophy was an important element." He was elected president of a World Press Congress and received many other honors. In 1934, a year prior to his death, the National Editorial Association held its convention in Columbia, Missouri as a tribute to Williams for his long service to the cause of Journalism and the American Free Press.[17]

Notes

1. Lucy Maynard Salmon, *The Newspaper and the Historian* (New York: Oxford University Press, 1923) pp. 116-17.

2. Harold Heard, *The March of Journalism* (London) pp. 178-81.

3. However, Patterson's column which began during World War II, entitled "Grassroots," was identified on the page as a Patterson-WNU product.

4. From interview with WNU staffers.

5. "Patterson Helps to Edit 12,000 Newspapers," *American* magazine, October, 1927. p. 157ff.

6. *American* magazine, ibid., p. 158ff.

7. Files of the Fenton, Michigan, *Independent.*

8. Records, Joslyn Art Museum, Omaha.

9. Omaha city records, and interviews with residents.

10. This democratic image in social life is part of the midwesterner's cultural value system and Joslyn, no doubt, helped pass it on to the rest of America. "Anyone who dressed better than his neighbors, put on airs, who flaunted domestic help, was looked upon with suspicion," stated Nevins and Commager in their *A Short History of the United States* (New York, Knopf, 1966) p. 355. The shunning of "high falutin " ways was a cultural habit, an anti-monarchist legacy of the immigrants who had left Europe. Americans still tend to shun royalty, military and diplomatic titles. Europeans, on the other hand, still invest themselves with military and diplomatic titles even after they have retired from service.

11. William H. Taft, "Walter Williams Founded Journalism School," *Publishers' Auxiliary* (June 6, 1965) p. 6.

12. *National Printer-Journalist,* 1893, p. 312.

13. William H. Taft, op.cit., p. 44.

14. James Creighton, "Patent Insides and the Missouri Editor," University of Missouri, unpublished monograph. Creighton is now the feature editor of the St. Louis *Post-Dispatch*.

15. Ibid.

16. Ibid.

17. Frank Luther Mott, *Time Enough* (Chapel Hill: University of North Carolina Press, 1963) p. 155.

Chapter Six

Ready-print Offers Tabula Rasa for Editors

At times, the newspaper proprietor is gripped by an omnipotent sense of power, knowing that his words were reaching the minds of the readers. This was especially true of the rural publisher-printers who wrote forthright editorials. Editors sometimes referred to the feeling as "changing the world, one county at a time." An example of this sense appears in this poem written by Thomas MacKellar in 1884.

> Pick and click goes the type in the stick
> As the printer stands at his case
> His eyes glance quick, and his fingers pick
> The type at a rapid pace;
> And one by one, as the letters go,
> Words are piled up steady and slow,
> ...Oh where is the man with such simple tools
> Can govern the world as I?...[1]

Through time, writers and country editors have disliked the distraction of business details, the management aspects of the business. The Chicago ready-print helped out. Newspapermen with the willingness and ability to write and too small a town to cadge much of an income, had a load taken off their shoulders when ready-print arrived to prop up the economy of their calling. It was a subsidization in time and hard cash. By offering all their editors a blank page, a tabula rasa, the ready-print service gave them opportunity to air their editorial bias, if they were so inclined.

Some editors sought merely to reflect the opinions of their readers. Others, a smaller number, stepped ahead and led their readership, offering sometimes radical, sometimes unpopular points of view to the still-forming nation. The ready-print gave birth to an extraordinary breed of outspoken country editors freed from many mechanical printing chores, and to a limited degree, freed from the choking grasp of advertisers.

There were those to whom "speaking out" came easily, and brought forth an aggressive editorial style. Country editor Frank L. Avery never forgot the front page streamer which the publisher had given him on his first day of work in 1896. It read: "WHOSOEVER SAYS THAT I AM OPPOSED TO THE FREE COINAGE OF SILVER AT THE RATIO OF SIXTEEN TO ONE, IS A DRIVELLING IDIOT AND A BLASPHAMOUS LIAR," signed "The Editor."[2]

Who were the editors who filled the blank side of the pre-printed sheets? Were they all outspoken? Definitely not—though it took moxie to operate even a bland country newspaper. The few who were willing to write fearlessly knew that they were risking their hides. A small number of American town editors were willing to endure the danger, year after year—as though they were the product of some older, more primitive civilization when knighthood was in flower. They were courageous men, these country editors, volunteers, working in a sometimes dangerous business.

American newspapers are not adequately protected by the ambiguous First Amendment to the Constitution; but a sizable number of country editors (most were ready-print subscribers) took matters into their own hands—writing freely, criticizing government and politicians, pursuing vigorously whatever came into their editorial sights. The lack of legal protection made more courageous the act of establishing and operating these small, independent newspapers.

Some large city newspapers spoke out just as forthrightly as some of the country editors, but city papers usually had natural protective assets such as establishment connections, power to command the support of the police and even the governor, scads of money to pay

libel lawyers. They also had the most practical advantage of all: a large, block long, protected, fireproof granite building in which the editor could (in safety) stare out calmly at frustrated, eyeball-bulging, angry readers unable to lay their hands on him.

As William Allen White pointed out, not all country editors were saints, but some obviously qualified for saintly martyrdom. A town editor, down on Main Street, operated his business while looking over his shoulder. Close at hand were two potent forces casting constant dark shadows over town journalism: (a) The federal, state and town politicians with their threats of invoking vague libel laws and (b) the irate reader who had merely to walk down the street, open the screen door, stride over to the editor's desk and take a swing at him (or on occasion shoot him). A commentator wrote in 1887 that in contrast to his city counterpart:

> ...the country editor is too near his people to entrench himself, when the storms come, behind heavy doors and an impertinent office-boy. He must face wrath or flattery with equal readiness, and assuage or defy the one and absorb the other with equal tact.[3]

When starting up, newspapers in that horse and buggy time filled their role as reporters of events. But the fire-breathing editorials came later as editors expanded their role, plugging into civic life in the community and attempting to shape the world around them—changing the world for the better, one county at a time.

It is the individual acts of "Kamikaze" editorial courage that captured publishers' imaginations and the American reader's interest, and seemed to drive the system onward.

What really counted toward the development of an American free press was that the "ideal of the outspoken editor" became a force within the trade, and was even grudgingly admired outside of it. This gave American journalism a moral tone that was carried into the larger papers as well, as towns grew into cities.

Like circus lion tamers, who voluntarily house themselves within the cage, armed only with determination and a flimsy whip, the risks taken by outspoken editors defies conventional logic and severely wounds the theory of free enterprise. Acts of courage are much admired in the trade down through the years and every country editor carries his own "bravery stories" around with him to be talked about at the next state press convention.

Though editors' accounts of their own heroics were occasionally exaggerated, there were real heroes aplenty. Cultural, altruistic,

The author, when editor of his Kentucky newspaper, injected his editorial page into many local issues. The above shows some of the result.

commandments took shape and gnawed the conscience of editors and reporters. Here are a few examples of the value system that arose: Do not flaunt your editorial power! Work long hours for low pay! Disagree editorially with your banker's politics even if he holds your mortgage! Expose the police department if it has the habit of taking bribes! Write *ALL* the truth about government officials! Tension, not a peaceful night's sleep was the reward for an altruistic editor. Editors dared not stray too far from the code.

Lonely editors sought assurance and approval from fellow editors in their state. State press associations were founded and filled a need. Their main reason for existence was the psychic, social benefit it gave lonely editors, offering them a periodic meeting of the clan where strength was gathered and editorial resolve pumped up. Almost all the country editors sought entry into these organizations.

Proud indeed, was the publisher who could point to his wall where hung a blessing in the form of a "Fine Typography" or "Courage in Journalism" award medal or plaque from a state press association. The typography certificates outnumbered the CIJ awards, but they looked a lot alike in shape and size.

Politicians, those anxious to get their hands on the public trough, sometimes owned newspapers and passed themselves off as "crusading" editors. However, these wolves in sheep's clothing would frequently find themselves under fire from competitive newspapers in their town. Newsmen believed that it was unethical to serve as a community editor while holding elective or other government office. Once an editor committed himself to putting his name on the ballot he was expected to leave the newspaper business by others in the proud priesthood. He was considered to have gone over to the enemy.

Also held in low regard were country editors who played the sycophant to those in power, giving free access to their papers to every political muttering ol' Senator Blowhard could muster. The suspected reason for their unwavering toadying to one political party or the other was the lure of good ol' hard cash channeled in one form or other to the newspaper.

The July, 1912 issue of *McClure's Magazine*, in an article about the two major political parties' attempts to control the town press, wrote: "The country press... has been, from the time of the Civil War, tied fast to the party machine by the county printing contracts and by cessions of county postmasterships to the editor." These well-financed party-line newspapers, whether Republican or Democrat, were held in check and made honest, however, by the existence of two or three independent competing ready-print newspapers in their towns, or in nearby villages.

In spite of peer pressure, some editors chose to run for political office. They found that owning their own paper, a potential propaganda machine, was a powerful assist in getting elected to local state or national office. Most successful at this was photogenic President Warren G. Harding, who, aided by his own paper and the mighty ready-print and a boilerplate propaganda campaign that featured his photogenic face at every opportunity, moved unerringly from his little Ohio town newspaper into the White House. Quixotically, despite the president's scandal-ridden reign, Harding was one of the country editor's favorite political figures.

Many a midwest town paper still proudly displays his official campaign picture on the office wall. The photo shows him working on an ink-covered type form in his grimy newspaper back shop— dressed incongrously in a tailored Sunday suit and patent leather shoes.[4]

William Allen White, America's most famous country editor in the nineteenth century, described the spirit of the ready-print papers of his time. He wrote: "The newspaper business in that far day was not a

The ready-print paper was cut to the size of standard presses

manufacturing enterprise. It was an artistic adventure...they lived as artists of old---partly by medicancy, partly by piracy, but always in joy...There was a flavor in those days about the printing office. Printers were supposed to graduate into editors, editors into statesmen, statesmen into leading citizens, and rise in the state and nation."[5]

White, himself, rose to be Assistant Secretary of State, one of his nation's highest offices.

Mark Twain also spoke of joy in country newspapering. In replying to European criticism of American newspapers as too irreverent, ex-country editor Twain wrote that dictatorial monarchical Europe's newspapers of that time had "a graveyard gravity of countenance: to laugh would expose the whole humbug." He compared the foreigner's dread of a newspaper that laughs, to the devil's aversion to holy water. Twain abhorred pretense, piety and "puttin' on airs" in newspapers, writing:

> Its frank and cheerful irreverence is by all odds the most valuable quality it possesses. For its mission...is to stand guard over a nation's liberties, not its humbugs and shams. And so it must be armed with ridicule, not reverence....to my mind a discriminating irreverence is the creator and protector of human liberty.[6]

THOSE WHO SPOKE OUT

There were times when humor was out of place, as in wartime or during the civil rights struggle of the 1960s. Southern country newspapers were frequent victims of advertiser boycotts during that period. Many southern editors, including this author, were heavily harassed for supporting President Lyndon Johnson's civil rights act of 1964. There were midnight phone threats, gunshots from ambush and newspaper plants were burned.

As it was, when the advertisers would boycott, the smaller southern papers had little recourse than to avoid the forbidden subject of Civil Rights. Glaringly apparent during that time was the absence of the Southern editorial voice in countering the racial fanatics and lunatics.[7]

There was almost a total editorial vacuum; and one could point to only a half dozen editors who faced the barrage and spoke freely. Those who spoke out strongly on the issue of civil rights in the sixties were editors of the newspapers of some of the larger southern cities. Most effective in the cause were Ralph McGill of the Atlanta, Georgia, *Journal-Constitution* and Hodding Carter, Sr. of the daily Greenville, Mississippi *Delta Democrat-Times.*

It might be theorized that, had ready-print existed, southern town editors might have spoken out occasionally for human rights, lessening, perhaps, some of the outrageous illegal actions of the politicians, Klans, and White Citizens Councils. With half the paper full of ready-print national advertising, the southern small town papers might, at the very minimum, have given the air of prosperity even if boycotted by the town advertisers.

Historically, proud editors have not wanted to be called "timid." No American editor wants to be called a slacker, a luke-warm editor, one who never calls a "spade a spade". But some went part of the way, employing the rule: "Never anger more than one-half of your readers at a time."

Poetry was sometimes employed in the trade magazines to fire up the journalists, to get them to speak out. This offering appeared in the *National Printer-Journalist* of 1904, written by O. Byron Copper, a DeSoto, Wisconsin editor of that time.[8]

THE LUKEWARM EDITOR

Luke Warm, a timid editor,
Once ran a country sheet,
Whose every line and local note
Was couched in tones discreet,

That none might take offense thereof,
Not register a kick,
Although his guff and red-hot air
Made all his readers sick.
Luke smiled on ev'ry face he met,
And wrote all things up right,
And never was he known to mix
In any righteous fight;
When any local renegade
Got in a nasty mess
Luke smoothed it o'er without a word,
And let his reader's guess.
And thus poor Luke went blindly on
With plan he thought discreet,
Until his patrons 'gan to ask;
"What good is Luke's old sheet?
Without backbone, nor e'en a mind
To stand by home and right;
Nor e'en the nerve to print the truth
In plain old black and white!
We'll stop our papers all at once,
Our sentiments to show!"
Then each into the sanctum stalked
And plainly told Luke so.
Thus poor L. Warm the lesson learned:
This honeysuckle fun
Of trying every class to please,
Displeases everyone.

Many new recruits lured to nineteenth century American newspaper publishing by ready-print were not daunted by the bullets, whips or epithets. Found in a relatively short time were the thousands of country editors and countless editorial assistants with the talent and audacity to face readers, at times passing only inches away on the town streets the day after the appearance of each issue.

Finding such talent would seem to have been an insurmountable task. Obviously it was not, thanks to the safety net of ready-print which assured that at least half of the newspaper would appear on time even if the editor had been shot dead in the meantime.

Many editors learned that if they were quick to display a critical pen, they had better back it up with a gun slung in their belt. One Southern publisher set a record by being horsewhipped by readers twice on his first day of publication. The pistol became as indispensable to some editors as the printing press.

Editor Arthur E. Pierce wrote about the problems of producing an outspoken newspaper in his account of the early trials of the *Rocky Mountain News,* printed in a village that became the city of Denver: "William N. Byers spoke the truth and spoke it fearlessly. He was unsparing in his denunciation of the rough element, the thugs and gamblers. They assaulted him and the office and captured him, taking him to a saloon; were about to hang him. I was a witness in this affair and saw one of the desperados, George Steel, shot from his horse and killed by one of the enraged citizens who came to the rescue of Byers and the *News* office."[9]

The big city press occasionally took note of their brother county journalists, isolated in the wilderness. "His heart and brain and pocketbook are in his work," wrote the Watertown, N.Y. *Daily News* in 1904. "This great army of workers in this nation are in close contact with their constituents...unlike their metropolitan co-workers, who write from the dizzy height of some great office building."

Courage, and a dependable pistol was a requirement of many pioneer editors, reported the 1965 *Publisher's Auxiliary,* the national journal of town publishers. "Life in many communities was violent, and the editors were in the midst of it. Newspaper plants were wrecked and burned, editors were attacked by word and blow..., a Nevada editor when he died in California is reported to have had a revolver with a half dozen notches on its handle, each representing a man killed in Arizona and other Far Western spots in the editing of a newspaper."

Salesmanship was important. A smooth talker could sell more ads and subscriptions. To have an accountant's mind, and the understanding of a profit and loss statement, was invaluable.

Violence visited upon editors was not limited to the West. Writer W. O. Saunders tells about his difficulties with the fanatic religious element in Elizabeth City, North Carolina. His paper, a ready-print user, was called the *Independent,* and he was prosecuted for libel in almost every term of the circuit court in that area. Repeated drubbings and threats of assault, even boycotting by local advertisers did not deter him from publishing the truth as he saw it. Things became violent when one of the church factions in town decided that he was an "infidel." Saunders,

We are "THE POWER BEHIND THE THRONE,"
  When FREEDOM'S clarion rings!"
To make the people's cause our own,
  And curb the greed of kings!
    CHORUS:—Join hands around, etc.

The lightnings flash our "NEWS" afar,
  Around earth's circling sphere,—
It yet may be that every star
  Earth's "TELEGRAMS" may hear!
    CHORUS:—Join hands around, etc.

May peace and harmony prevail,
  And wisdom guide our laws;
United we shall never fail
  To spread our noble cause.
    CHORUS:—Join hands around, etc.

T' the Ladies who have taken part,
  "God bless their loving hearts!"
Their smi'es lend success to—"THE ART
  PRESERVATIVE OF ARTS!"
    CHORUS:—Join hands around, etc.

This was a welcoming song sung at a convention of American and Canadian editor-printers in 1892. No ordinary conventions were these gatherings. They were designed to invigorate the editors and the free press.

on the whole a rather religious man, believed that the furor was more political than religious. At any rate, the entire adult male portion of the congregation marched from a church to his house. He writes:

> They were inspired by the hatred and animosity of some of the members of the church who had been attacked in *The Independent*. I pulled a gun on the crowd assembled in front of my house and ordered them to disperse. The answer was a threat to take me, then and there. To this I replied with three shots fired in the air....
>
> I did not think that a host of Christian brethren, right out of the sanctuary, would be armed with guns. But I was mistaken. the answer to my shots, fired high in the air, was a fusillade of bullets, fired into my house. Neither my wife, standing in the doorway, nor myself, standing on the front stoop, was hit. Miracles do happen.

Apparently the shots cooled the crowds ardor and they finally let the editor alone.[10]

Other courageous acts came at times from unexpected sources: ex-ribbon clerks with metal-rimmed glasses, not previously known for their boldness, upon becoming scribes, would suffer a transformation and, willy-nilly, throw stinging, intimidating words at crooked politicians, town bullies, fools, the fatuous and the boring.

Things would really heat up when politicians, to cover their tracks, used editors as favorite whipping boys. Cries for assaulting the editor (or the "media" in current terminology) have echoed across the land, coming mostly from editorially bruised politicians, ranging from presidents to county sheriffs.

Some of the outcry was inbred in the community. Charles Harger wrote, "It is characteristic of the country town to engage in community quarrels. These absorb the attention of the citizens, and feeling becomes bitter. The cause may be trifling: the location of a schoolhouse, the building of a bridge, the selection of a justice of the peace, or some similar matter, is enough. To the newspaper office hurry the partisans, asking for 'ex parte' reports of the conditions. One leader is, perhaps, a liberal advertiser; to offend him means loss of business. Another is a personal friend; to anger him means the loss of friendship. The editor of the only paper in the town must be a diplomat if he is to guide safely through the channel."[11]

Among the colorful figures (riding along on the financial assist of ready-print) of the predominant small town press was Thomas Parker "Tee Pee" Fulton, editor of the Eldorado *Democrat* in predominantly Republican Kansas in the 1880s. His chronicler wrote:

> He stands something under six feet and wears a slouch hat, under it his black hair (for he was only thirty-five), black eyes glistening under black eyebrows with a military mustache, and a goatee surrounding his large, generous mouth. No slouchy sloven is he, but a scholar and a gentleman, and also at proper times a judge of good whiskey. Tee Pee could sling a pen. His was known as a vitriolic pen. And he was always ready to back it up with his trusty gun. It mattered little that he was the world's worst shot.... He wrote rapidly and well. His copy was as meticulous as his clothes and manners. He leaned to editorial rather than news. His paper had only four pages; and the two outside pages, printed in Kansas City, (the ready-print) contained news of the world on the first page, a love story and miscellaneous items on the fourth. So the editorials and the local items, on the paper's inside pages were all that Tee Pee contributed to the news end of the paper. He solicited advertising and, after the manner of editors of his day, as a solicitor he was half blackmailer and half mendicant—from Democratic merchants he begged, from Republicans he mildly insinuated threats! Also he solicited subscribers and job (printing) work. He intrigued diabolically for the county and city printing and was in politics heels over head. His little office would not have invoiced more than 1,500 dollars; yet with that weapon he wielded much influence in his town and county and state. He was an artist who owned the tools of his trade. [12]

The most peaceable editor would stir passions for even slight matters, such as the misspelling of a reader's name. Even when a cowardly, overly-mild mannered editor sought desperately for community approval and his own personal tranquility, he could be caught up in a maelstrom as the result of an innocent mistake. Take the case of the two headlines that were inadvertently transposed at the top of page one of a newspaper in the upper South. One headline read "CIVIC LEADER DIES"—over a photo of a well known society leader in the town; and the other headline read "OLD EYESORE GONE AT LAST"—over the picture of a demolished building. The heads got switched, and the resultant furor put the mild editor's life in jeopardy; and was the subject of controversy in the community for years.

READY-PRINT TRIED TO BE
NON-CONTROVERSIAL, PROFITABLE

Later, around the turn of the century, things began to change in the shoot-'em-up school of rural journalism, nudged along by ready-print editorial policy, the increase in one-paper towns and the threat of competition from big city dailies. Subject matter shifted to religious themes and "safe" editorial campaigns, promoting "family," "motherhood," "home safety," and "shop-in-your-hometown".

Prior to the turn of the century, rural editors, with few local stores around, earned most of their income from subscription sales, not advertising lineage—and they therefore felt obligated to produce lively, controversial newspapers aimed only at gaining readership. But, as advertisers grew in number, the tendency was to tone down editorial debate and devote more attention to buttering-up the advertisers.

The ready-print side of the newspaper was a poor role model for a journalist seeking to operate a government-watchdog, investigative publication interested in improving society. Exposes of government malfeasance or shady business practice were not for the ready-print, even at a time when the government Teapot Dome or Tammany Hall scandals were the focus of the city newspapers.

Many town editors simply ignored (and sometimes participated in) political shenanigans in their area. The selling of votes was a practice that rural districts specialized in. Counties in Ohio, Kentucky, and Tennessee contained a massive citizenry that regularly ignored the civic privileges given to them by their country and routinely added to their income by selling their vote to whatever politician offered the most money on election day.

The practice, which struck at the roots of the democratic idea, was so widespread at the turn-of-the-century that national magazines began to publicize it. But it caused hardly a murmur in the ready-print—even when muckraking *McClure's* magazine wrote about a county in Ohio where a judge (a reformer) placed 1,700 voters under arrest, over one-quarter of the eligible voters in the county. They were all fined or given jail sentences for selling their votes, and most pleaded guilty.[13]

An example of ready-print

Chicago ready-printers, cheerfully amoral since they saw themselves as a service to, rather than a member of, the newspaper fraternity, made large profits from advertisers of harmful patent medicine. The mostly inoffensive editorial matter was incongruously set alongside sleazy sexual-potency and harmful drug advertisements. The use of the words "patent insides" to indicate ready-print came from the practice of the ready-printers to clog their pages with this type of tacky, but highly profitable, patent medicine advertising.

Many of the ads were attacked by state press associations and various health organizations without result. Cocaine and equally dangerous drugs were openly advertised on ready-print pages (though beer and liquor were not advertised since they were opposed by the Protestant bible belt churches, especially the Methodists). The ready-print featured advertisements containing clinical discussion of venereal diseases and masculine impotency that obviously resulted from syphilis and gonorrhea. Thomas Clark, in his book *The Southern Country Editor,* commented:

> It is a queer commentary of the sacred American guarantee of the freedom of the press that it can be thought of in terms of medical advertising. Yet seventy years of the country journalism of the nation were one long dose of senna leaves, royal gentian, purgatives, narcotics and alcohol (hidden in the medicine).
> Without a doubt the advertisers filthy hands were clutched tight about the timid publisher's throat. Local advertising, public printing and subscriptions income were insufficient to free the local pages from them. The two types of income from the medicine trade, though meager, were more than any editor could resist. When they bought ready-printed sheets with advertising they got their paper stock for a negligible sum,...and when they printed original ads themselves they were paid low rates for long runs. Advertising agencies were shrewd. They understood from the start that many an editorial hand could be reached with a subsidy, almost regardless of the validity of the product advertised.

THE JOINING OF TWO MOVEMENTS, ANTI-LIQUOR AND RELIGIOUS FUNDAMENTALISM

Ready-print wanted to please everybody, their readers, the country editors but they especially tried to please the subscribers in the Bible

Belt. "We are never controversial," the ready-print companies would proudly announce—giving the impression that "controversy" (the life's blood of a large number of newspapers and an essential element in the democratic process) was always wrong.

Ready-print and boilerplate showed a knack for promoting safe, already-popular causes. Their vast circulation and monopoly of reading matter in American homes gave impetus to deserving and undeserving causes, alike. Not surprising, since it served a rural clientele, national prohibition became one of its campaigns.

Religious fundamentalism was another. The joining of the two causes created a surge that brought about the oddest of the amendments to the Constitution, the Eighteenth—which made illegal the production and distribution of alcoholic drinks. It did not, however, outlaw the other equally harmful substances like opium, cocaine, and marijuana that were even then menacing the country.

Early on, ready-print editor Wright Patterson and the provincial churches steadily propagandized against drinking alcohol. Most American town newspapers found themselves with increasingly aggressive news stories and editorials against drinking. Temperance and religion always ran side by side on the page.

The "Temperance Notes" column and others like it dominated the pages until the passing of the Amendment in 1919. The variety of stories was endless. An example was a 1909 issue of the ready-print with this poem (yes, more poetry!) at the top of the page, under the head THE WARFARE AGAINST DRINK:

> Our Temperance band is marching strong
> And shouting victory all along,
> We fight the king who soon destroys
> The happiness of girls and boys.
> And gladly we will go and fight
> To win for temperance and the right,
> And ah, some day what news we'll bring,
> For we'll dethrone the Liquor King.
> Now won't you join our Temperance band,
> And stand for freedom in this land?
> And ah, how happy we will be
> When from King Alcohol we're free.

Next to it was a column titled "The Pulpit, An Eloquent Sunday Sermon by A. H. Lewis, D.D ...God alone has absolute power to create...Much the larger share of human suffering comes through impaired physical health. Weakness and disease make men a burden on society, lead to poverty, drunkenness, social impurity, larceny and kindred evils...."

Another religion/temperance page had these:

WHY A TOWN LOST OUT
Saloons From a Business Man's Point of View.

DR. TORREY'S TESTIMONY
Why the Great Evangelist Signed the Pledge.

AN ENCOURAGING OUTLOOK
Probability that Temperance Will Be Taught in British Schools.

When that ambitious (and successful, since drinking of alcohol during Prohibition diminished by more than one half) American social experiment in one of the world's hardest drinking countries, swept down from the prairies and became the law of the land, it revealed the existence of an opinion-molding mechanism that carried the message of prohibition swiftly and effectively through the provinces. The information carrier that served everybody was the country editor's paper, and its ready-print columns.

The history of the Prohibition legislation began with immigration and the growth of the cities. Between 1860 and 1890 the liquor business in America grew sevenfold as cities grew and the habit-forming substance captured the drinkers. What started as "Temperance" grew to outright prohibition of alcoholic beverages.[14]

By 1906 after years of ready-print articles, columns and the linking with religious causes, approximately 40 percent of the country was "dry." Twenty three states already had some form of local option prohibition. The impetus behind the movement came from the midwest, the stronghold of ready-print and religious fundamentalism. Bernard Weisberger has written: :"All those who debate Prohibition and Repeal carry the stigmata of our combined frontier and evangelical heritage."[15]

The South and East followed. Page Smith noted that the rural towns and counties went over, one by one until the cities were surrounded: "Often conflicts developed where the rural populations of counties forced cities within their boundaries to go dry."[16]

Aided by the distraction of World War I (preparedness for war and sobriety were made companion causes), on December 18, 1917 the Prohibition Amendment was passed by Congress and submitted to the states, outlawing the sale and manufacture of any beverage having an alcohol content of more than one-half of one percent. After ratification by the required number of states, over President Wilson's veto, the Congress passed the Volstead Act in October 1919.

Not until August 26, 1920 did the Congress finally pass the bill giving women the right to vote. Women's Rights was never a favorite editorial topic of Wright Patterson, the ready-print editor, though he never openly opposed it.

THE SOCIALIST COUNTRY EDITOR

The ready-print newspaper found itself for a while among the Socialists when it seemed that that cause was becoming popular —and for a considerable time was more than willing to please this political faith if there was a profit in it.

Until the time of the first World War there were many Socialist papers being serviced by the boilerplate and ready-print, especially in the upper midwest, most prominently around Milwaukee. The Nonpartisan League, a Socialist organization and an offshoot of the Wisconsin Progressives of Robert La Follette, bought boilerplate and ready-print and operated more than 50 papers in Minnesota alone.

Ready-print regularly ran the publicity releases from the Social Democrat party, which won important electoral offices in Wisconsin, the Dakotas, Oklahoma and other states. Towns like Albert Lea, and Marshall, Minnesota; and Aberdeen, South Dakota and Grand Forks, North Dakota were strong Socialist areas and established Socialist weekly and daily newspapers.

A typical ready-print example, datelined Milwaukee, April 1, 1910, read: "SOCIAL DEMOCRATS ACCUSE PRESIDENT ROOSEVELT", the story charged that the Republicans were stealing all the socialist ideas. (Socialist leader) Victor L. Berger stated that he was formulating plans to spread socialism into twenty-six states of the Union. He said, "The people are awakening. They are becoming more liberal and beginning to understand social conditions better. Why, look at President

Theodore Roosevelt. His agitations and exposures are helping us immensely. He is paving the way for socialism. While he is not of our faith, nevertheless he is helping us. He is convincing the people that we know what we are talking about. Why, he has even stolen some of our ideas."

Though socialism had already come under heavy fire in the U.S. at that time, ready-print was willing to run this story despite Berger's known support of armed revolution in America. In a July 31, 1909 issue of the *Social Democratic Herald,* Berger stated: "...it is easy to predict that the safety and hope of this country will finally lie in one direction only, that of a violent and bloody revolution....Each Socialist and worker should also have a good rifle and necessary rounds of ammunition in his home and be prepared to back up his ballot with his bullets if necessary."

Though many currents of socialist thought were forming themselves, mainly in Europe in the late nineteenth century, the open discussion of socialism in ready-print did not last past the early part of the twentieth century once Wright "Pat" Patterson learned that socialism, of whatever type, was not well regarded among most of his customers. Patterson and his boss, Joslyn, never wanted to put company profits in jeopardy; thus the searching, social ideas being discussed widely and openly in London and elsewhere in Europe, would no longer be spoken of in the nation's dominant ready-print, the U.S.A.'s only national newspaper publication of the time. Sidney Webb, Bertrand Russell or George Bernard Shaw would never appear in its columns if Pat Patterson could help it---thus the Fabians and the dozens of debating, philosophic groups rising in the wake of Darwin were to be little known west of New York City.[17]

Ready-print editors always went with the tide. This suited the main office operation since it was much more profitable to write stories that would fit in most of their area editions around the country. Stopping a press and resetting type to change a story to accommodate local custom or prejudice would shorten the press runs thereby making it more expensive.

The watered down WNU editorials of the early twenties caused comment in many national publications. The *New Republic* magazine, in its April 11, 1923 issue, denounced country newspapers as "without purpose" and criticized ready-print and boilerplate canned editorials, stating: "The editorial page, once the battlefield of charging opinions, is now filled with cheerful, watery blurbs prepared for a hundred papers...one can glance through the entire issue of the Northfork *Times* without once detecting a glimpse of the editor's personality...."

The unschooled fledgling editors tended to imitate the main office ready-print editorial staff. As town businesses updated merchandising methods by running more display advertising in the papers, their conservative leanings began to influence editorial policy even further and the watered-down style of journalism began to dominate rural news columns.

Notes

1. *Inland Printer,* July, 1884, p. 19.

2. Frank Avery, "Early Days of a Printer in the South," *Publishers' Auxiliary* (September, 1965). The very literate Mr. Avery writes about his days in the Banner-Advertiser of Ozark, Alabama (edited and published by Ed M. Johnson). Avery was the son of highly educated parents who were made destitute by the War Between the States. His schooling was cut short and he began work at age 12 as a printer's devil and hand compositor.

3. Edwin A. Start, "The Country Newspaper," *New England* magazine (November 18, 1889) pp. 329-35.

4. I worked as a reporter in the office of an Indiana newspaper for three years with that odd picture of Harding staring at me from the wall.

5. *The Autobiography of William Allen White* (New York: The MacMillan Co., 1946) page 118.

6. A. L. Scott, *Mark Twain at Large* (Chicago: Regnery Co., 1969) p. 140.

7. The Pulitzer Prize was given to country editor Hazel Brannon Smith of the Lexington, Mississippi, *Advertiser,* who editorialized for voting rights for all Americans. It cost her every single advertiser in her newspaper. She continued to publish, however, with grants from outside of the South. Mrs. Smith was a fellow member of the International Conference of Weekly Newspaper Editors.

8. *The National Printer-Journalist,* 1904, p. 833.

9. "Sixty-two Years in the Service," *National Printer-Journalist* (June, 1921) p. 280. For a view of widespread shootings, whippings and general editorial combat, the reader should seek out Charles Carver's

Brann, *The Iconoclast,* John Myers' *Print in a Wild Land,* and W. H. Winan's *Live and Lively Experiences in the Life of an Editor.*

10. W. O. Saunders, "The Autobiography of a Crank," The *American* magazine, date unavailable, p. 132.

11. Chas. M. Harger, "The Editor of Today," *The Atlantic Monthly* (Jan. 1907).

12. White, op.cit., pp. 111-12.

13. A. Z. Blair, "How We Disenfranchised a Quarter of the Voting Population of Adams County, Ohio," *McClure's* magazine, 1911, pp. 29-39.

14. *The Heritage of America,* edited by H.S. Commager and A. Nevins (Boston: Little Brown & Co., 1949). p. 99.

15. Weisberger, *American Heritage,* May-June 1990, p. 30.

16. Page Smith, *America Enters the World.* (New York: McGraw-Hill Publishing Co., 1985) p. 786.

17. Patterson and W.N.U., would remove articles that would offend certain sections of the country. He and his printers had devised the system of dropping into the ready-print press form a galley of type exactly the size of the articles to be replaced.

Chapter Seven

Mail Order News From Chicago

> This is America—a town of a few thousand in a region of wheat and corn and dairies and little groves. The town is, in our tale, called "Gopher Prairie, Minnesota." But its Main Street is the continuation of Main Streets everywhere. The story would be the same in Ohio or Montana, in Kansas or Kentucky or Illinois, and not very differently would it be told up York state or in the Carolina hills.
> —Introduction to Sinclair Lewis' novel *Main Street*[1]

> **Read'y,** adv. In a state of preparation so as to need no delay.
> —Noah Webster's Dictionary, 1870.

The eleven Southern states were brought back forcibly into the Union. With the bloody war between the states now safely over, the South was readmitted, but given a status some would describe as colonial. The North now firmly held the pursestrings and the source of mass communications.

But America was in the process of re-unification. How would it be possible to accomplish the miracle of putting the nation back together despite deeply held bitter feelings by both North and South? Ready-print would become an instrument in the process.

With an irony of record proportions, the hidden northern-based (Chicago) ready-print became invisible "carpetbaggers," working for the Union so dearly fought for by northern states. Though it came from

Yankeeland, southern country editors flocked to buy the northern ready-print and boilerplate. Southern newspapermen seemed more willing than their fellow citizens to bury wartime feelings and begin anew. Chicago played along, sending on down a mix of recipes, jokes, sermons and a number of mildly anti-Yankee stories.

With a press devastated by the war, there was a necessity for an economic stimulus for new newspapers to start up in the South. A surprising number of Southern editors contracted for a ready-print franchise, and later boilerplate, from Chicago---but not without complaints from some of their less reconstructed fellow journalists from the area. One southern editor wrote: "...no newspaper which has half of the editing done in Yankeedom can lay any claim to legitimate journalism; it cannot win the full respect and esteem of its home people; it cannot consistently urge the patronage of a 'home institution' and honestly boast of 'being here to stay.'"

But ready-print filled a need. The professional-looking pre-prints hastened establishment of newspapers in many Southern cities and towns. The journals served a variety of purposes: to recruit voters, black and white, for the Republican cause; to give the newly enfranchised negroes a newspaper of their own; to give southern country editors a firm economic base with a low cost supply of printed newsprint; and served as a voice against the threatened mass migrations from the south into foreign countries or far western territories. Many political organs came into being quite suddenly, some edited by carpetbaggers newly arrived from the northern states.

Historian Thomas D. Clark noted that the Chicago ready-printers were able to lure many of the conservative Southern newspapers into the fold with a bold stroke: they signed up writer Bill Arp, the sage of the South, their most respected newspaper columnist and a decided influence on the Southern mind-set after the war. The move served the ready-printers well and it gave Arp a sounding board throughout the entire south.

During the war Arp was an occasional columnist for the Rome, Georgia newspaper *The Southern Confederacy*. After a stint as writer with the Atlanta *Constitution* following the peace at Appomatox, Arp signed on with the Chicago ready-print company which ostentatiously called itself "The Western Newspaper Union" ("Union" being a popular word of the time).

Arp became the most popular columnist in all of the South. His alliance with the Yankees in Chicago who ran the ready-print company

Rather a child would pray for me
Than some one in a marble shrine,
For the love that lisps at a mother's knee
Is so wondrously fair and fine
That the words go straight and the words go far
With a grace that they have alone—
Go out and onward past star and star
Till they tremble unto the throne.

Rather a child should lisp my name
In a blessing when comes the night
Than to hear it breathed while the candle flame
Lends the altar a holy light,
For the shrill, sweet voice of a child can rise
On the mystical wings of love
And cleave the silence beyond the skies
To the listening Ear above.

The bedtime prayer, the white, white gown,
And the light that is low and dim,
The fair, wee head that is bowing down,
And the message sent up to Him!—
Then you know somehow that the pure child-heart
Is nearer to the Soul of Things;
For sighs that rack and for tears that smart
A Gilead-balm it brings.

Wonderful, too, the simple trust
Of the child in the love it asks—
It can lift us up from the shreds and dust
With a strength to renew our tasks—
For a child asks not as we older ones,
But it asks with a heart that knows
The Hand that bestoweth the fairest suns
Lent the grace to the climbing rose.

Rather a child should pray for me
Than the godliest man on earth,
For the prayer made in the childish key
Is the braver of greatest worth—
And I sometimes think that the good God sees
How we trust, and has gravely smiled
At the simple words and the bended knees
And the faith of a little child.
—Wilbur D. Nesbit in Chicago Record-Herald.

THE =YOUNG MOON'S= GIFT.

Cassy, in an old brown shawl, sat on the steps enjoying the early spring twilight. The maze of maple tops seemed to have caught the crescent of the young moon. It was bright as a bit of new silver, and a childish desire to wish by it came to Cassy.

"I wish he'd come back," she said.

The words came suddenly and they set astir a host of memories she had been wont to fight against. Why should he come back, and why should she want him to come after he had done as he had? And yet—and yet, after 20 years, her heart was still full of him.

It all came back to her now, not so much in facts as in feeling. It had all happened in the spring. There was the day she bought her wedding dress and that other when it came home and she tried it on for the last time before wearing it, and afterward a great flurry until that last evening. She had dressed early and most of the guests were there. Everybody was laughing and talking and expecting the tardy old minister. Suddenly Gordon bent over her.

"If you don't mind, Cass, I'll just step out for a five-minute walk. I—I don't feel well and the air may do me good."

Then came the old minister, but Gordon did not return. They waited for him, they searched for him. Had something terrible befallen him? that Cassy, clamour of them all, went to her room and took off her wedding dress.

"Tell them to go home," she said.

...down again, and her took Zack's place beside her; but though they were so near they did not look at each other.

"I always thought, Gordon," Cassy went on, quietly, "that if I ever saw you again I'd tell you something. I had a feeling that night when you went out of the house that you'd never come back. And I had a feeling before that you wanted to tell me some thing and didn't dare. What was the trouble?"

The man drew his breath hard. "I had a wife," he said. "I tried to persuade myself that she didn't matter—she was a thousand miles away and she'd never know it. And I did want you so. Can't you see how it was?" he turned to her almost fiercely.

"What made you come back?" Cassy asked.

"It's the first time I've had a right to. She died last month." He buried his head in his hands.

"Maybe you loved her?" Cassy suggested, strangely.

He flung up his head. "Love her! Why, I hated her. She married me because I was a boy and a fool, and I never lived with her a day after I found her out. But I had to take care of her, and I did, for 20 years."

Suddenly he saw that Cassy was barebeaded. He picked up the shawl and put it about her. "I had to come back and tell you," he said. "I didn't expect you to forgive me, but I wanted to tell you by word of mouth. And—and I wanted to see you, too. I wanted to know if you were happy."

He twisted his fingers piteously. "I've told about everything I came to say," he said. "But there's one thing more. If—if you could forgive me, Cassy! know it's a lot to ask, after a man's—and—I—Go wish—"

Cassy looked at him. "Why don't you wish by the moon?" she asked. "She was particularly amiable to night. I made a wish and she granted it. Maybe she'll grant yours."

He looked up at the moon and for the first time Cassy saw his face plainly. How old and haggard it was! He must have suffered, too, for, after all, he had loved her. Her throat swelled and she laid her hand across his.

"Gordon!" He turned with a start. "I just want to say that I've never borne you any grudge and don't now. But I loved you." Her voice was steady. "I'm just as free as I ever was and if you are I don't see why we shouldn't be happy together yet."

For an instant he stared at her seeming not to comprehend. Then he buried his face on her shoulder and sobbed like a woman. And thus, holding each other, they sat a long time while the moon smiled and Zack kept watch over them both.—New Orleans Picayune.

WEST POINT OF THE SOUTH.

Virginia Military Institute Has a Brilliant Record.

"In all the professions and vocations of life," says a writer in the National Magazine, "the men trained at the Virginia Military Institute have won for themselves honorable distinction. The record of services rendered by her sons in the Civil, Spanish and Philippine wars has established the reputation of the Virginia Military Institute..."

New York City.—The pointed yoke is always a pretty one. It allows of treatment of various sorts, and its lines are very generally becoming. This one is made of strips of material embroidered with French knots combined with simple Irish insertion, while the blouse is made of linen lawn, but Cluny laces are being much

Foulards in Style.

Foulards are always good style, and a foulard frock is a most useful asset in the wardrobe.

Lingerie Trimming.

Footing makes attractive trimming for lingeries, and it is durable, too. The plain, as well as the point d'esprit, four inches wide, makes dainty ruffles for drawers. Finish the edge of the drawers with seam beading and to this overhand the footing ruffle that has been gathered on its own thread.

Embroidery Galore.

Embroidery is being used on all the newest gowns, and is losing no whit of its popularity. In embroidery original and personal touches may be put on the simple frock that will give it distinction and, as hand embroidery is never cheap and cannot be copied by the masses, there is good reason for its hold on the modish woman's fancy.

Odd Yoke For Gown.

A novel yoke that might be copied at home, if one has plenty of time and patience, was made of small pieces of the material of the gown cut haphazard fashion, and then joined together with fancy feather and fagotting stitches. It reminded one of an attempt to put a jigsaw puzzle together, and where the pieces would not exactly fit in the fancy stitches were employed.

Youngest Great-Grandmother.

Mme. Edna Bertonelle, a seamstress in the Quartier Montmartre, Paris, is held to be the youngest great-grandmother in the world. She was married at the age of fourteen, and her first child, a girl, married at the same early age. When Edna was 31 she was a grandmother. Her grandson married at 17 a young woman a few days his junior. On her 48th birthday Mme. Bertonelle was a great-grandmother.—New York Sun.

Wide Waist Lines Still Popular.

Practically all the street gowns, whether in linen or tussor, are made with the wide waist line that lends an uncorseted appearance to the figure. Women who have taken up and gone to the extreme of this fashion are wearing under such garments an elastic band form in lieu of the batiste or couille corset. This is the newest of Paris fancies, and may or may not become popularized. It will hardly be a practicable garment for the average summer dress, but with some of the tussors and heavier materials in which silk and linen are combined, such bands undoubtedly will aid in a perfecting of the "Middle Age" dress forme that now seems to be coming in.—Harper's Bazar.

Miss Marbury Raised Poultry.

Miss Elizabeth Marbury, who acts as agent to sell plays in America, England, France and Germany, is proud of the fact that she once made a success managing a poultry farm. It was when raising chickens near Oyster Bay that she first got literary ambition. She made several translations of French comedies and gave up the poultry farm when the first in the series had been produced successfully. Miss Marbury holds the distinction of being the first play broker in this country. She was the personal representative of Sardou, and now has her business so well in hand that she is enabled to pass about half the year in her villa in the south of France. She has made a fortune as a play broker and has earned it, as her work entails the reading of about 300 plays a year.—New York Press.

All Hatless in Church.

Nearly all the 400 women in the First Baptist church at Elgin, Ill., went hatless to services. The following special announcement appeared at the head of the weekly calendar:

"By a vote of the church all ladies are requested to remove their hats before the beginning of the sermon."

Only 50 women showed unwillingness to comply with the request, and for their benefit the Rev. A. F. Purkiss, the pastor, said:

"Those who want to see have as much right to ask that the hats be removed as I would have to ask the chickens to keep out of my garden. If we can see each other we will get a religious force and power which we can get in no other way. I see some faces today which I have never been..."

An example of ready-print

lasted for over 25 years until his death in 1903. Using this northern media instrument, Arp solidified many of the southern cultural values. He never editorially "went over" to the North, but his joining with WNU taught many southerners that partial accommodation with their conquerors was better than no accommodation at all. He was single-handedly responsible for the popularity of ready-print in the South, and thousands of new and old southern papers signed on both on boilerplate and ready-print and the number of newspapers in the south grew tenfold.

Clark, one of the few historians to get a grasp of grassroots journalism, wrote of Arp in his book *The Southern Country Editor:*

"Too long this significant figure in country journalism has been neglected in the history of Southern thought. Bill Arp, like many syndicated writers, spoke for large numbers of inarticulate people. He expressed a devotion to home and family. He loved the changing seasons of the year. He held a typical Southerner's views on religion, education, racial confusion and politics. Sometimes he wrote whimsical dialect, but his most effective columns were those in which he used colloquial English to express positive opinions. He spoke in ardent defense of the impoverished South. Arp revered the Democratic Party and often attacked Republicans with venomous tirades which caused them to appear as gory monsters. His observations on Teddy Roosevelt's (moderate) racial attitudes were sharp and pointed. Arp was not a racial liberal and his narrow views on the question helped to harden racial extremism, and the heaping of indignities on negro citizens.[2]"

Bill Arp helped to preserve many of the Southern feelings about the war and promoted their struggle against the oppressive Reconstruction policies from Washington. But his attitudes were placed within the framework of being an American first, and then a Southerner. There was a need to get the North and South back into a more friendly relationship, was the perception of the Chicago ready-printers. They responded to the perceived need with a flood of articles. A typical ready-print Union-building "reconstruction" article was this one, sent to over one thousand Southern newspapers, (indelibly printed on the back side of the ready-print sheets) was this example, which appeared under the large headline: "CONFEDERATE MONUMENT To Be Erected in

Mount Hope Cemetery in New York City."

> Members of the Southern colony in New York are taking great interest in a proposed Confederate monument to be erected in Mount Hope Cemetery under the auspices of the New York Camp of Confederate Veterans. The money for the monument, about $10,000, has already been arranged for, and the design was completed and accepted recently. It is proposed to dedicate the monument next Decoration day, with exercises lasting three days. There will be a parade of Confederate soldiers, and the boys in blue will march in alternate companies with the veterans in gray. It is announced by the officers of the local Confederate camp that there will be 50,000 confederates in line, and it is hoped to have as many New York state troops, detachments from the army, and distinguished ex-Union veterans. It is believed that the occasion will do much to strengthen the bond of fellowship and good feeling between the north and the south.

THE NEW AMERICAN

Until the complete establishment of RFD postal routes in 1910 Americans were using weekly newspapers for most of their reading matter. Few books and magazines were available and only one farmer in 300 took a daily newspaper.[3]

Many have commented on the role of the newspaper. The country editor's product with its hidden ready-print was welcomed into the American home, mind and heart as the "local" paper, the town's pride and its archive. It was the clock that tolled every Thursday, signifying that all was well; "the little journal that shared a place in the home next to the family Bible," as one small-town editor put it.[4]

Henry Steele Commager, in his *The American Mind*,[5] wrote: "The transformation of the newspaper was, in fact, far more than editorial; it was physical, it was economic, it was psychological, it was moral. It was part of the transformation of America itself---of the process of mechanization, urbanization, and centralization, of the concentration of economic control, of the emancipation of women, the broadening of social interests, the standardization, democratization and vulgarization of culture."

Rather than books, book-length serial stories were disseminated. Despite the propaganda and hidden advertising, the amount and high quality of informative material made ready-print a national educator.

Many families regularly clipped the novels, short stories and other entertaining and educational matter from the ready-print and kept it in scrap books for reading and reference. Nineteenth century mothers, north and south, taught their children from scrapbooks thick with clippings from the ready-print.

The ready-print could boast of a remarkable number of contributors of articles, novels and features, including: James Whitcomb Riley, Opie Read, Albert Payson Terhune, Mary Roberts Rinehart, Jane Addams, Albert Bigelow Payne, Jules Verne, Bret Harte, George F. Butler, Lyman Abbott and Carolyn Wells.

There was little else to read. Theodore Tilton, editor of the New York *Independent,* lecturing in Tiffin, Ohio in 1869 stated that not enough books could be found locally to make one respectable library.[6]

In his *History of Wisconsin,* Richard N. Current wrote: "As late as 1873 Wisconsin still lacked public libraries (in the sense of tax-supported ones) except for the library in the state historical society in Madison."[7]

The average farm home contained farm almanacs, and a religious book or two. Even homes with intellectual pretensions had at best three books, *Robinson Crusoe, Pilgrim's Progress* and *Tennyson's Poems.* The majority, living in countryside isolation, obtained most of their information from the local weekly or small daily papers with an infrequent glimpse at a big city paper. What they were reading can offer clues about the "programming" of the nation's character. Stolid New Englanders, casual Midwesterners and embittered Southerners with Civil War feelings buried only shallowly, are each unique in their cultural appearance. But, despite the massive bloodletting of a national rebellion, a uniform national identity could be discerned. In spite of the obvious difference between North and South, a form of political and cultural union was established.

Sociologist Vianna Moog wrote: "If it is true that one can still talk of a Northern mentality distinct from that of the South, of a Protestant mentality different from the Catholic, of liberalism in the Midwest and reaction in the South, of universalism in the East and isolationism in the Center, or of one American civilization of the Atlantic and another of the Pacific, as of social entities to which climate, geography, and form of production lend peculiarities that make them unmistakable, it is no less certain that, in general, one American is becoming less and less distinguishable from another American.

"The Yankee, subordinating men to things and not things to men, at the same time that he is extending his commercial chains, his trusts, his assembly lines, offering to all, from North to South, from East to West, the same clothing, the same foods, the same reading matter, the same radio and television programs, the same columnists, the same slogans, is slowly and gradually achieving, both on the international and on the national plane, what used to seem impossible."[8]

Given the information that respected national newspapers did exist in America from the late nineteenth century, social scientists need to dig further. Similarity reigns beyond the narrow cultural strip on the northeastern seaboard—America's old guard. Study of our grass roots will lessen future surprises such as recent national elections that show a bedrock conservative, nativist feelings, the persistence of the messianic, the spiritual, the Bible Belt, or the continuing plastic "small town" atmosphere of American suburban houses and shopping centers.

A SURVEY OF THE W.N.U. READY-PRINT

George A. Joslyn's W.N.U., under the editorship of Wright A. Patterson, in its heyday offered a wide variety of reading matter in the ready-print. Here is a sampling, beginning with the June 6, 1894 issue:

The weekly newspaper it appears in costs 50 cents per year and the amount of ready-print matter per issue would amount to a small book---it was a bargain offered for only one cent per copy. The temperance column was listed prominently on the front page. The local advertisements were scattered equally through the issue with the Chicago side using the same type-face. One of the "articles" headed A MIRACLE OF MEDICAL SCIENCE turned out to be an advertisement in disguise, another headed "Secret Societies" and was hand set by the local paper. Local news was sparse in the issue and ready-print, boilerplate and advertisements dominated.

October 10, 1894 issue: Ready-print was on the front and back page. A poem appeared on the front, beside a serialized novel printed three columns wide. Headlines were gaudy. Here are some examples: "EXPLOSION IN W.VA. SAWMILL, CYCLONE IN LITTLE ROCK, FLOOD IN CUBA, CHINA POLICY." The news stories tended to be short and the fiction long. Advertising on the ready-print side was of rather high quality given the reputation of "patent insides" advertising (books, chocolate, Scott's Emulsion, consumption cure---a total of one and one-half columns. A book was presented in segments, "Betrayal" by Mrs. A. P. Carriston (a romance of love, intrigue and crime).

December 26, 1894 issue: "Chat," a romance of West Virginia by

David Lowry. No photos, just line drawings. Royal Baking Powder was a constant advertiser, large three column by seven inches.

October 12, 1898: Switched from Patent Insides to Patent Outsides, four local pages, four ready-print.

January 30, 1901: First photo appeared. Women's Christian Temperance Union column appears regularly on the front page.

May 27, 1901: A boilerplate sheet music piece appeared with both words and music. This feature ran regularly.

September 17, 1902: Fiction story by Bret Harte running regularly. The quality of the newsprint improved suddenly. Probably a promotion gimmick by the ready-print supplier.

Jan 2, 1907: Two editorials appeared, both wishy-washy boilerplate: "Teachers Are Not Paid Enough" and "The Labor Union in American Politics."

June 3, 1908: Big news story on the Wright brothers new plane.

The writing style of some of the ready-print articles was of the "thumbsucker" variety—with little research and much speculation. A journalist of the time could write an article on just about any subject.

Hidden ads: A news story headlined "A Miracle in Missouri," appears to be a disguised advertisement for "Pink Pills for Pale People," but is not identified as to source.

The typefaces of both the ready-print and the home side were identical. By 1905 advertisements began to enlarge from the previous one-column size. This was linked to the equipment now being used by the ready-print printing house which allowed the use of wider heads and the removal of the one column spacing rules.

There appeared an excellent eight page insert to the weekly, giving the paper twelve pages of ready-print and four of a mix of local news and ads. A small, eight point type is used throughout giving the reader an immense amount of reading matter for his one cent, unmatched in latter twentieth century newspapers.

This ad was typical of the time:[9]

> "THE YELLOW FEVER GERM---has recently been discovered, bears a close resemblance to the malaria germ. To free the system from disease germs take DR. KING'S NEW LIFE PILLS. Guaranteed to cure all diseases due to malaria poison and constipation, 20 cents."

Library of Congress

FORMS OF THE WESTERN MIGRATION

Historians tend to disagree as to the form of the western migration; whether the group colonizers were more influential than the random, loosely organized groups and families. The evidence seems to be on the side of the highly motivated, disciplined, organized bands of migrants who formed their own communities.

The similarity that seems to cover the bulk of midland America arose despite migratory elements of considerable diversity. One has only to glance at a sampling of the communities that were organized by those seeking to perpetuate strong religious, national or social causes to realize that it must have taken a high cultural heat to create the melting pot that exists today.[10]

During the settling of the West this cross-fertilization of culture could only have existed if the barriers of isolation were removed and strong communications links existed.

Some of the communities and the strikingly different groups that founded them are as follows: Greeley, Colorado (Temperance, Religion), Springdale, Iowa (Quakers), Salem, Iowa (Quakers), Angola, Indiana (Spiritualists, Free Love), Zeeland, Michigan (Dutch Reformed Church), Newport, Indiana (Quakers), Harmony, Pennsylvania

(Celibacy, Religion), Salt Lake City, Utah (Polygamy, Religion), Texas, Ohio, and Wisconsin (Organized German colonists). In many states there were: German Baptist "Dunkers", Celibate "Shakers", Communist Owenites and Phalanxes, naturalists, German Pietists, and there were many more.

Page Smith wrote in *The Town In American History:* "While many towns preserved the dominant characteristics and ideals of their founders, others of course did not develop along the line suggested by their early settlement. Towns, whatever their origins, grew more and more alike, not because of any logic inherent in the towns themselves but because they came increasingly under the influence of urban culture and urban values."[11]

Then, of course, readers of small town newspapers and their ready-print sections were never aware that their stories were written, edited and printed in Chicago. The rural culture was being influenced by a big city media mistakenly believed to originate from their beloved home town paper.

The miracle is how quickly, in the main, their cultural bonds were formed and the old broken away. The more radical Amish and Mormons and a few other religious sects who doggedly held onto their traditional life patterns, were the exceptions.

Newell Sims, in his study of an Indiana town that had been founded by Spiritualists from the state of New York, estimated that in 1865 ninety percent of the population were believers in Spiritualism and free-love. He said: "Men frequently traded wives for a season. Women took delight in flaunting their disregard of marital vows, and openly declaring their 'right to choose the fathers of their children, regardless of marriage.'" Public dances were numerous as were drunken debouches and Saturnalian revelries.

The town newspaper at this time was tolerant of these practices by its readers. Not until the establishment of a Christian church and a ready-print newspaper in 1870 did things begin to change. Ideas brought in from outside began to eat away at the established beliefs. Organized Christianity and its ready-print ally quickly moved in on these "forces of pleasure" and the town became indistinguishable from the hundreds of those around it. By 1910, the year of Sim's study, the Christian church, he said, "had become the most dominant social force in Aton, leading reforms, promoting improvements, and directing pleasure." Three-fifths of its citizens were regular church attenders and the town was as booster minded and orthodox as any in the middle west.[12]

GENERIC RELIGION, THE BUILDING OF THE BIBLE BELT

America is one of the most religious countries in the world. If you would climb a hill and view the clusters of American villages and towns around you, the most distinctive feature that you would note are the great number of tall steeples. If you could extend your gaze beyond, to the national borders, you would see 360 thousand churches of a hundred religious varieties, sometimes two or three in a single block. The denominations vary from one extreme to the other—from Biblican fundamentalism and other-worldliness to some sects that are hardly religious at all.

When the isolated villages of America (to visit a neighboring county seat town by horse-and-buggy took an entire day) formed a fervent Bible Belt in a relatively short time, it was the local newspapers that furnished the ready-print *Sunday School Lessons.* Written in "King James" English, *Sunday School Lessons* was the longest surviving column in the history of ready-print, lasting until the demise of the service in 1953.

Since people tend to believe what they see in print, ready-print gave legitimacy and mainstream status to some religions, but selectively excluded others.

The centerpiece of worship for Catholics is the Mass. For Baptists, it's the Bible. For Episcopalians, it's the *Book of Common Prayer.* For the bible-belt ready-print readers it was the common, populist, Sunday School column that appeared in every issue. In Europe it was recognized that printing was the death of the cathedral, but, through print, Americans raised their religion to new, record, heights.

In the handling of religious journalism and the diversity of denominations there were bound to be problems. The editors of ready-print discovered that frontier fundamentalism, with its multitude of sects, were difficult editorial subjects.

Ready-printers in Chicago found themselves trying to determine a middle position on religious quarrels. Was it preferable to baptize by dipping new converts under water or merely sprinkling their heads? Should fundamentalists be allowed ceremonial excesses—to faint and hypnotically "speak in tongues" during their ceremonies? What kind of music, which hymns (if any) should be allowed in the sanctuary? What about the newly arrived sects, the Christian Scientists, Mormons, Mennonites, Amish and other smaller off-shoots of the religion? Was everything to be treated as holy on face value alone. Protestantism had become wildly fragmented, but it was obvious that the ready-print editor could not be Baptist, Episcopalian, Catholic, Seventh-Day Adventist, Congregational, Presbyterian, Lutheran, Church of God and Methodist, etc. all at the same time.

Ready-print's decision was to to try to accomodate all churches, rather than re-set the news type (by hand until they bought their first line casting machine in 1900). But this meant having to "make-ready" their presses over and over again. Ready-print then, turned to issuing a functional one-size-fits-all editorial approach. In this they were surprisingly successful, demonstrating to some of the more quarrelsome sects that they had much in common and could cool down their heated inter-faith arguments.

Ready-print, of course, favored its largest circulation market, the dominant Protestant religious majority, and served the adherents long and faithfully. Wright Patterson, son of a circuit-riding fundamentalist minister, always liberally sprinkled the ready-print pages with writings and quotes from prominent ministers of the gospel. He wanted people to be like him, devout in the fundamentalist Protestant faith.

He made no room for Deism.[13] Many of America's founding fathers would have had a rough time of it in the ready-print era. In America, Franklin, Washington and Jefferson were deists and Madison and Monroe were probably not much more orthodox. Washington openly avoided church services and refused the Eucharist, while Jefferson made disbelief a fashionable heresy.[14]

The term "Bible Belt" is well known as the area, stretching from Pennsylvania down through the South and over to Texas, where tent meetings, and fundamentalism lived with a special intensity. A majority of the issues of ready-print at the turn of the century contained a massive amount of religions and temperance editorial material (at times close to 25 percent).

Religion received regular, cost-free, public relations assists in the form of the ever-present "Sunday School Lessons" in almost every issue and a Christian spin added to many editorial messages. The Protestant Jesus and God were always given preference in print; capitalized with a "He" or "Him" while other minority religious made do with lower case "he" and "him."

The impact of such widespread religious columns appearing in

Example of ready-print.

America's newspapers upheld the religious message with its display of clean, crisp print. Literacy was solidly linked to religion. More appropriate then, than now, was the maxim: "It must be true, I saw it in print!"---and the print that American's saw the most, was that of the newspapers.

A typical example was the April 7, 1907 issue of ready-print, sent to millions of readers and thousands of newspaper offices. It contained the column headlined *"JACOB'S VISION AND GOD'S PROMISE. Specially prepared for this paper."* The headline disingenuously stated that the piece was written specifically for the spiritual needs of that particular town, but thousands of the papers received the same column---though on different dates. Here again, the technique of disguising the source of ready-print gave the words added impact in the towns, readers believing that what they read was locally written.

Usually the longest column on the page, the religious matter with fundamentalist themes, repeated in a mix of King James and contemporary English such statements as: "In no way do men show their characters more clearly than by the response they make to the goodness of God....It would be well for Christians if they also took heed to be not unequally yoked together with unbelievers (2 Cor. 6:14)."

Strict adherence to the faith was the theme of column after column. Patterson's weekly stories were carefully stitched together by religious specialists, weaving in the main themes of the leading Protestant religions, skillfully allowing for the differences in interpretation that had spawned the hundreds of separate sects across America.

Moral messages abounded, such as: "The best start in life a young man can have is the benediction of a godly father or mother." Or, in the regular Methodist Epworth League column: "Is it not of God's grace that there has been such an upheaval in civic matters in the past few years?"

Perhaps even more penetrating into the national psyche was ready-print's habit of moving religious belief into the editorial pages, as well. WNU caused a stir in 1917 when it offered Rinehart's novel *"The Girl Who Had No God"* as a serial. It quickly explained that this was not an atheist tract but actually a pro-Christian story, explaining in a large promotion ad: "To have no God! To go through childhood motherless, and with a father who taught her his unbelief and pointed out Christians as slaves to a myth. To come to womanhood a dreamer, shut off from her kind, calloused to robbery and violent deeds...If one is

to live through great crises one must have a higher power to turn to."
A large source of income for the ready-print publishers were the religious weeklies sprouting up over the midwest and south. Many of them signed on with the ready-print service.

Infrequently a local editor would lash out at the boilerplate- and readyprint-assisted wave of religious fervor. But such editorializing was seldom seen in the face of the organized wrath, usually applied in economic form, meted out by church members.

A colorful campaigner against Bible Belt religion was Edgar Watson Howe, editor and publisher of the Atchison (Kansas), *Globe.* Operating from his bustling railroad town located on the Missouri River, he proclaimed that he was intolerant of liars, hypocrites and religion. Calder Pickett, his biographer, wrote: "He did this in a time of intense national piety, and in a section of America often regarded (and so referring to itself) as the Bible belt." His technique is illustrated in this item he wrote for his paper: "In Missouri, the other day, a mule deliberately committed suicide. He put his head through a post-and-rail fence, slipped his neck down to a narrow place, pulled back, and choked himself. The cause of the suicide is not known. He had not been drinking, and there was no trouble with his family. It is thought by some to have been the result of religious excitement."[15]

He also wrote: "To me, the most wonderful thing in civilization is religion. That people should have advanced so marvelously in everything else, as they have done, and carried along with them a doctrine they know to be untrue, is a fact I have marveled at all my life." He also took aim with: "Never have I known a sincere religious man or woman."

It took boldness, sitting in mid-Kansas, to write: "After a man has said grace at a meal some time is required before those around the table become comfortable again."

His novel *The Story of a Country Town* was well received wordwide.[16] In Europe he was feted in high literary circles. He would, in time, be placed alongside Sherwood Anderson, Theodore Dreiser, Mark Twain and Sinclair Lewis as a premier American novelist.

COMMUNICATING WITH OTHER ISOLATED AMERICANS

And how about the other cultural factors, how did they move across the land, the musical tastes, dress, humor, manners, sports, housing, competitiveness, educational methods, prejudices, facial expressions, merchandising methods, funerals, agricultural techniques, marriage ceremonies, eating habits, and so on.

It is evident that an efficient method of communication existed between the isolated communities of the frontier and the opinion makers and trend setters of the metropolitan areas and the newspaper becomes the most likely carrier of this information. Lonely American frontier towns and rural dwellers eagerly turned to their local newspapers to achieve group-awareness as a counter to isolation.

The reading of small town newspapers was all the more avid since there was little else to read. The national magazines were still in their infancy and of little interest to the average reader. For example, in 1890 the *Women's Home Companion* had only 80,000 circulation, and the *Atlantic Monthly* had a circulation of only 10,000, nationwide.[17]

National characteristics are quite apparent in the American people. In 1929 Robert and Helen Lynd reported that they could see a pattern. In their book, *Middletown* they described the civic club members' facial expression as follows: "Look at their faces. Oddly, they seemed all of one type. Fat or thin, old or young, one mark was on them all. Not dullness; not exactly; these were successful men. The keenest of them showed the mark most plainly. Moderation---the keying down of all spiritual force to the general level. No deep calm lines of single purpose, no steady driving set of jaw, no eyes of meditation. Rather a harassed and a scattered look, the mark of a thousand small habitual restraints, the price of living comfortably with neighbors."[1]

Lord Bryce, after studying America at the end of the nineteenth century, wrote about the "enormous ratio which the reading of newspapers bears to all other reading, a ratio higher than even in France or England...Although the leading American newspapers contain far more non-political matter than those of Europe..."

Bryce could only summon up a few paragraphs on newspapers in his two volume, two thousand page work *The American Commonwealth*. He stated that the newspapers needed a whole chapter, but did not write it.

He also wrote: "Americans are surprisingly alike in appearance and values, considering the startling size of the country and number of remote areas. Unlike China, the Soviet Union, Nigeria, Britain, France and many other countries internal cultural differences in the U.S. are at a minimum---with the exception, of course, of the residents of the South. But North or South, what one notes in the United States is a sameness that quickly and efficiently changes immigrants to its ways, usually within two generations."[18]

AN AMERICAN LANGUAGE

The course of the English language still needs much mapping. Midwest English has become standard American English. To verify, one need only note the nationwide radio, television, movies and the stage. All now speak (or attempt to speak) as they do in the inland---midwest and western areas of the United States. European-sounding southern, New York City and New England ways of speech have remained localized while this newer form of speaking and writing moved across the West. American English has changed rapidly.[19]

Reading and linguistics are linked. "Dialect" writing, as displayed by Mark Twain, Petroleum V. Nasby, and others pictured the speech of the developing areas. As the country moved west, writing, once it appeared in print, legalized the way Americans talk. New expressions were added in the press' political coverage, in the fiction, in the features of the ready-print and boilerplate that showered the continent. There developed a special character to the American language as it moved westward, new words for a new nation.

As Mary Helen Dohan has written: "It was inevitable that those who sought the frontier—discontented Anglo-Americans, adventurous Scots, devout Germans—set out..., leaving behind not only British accents but also British loyalties, which most of them did not have in the first place, the separation between them and the seaboard people should be not only geographical, but political and cultural as well."[20]

Newspaper English and common English have become close to one another. American town editors, early on, showed a knack for inventive use of the English language, though their output was full of euphemisms and airy, flowery phrases.

The large influx of new editors and reporters to man the ready-print and boilerplate newspapers revealed a shortage of good writers in America in the latter nineteenth and early twentieth century. A shortage of writers meant that there was much copying back and forth, spreading the new words and expressions in the more coveted "printed form" across the country. It also meant that much creation of language was going on, with the improvisers boldly staking new linguistic ground. Western and Midwestern speech in the United States could hold its own in originality and colorfulness with the Southern and Appalachian. An example of original use of the language and a penchant for poetry was this obituary written by an Arizona editor on the death of a highly esteemed gambler (you can picture the editor standing in the press room pulling each letter of type out of the typecase before him, thinking up the words and setting the type in a continuous motion):

> ...Death loves a shining mark, and she hit a dandy when she turned loose on Jim. He never played a short card nor overlooked a bet. A fact that is recorded on the unsullied pages of the BOOK OF LIFE above. He was square and open in all his dealings and never weakened on a bluff as long as he had a chip to back it up.
>
> Our camp is in mourning today, the somber emblems of death being displayed on every hand. All is black and gloomy, and nearly all the boys drink black port wine in honor of his memory.... But why should we mourn now, for he is happier now. A way up beyond yonder shining, star-studded battlements of glory, Jim is standing today with his breeches in his boots, listening to the music and trying to catch on to the points of the game. We lost and heaven took down the bet and why should we kick? If the cards run agin' us, it isn't on account of any funny business of the dealers.
>
> > Dear Jim, thou art gone from our midst
> > And thy loss we sincerefully mourn—
> > No one lived more square than thou didst,
> > And hence our hot tear-drops are pour'n.
> > We laid thee to rest 'neath the sod,
> > And grievously bade thee adieu,
> > And we know that the merciful God
> > Hain't no squarer angel than you.
>
> Good bye old boy, and may your last sleep be as quiet and peaceful as the noonday snooze of a babe. And when the last horn shakes up the earthly echoes and Gabriel calls court up above, may you go through the cross-examination without making a bad break. Requi 'scat in peace.[21]

One of the favorite poets to appear in the ready-print columns in the early part of the twentieth century was Edgar A. Guest. Inlanders loved his melancholy, sentimental poems. The hard, agricultural existence could absorb only a minimum amount of fancy cultural trimming. Besides the farmers and their town-dwelling compatriots never missed a chance to distance themselves from Eastern ways. So, they set out to adjust the language to suit themselves, giving English a most violent wrenching in the process.

Inland village front porches seemed just right for reading Guest's poems out of the country newspaper. His sentiments and values meshed precisely with the reader. The poems seemed to be written to the beat of a metronome. Grammarians cringed as he twisted the language to fit.

The most obvious casualty of Guest's poetry was the letter "g." Mid- and far-westerners have always avoided pronouncing "g" if it appeared at the end of a word. His readers could repeat from memory long passages of his poetry, especially those written in the concentrated midwestern dialect. Most popular was the emotional "It Takes a Heap O'Livin' in a House t' Make it Home." All could recite the long poem without missing a word. This was inland, mainly midwest, spoken English, words like: ye've (you've), an' (and), 'em (them), 'round (around), jes (just), t' (to), o' (of).[22]

The attrition of printing type had its impact on language. Type wore out, got lost, and was expensive. Before the invention of the typewriter most country editors wrote their copy directly into type and this sometimes dictated their writing style. A shortage of type in the case forced them to use shorter words and descriptions. Prosperous printer/editors with type cases filled to overflowing with the fairly expensive type pieces, could ramble on endlessly in their articles. Parsimonious editors, or those near bankruptcy, if they found, for example, that they had run out of the letter "W" they would substitute two letter "V" pieces of type, butted together.

Ready-print editor Pat Patterson's love of poetry of the typically American home-spun variety caused a lot of it to appear on the ready-print pages. Every issue had an immense amount of it, good and bad. Deep-felt feelings came to the fore when rime or verse was used and the WNU editorial rooms in Chicago sported a number of cigar-chomping, hard bitten types with a talent for the delicate phrase.

The use of the telegraph and the increase in size of advertisements in newspapers at the end of the last century shortened the language of print. Long rambling sentences wouldn't do since space was at a premium on the newspaper pages. At first the papers turned to small print, to agate size type, but complaints, especially from elderly readers, required the editors to trim excess words, and use short words—those who stayed with the old flowery style and did not adopt the terse, idiomatic new style ran the risk of doing a very un-American thing: making a distinction between social classes, "puttin' on airs."

Notes

1. Sinclair Lewis, *Main Street,* (New York: Harcourt, Brace and Co. Inc., 1920) Introduction.
2. Thomas D. Clark, *The Southern Country Editor,* (Indianapolis: New York: The Bobbs-Merrill Company, 1948) p.58.
3. Wayne E. Fuller, *RFD, The Changing Face of Rural America,* (Bloomington: Indiana Univ. Press, 1966) p.291.
4. Boorstin, *The Democratic Experience* (New York: Random House, 1973) p. 136.
5. Henry Steele Commager, *The American Mind,* (p.69-70)
6. Lewis Atherton, Main Street on the Middle Border, (Bloomington: Indiana University Press, 1954) p.119.
7. Richard N. Current, *History of Wisconsin* (Stevens Point: Worsalla Publishing, 1976) p.535. Richard N. Current
8. Vianna Moog, *Bandeirantes and Pioneers,* (New York: George Braziller, 1964) p.146.
9. The survey was taken of the issues of the Chestertown, Maryland "Enterprise," an independently owned newspaper that existed until the 1950s. It suspended operation about the time that ready-print went out of business, as did many papers around the country.
10. Page Smith, *As a City Upon a Hill,* The Town in American History (New York: Knopf, 1966,) p.101 ff.
11. Ibid, p.18 ff
12. Newell Sims, *A Hoosier Village* (New York: Columbia Univ. Press, 1912) 28-63 ff. This study of Angola, Indiana, (named Aton in the book.) speaks of the influence of the local papers on the character of the city. Begun as a spiritualist and free love community, Angola grew to become the typical midwest county seat town.
13. Deism is defined as: Belief in the existence a God on the evidence

of reason and nature only with rejection of supernatural revelation.

14. Homer W. Smith, *Man and His Gods* (Boston: Little Brown and Co., 1955) p.400-01.

15. Calder M. Pickett, *Ed Howe, Country Town Philosopher* (Lawrence: The University Press of Kansas, 1964) p.33.

16. Edgar W. Howe, *The Story of a Country Town* (New York: Dodd, Mead & Company. 1927).

17. Lynds, op.cit., p.231.

18. Bryce, *The American Commonwealth,* (New York: MacMillan Co., 1920) p.276.

19. See *Phonology of the Lost Cause* by Michael Montgomery and Cecil Melo in *English World-Wide,* fall, 1990.

20. Mary Helen Dohan, *Our Own Words* (Baltimore: Penguin Books, 1974) p.152.

21. In author's collection.

22. Edgar A. Guest, "It Takes a Heap o'Livin' in a House t' Make It Home," , *The American Magazine* (April, 1922) p.7.

Chapter Eight

Evidence of Propaganda

> The U. S. has "a population reading on the average at the sixth grade level...its reading is newspapers, and very little else."[1]
> — *McClure's Magazine,* July 1912

GOVERNMENT AND PRIVATE SUBSIDY

Many governments of the world, totalitarian or democratic, do not share the British and American tradition of the press as an independent watchdog and adversary of government. Examples are the several western democratic European countries where the press receives direct government subsidies.

In the U.S. especial commitment in communications and media to private ownership and to the profit motive is unique world-wide. These were the findings of a 1979 joint Ford Foundation/International Communication Agency report.[2]

Historically the private enterprise free press system in the U.S. has worked remarkably well. But why has it succeeded in a scandal-marked U.S. society where a lot of political shennanigans and "back-scratching" prevail. U.S. is a society where many legislators even admit that they can be influenced by campaign contributions.

Newspapers have been allowed to proliferate, to offer competition to each other. The system has been automatically self-cleansing. There simply have been too many papers, too many separate proprietors to bribe (though, nonetheless, bribery has occurred). However, even the most well-heeled national political organization or special interest would face bankruptcy attempting to "grease the palm" of many thousands of publishers.

Influencing a central news source by the bribers would seem to have made more "economic" sense. This was shown in New York city in the 1870s when the notorious political "Boss" Tweed Ring, which dealt directly with many papers, came under fire from The New York *Times*. The *Times* editorial campaign destroyed the generous advertising subsidies paid by the political machine to many nearby newspapers, with the effect that 27 of 89 newspapers on the payroll of the ring suspended operations and others changed in ownership, management, personnel, and politics.[3]

America, like some of the other countries, has looked away from its endemic bribery, especially that openly practiced in the political field. Those indulging in bribery use ambiguous words, prefering the more innocent, and legal-sounding expressions like: "gifts," "campaign contributions," "points," and "finder's fees." By whatever word, much of the money passed on is in return for favors or influence, a bribe by any reasonable definition. Bribery can be a threat to the free press as well, with "institutional advertising" one sees now and again in the papers, designed to influence the editor's pen.

Also, it stands to reason that, with one exception, the U.S. has historically lacked "one-reaches-all" national newspapers with circulations large enough to reach a majority of the readers. The one exception was ready-print. It was dominant, it was a "national newspaper." Was it, then, a target for bribers? Alas, the U.S. Senate and the courts charged that it was.

In the U.S. "press code" a newspaper that beds down with the enemy (politician for example) jeopardizes its role as honest independent watchdog and adversary of government. This, in the American cultural scheme, would be a serious breach of confidence with its readers, in theory causing circulation to fall and advertisers to withdraw and the paper, justifiably, could pay with its very life.

Of course this punishment would be more easily applied in the ambience prevailing at the turn of the century when newspapers were locally owned, and possessed reasonable resources unlike the diversified communications conglomerates of today who would barely feel the sting of having a few of their papers driven out of business by the lack of public support.

In the case of ready-print, news historian Lucy Maynard Salmon, writing in 1923, warned of the dangers of ready-print propaganda: "Yet as no field can be absolutely free from dangerous germs, the 'ready-print' matter may have danger concealed beneath an apparently innocuous exterior. If 'eternal vigilance is the price of liberty' in the state, it is equally the price the historian must pay for truth and the advertising carried with 'ready-print' matter may be less innocent than the unwary suspect."

But Salmon, while acknowledging that two-thirds of Americans were readers of ready-print and boilerplate, could only find two pages to give to the subject in her estimable 500 page work *The Newspaper and the Historian.* Quixotically, the balance of her study was centered on the newspaper as a historical document, but she defined "newspaper" as something that came out every day—not weekly, and came from a big city; not from the outlands and wilderness where most Americans actually lived.[4]

There were some occasional victories for the guerilla forces of the free, unpropagandized press in America. An editor of an Indiana semi-weekly, with whom the author was acquainted, closely scanned all of the incoming boilerplate before inserting it into the pages and he would sometimes find propaganda or advertising tucked into a corner of the article or picture. Even if it got by him at the first reading and was locked onto the press the editor was not deterred. In one case he stopped the Country Campbell press in mid-run to scratch part of the soft metal of a photo to remove the name of an insurance company, leaving a jagged scar where the name once stood.

Only on one occasion did the W.N.U. brag about its propaganda. In World War II the company threw its shoulder into the war effort. Noting that the farmers and villagers did not buy enough "Liberty" Bonds used to finance the war effort, Wright Patterson was contacted by the Federal Reserve Board to help them out. Patterson defined it as "propaganda for a good cause."[5]

He put his writers behind the effort, writing it up in the news columns and advertisements. Patterson was bragging about it even ten years after the war, saying: "In a sense this was pure propaganda. But the cause was legitimate. In the next Liberty Loan campaign, per capita subscriptions in the country districts rose to twenty-three dollars (over 100% increase).[6]

MR. COUNTRY EDITOR, IF YOU DON'T PLAY ALONG, WE'LL RUN YOU OUT OF BUSINESS!

The national anti-trust law was enacted to counter the inability of the states to handle the problem of corporate monopoly that was plaguing the country. It was the era of editorial muckraking, books like Ida

Tarbell's *History of the Standard Oil Company,* and *Collier's* and *McClure's* magazines led the way with revelations of corporate chicanery and the building of trusts to monopolize trade in dozens of industries. Under Theodore Roosevelt the government finally went into action bringing suit against the trusts in the first decade of the new century. Railroads, steel companies, the meat packers and oil barons were burned by the publicity arising from the court cases. Though few were prosecuted the government moved successfully against some of the biggest violators.

Increasingly the U.S. population was being editorially dominated by the Western Newspaper Union. Despite the existence of a dozen branch offices, the bulk of the W.N.U.s editorial product was written in Chicago, edited by Wright A. Patterson. Branch offices were mainly gladhanding regional sales offices seeking to sell the company's products which also included printing equipment and ink. The editorial matter was left almost totally to the Chicago headquarters, with its staff of 25 reporters and feature writers.

Beginning in 1900, W. N. U., under the leadership of George A. Joslyn, began the takeover of the entire ready-print and boilerplate business in the United States. By 1912 only the small American Press Association still stood as a serious competitor---and only in the boilerplate side of the business.[7]

There were reports that unfair business methods against some newspapers by W.N.U. began to appear in America's heartland. The scene was repeated in hundreds of the colorful small city and town newspapers from the Atlantic to the Pacific: publishers toiling over their type cases and editorial pencils were called away to the front office to be confronted by visitors from W.N.U. threatening to run them out of business if they did not drop a competitor's ready-print or boilerplate service.

The stern-eyed intruders from W.N.U. meant business, and the country publishers knew it. W.N.U. threatened them with starting competing newspapers (in towns that barely supported one or two papers) if they continued to patronize competitors.[8]

The methods worked despite counter measures by the publishers and the American Press Association (which was working to share the advertising profits among all the town publishers rather than keeping them—which was W.N.U.'s policy).

In 1910, after buying out his last major ready-print competitor the New York Newspaper Union, Joslyn became the czar of the

| The Old Home Paper | The Sterling Kansas Bulletin |
| Vol. 27 May 1, 1903. No. 18 | |

The Bulletin is printed on No. 1 paper, so as to stand the wear and tear of family reading and borrowing by the neighbors.

This Kansas newspaper was home-print, except for the boilerplate

ready-prints, in effect he became the co-publisher of over 6,000 ready-print newspapers, most of whose pages and news stories looked surprisingly alike.[9]

Thus W.N.U. was the dominant "Free Press" in America since it held the overpowering lead in readership—many times the circulation of any other publication. The prevailing wisdom has been that the bulging, concentrated press of the big city was the only "press" around worth mentioning—yet very few Americans west of the Alleghenies or south of Philadelphia ever saw a copy of these city papers.[10]

George Joslyn was "boilerplating America" and he knew the effect of his gigantic circulation and its money-making potential---as did his patent medicine advertisers and propaganda customers. More than just Bible lessons and news appeared in the folksy ready-print and boilerplate. Many of the members of the United States Senate were convinced that W.N.U.'s ready-print was not a straightforward honest news sheet as that company's publicity handouts pictured it.[11]

Joslyn, not satisfied, moved to take over the boilerplate business as well, but the surviving American Press Association put up a fight. In W.N.U.'s official company biography the attempted takeover was hailed as the "Era of Consolidation" without giving details. But town publishers worried about getting their ready-print and boilerplate from a single supplier. The danger of hidden propaganda also was a concern.

The laws of the nation forbade the licensing of newspapers, but the Chicago ready-print suppliers (especially in the 1890-1920 period) dispensed a form of commercial licensing in offering (or not offering) franchises. The ready-print suppliers, even though they were the partial publishers of the nation's town press (or publishers of a national newspaper, if you view it that way) chose to remain in the shadows by always referring to themselves as a "service to the newspapers" much as a paper, ink or a printing press supplier would define itself. While this moved them out of the public limelight, their self-description as a business made them vulnerable to the Sherman anti-trust act passed by the Congress in 1890 and placed the company outside of the protective legal umbrella of the First Amendment.

The Western Newspaper Union had become completely dominant. With only a few dozen exceptions, almost all of America's town newspapers used WNU ready-print or its near-twin, the boilerplate.

CHARGE READY-PRINT AND BOILERPLATE WITH "FORMING SINISTER MONOPOLY" TO INVADE THE MINDS OF AMERICANS

There was one of those periodic Red Scares in 1912. The Department of Justice landed in the newspaper headlines when it filed a suit against W.N.U. The government, in the deposition, stated that forces were under way to sell the national ready-print newspaper to "those interested in instilling certain economic ideas in the minds of the public." The "economic idea" referred to was socialism, but this was not revealed in the deposition. The Department of Justice could ignore Joslyn but the spectre (highly unlikely) of a possibly dominant Socialist news source was enough to incite action against the monopolist ready-print.

After decades in which W.N.U. ready-print seemed to enjoy throwing its political and financial muscles around in what was clearly a violation of anti-trust laws, the U.S. Goverment intervened and took action against the Western Newspaper Union in an attempt to stop the takeover of its only remaining boilerplate competitor, the American Press Association.

The charges against the Western Newspaper Union revealed that the company, despite picturing itself as a sort of cooperative group devoted to the cause of the town press, was actually a heavy-handed monopoly that would not hesitate to twist the arms of individual newspapers if it would help the cause of W.N.U.

On August 3, 1912, a petition was filed in the U.S. District Court. Under the anti-trust act of 1890 the defendants were ordered to stop acts of unfair competition such as threatening a publisher with starting a competing newspaper in the same town if he did not buy the ready-print or boilerplate from them; or undercutting prices to achieve the same ends. The judgment was made by Kennesaw Mountain

Landis, whose fame from this and other cases caused him later to be titled one of the nations most liberal judges. Landis also sat in judgment on the Standard Oil Company, fining it $29,000,000 for anti-trust violations. Later in life he retired from the bench and became the first Commissioner of Baseball.

The court decree charged also that in 1909 and before, W.N.U. acted in concert (with A.P.A.) to destroy competition and attempted to prevent additional competition from arising. The details offered in the government's suit gave a less than pretty picture of the way the way W.N.U. (also called the Central-West Printing Co., the name of its holding company) did business.

Using the words of the deposition, the suit listed the following unfair acts of the Western Newspaper Union:

"Gross underselling of their competing services in the chief field of operations of such competitors; (2) sending out traveling men with instructions to call only on the customers of such competitors and to get the trade of such customers regardless of the prices which it might be necessary to quote; (3) summoning such competitors to conferences and openly telling them they could not continue in their competing business, but that they must either get out or sell out, and coupling such demands with threats of still fiercer unfair competition, including the installation of competitive plants in their territory, and a recitation of plants already bought out or put out, ..."

Central-West Publishing Co. and its subsidiary companies also were accused of these other counts of unfair competition:

(1) While maintaining their old prices to political committees, and in the territory where they are not in competition with the American Press Association, they sell to their other customers stereotyped plates below cost for the purpose of destroying the trade of their... competitor. However, they refuse to enter into long-term contracts at such prices, thus showing that these prices are but temporary.

(2) They have caused certain persons to purchase small blocks of stock of the American Press Association for the purpose of harassing said association by unconscionable and unreasonable demands for examination of books, accounts, and records of said association, and for the purpose of obtaining other inside information of their competitor's business.

(3) They are either causing or permitting their agents throughout the country to persistently circulate reports to the effect that they will put the American Press Association out of business in a short time; that the

competition; that a combination by them with the American Press Association will be formed, and other similar reports; and that unless the country publishers to whom these statements are made patronize them at this time they will be made to suffer as soon as the American Press Association is out of the field.

(4) They have threatened papers located at points that can not support two small newspapers to start competing papers unless they patronize defendants.

(5) They promise to protect publishers against suit for damages that may arise because of repudiation of contracts with their said competitor.

(6) In connection with the last stated, at times they offer free paper and free plate for thirty days in order to enable customers to change temporarily to a home-print paper, and thus to avail themselves of the clause in the American Press contracts permitting cancellation of contracts by papers becoming "home-print" papers and coupling such bonus thus given with an agreement to change back to Western Newspaper Union's ready-print at a cut price with free plate service continued for the home-print side.

"They either instruct and authorize their agents to retain or permit and acquiesce in their retention of plate metal belonging to the American Press Association."[12]

In the suit the Federal Court zeroed in on the ready-prints from two angles. It defined the service as both a business seeking to eliminate all competition and a dangerous propaganda menace.

The U.S. defined the town newspapers and their news sources in this fashion:

> There are in the United States approximately 16,000 smaller or so-called "country newspapers." With an approximate average circulation of 800 per paper, and making a reasonable allowance for duplication, said papers have an aggregate circulation of about 12,000,000 copies; and if each paper is read by but one household, said 16,000 papers reach about 60,000,000 of the people of the United States, or nearly two-thirds of its entire population. Because of the very limited circulation and number of copies of each issue printed by each separate one of these so-called smaller country newspapers and because of the large expense necessary to the gathering of news and the acquisition of miscellaneous matter necessary for the composition and make-up and in the printing of such papers entire in each

The ready-print and boilerplate (example above) reached 60 million people office, for the purpose of gathering news and miscellaneous matter more extensively, to distribute and furnish the said matter and service to all of such smaller papers in a form already made up for the individual use of each of them, and to do this at a less price for such service than it could be done individually by such papers, there have grown up in the United States two competing industries and services known in the newspaper world, respectively, as (1) plate service and (2) ready-print service. Plate service consists in furnishing such news and general matter in the form of metal type plates cast in newspaper lengths and shipped from the several distributing points of the plate concerns to the issuing offices of the papers using it.

Ready-print service is the furnishing of newspapers printed on one side, or on two or more pages, to the several newspapers from the distributing office or offices of the ready-print concerns. Both of the two service are generally known and frequently referred to as the patent insides of the newspaper.

This service is supplied to and this action refers only to what is known as general newspapers and does not take into account papers devoted to a special service, such as the farm and religious papers. Probably 300 out of the 16,000 of these country newspapers are issued without any of either plate or ready-print in their make-up. Many use plate matter alone, in addition to what is set up in each office locally. Few, if any, use ready-print alone, but nearly, if not quite, all who take a ready-print service also use some plate service for special features or for filling up. This for the reason that the ready-print service must be put out in full pages, while the plate service is put out in columns which may be used as sent out or sawed up and rearranged in the local office. Papers using the plate service only, or such combined arrangements, are known as "home-print."[13]

The U.S. Government claimed that a plan had actually been proposed by W.N.U. to sell the profitable combined enterprise to the undisclosed purveyor of controversial economic ideas, but offered no specific evidence for such a charge. The court decreed that the nation should not allow the joining of two major news distributors since two-thirds of Americans read the centrally published ready-print and/or boilerplate produced by the Central-West Publishing Co. and a much smaller, privately owned corporation grandly named "The American Press Association." Central-West Publishing Co., a holding company, was better known in the newspaper industry by the equally imposing title "Western

Newspaper Union." In the event of a take-over the only news not disseminated by the W.N.U. to the majority of Americans through their town newspapers would be the items of local news.

A segment of the decree read as follows: "If all plate and ready-print matter were supplied by one concern, then the news thus distributed and the discussions of economic and other important questions thus supplied would all be designed to mold the sentiments of the readers to one particular view, and that presentation of diverse views and full and free discussion of important questions from different standpoints which is essential to their proper understanding and hence necessary to the best public interests would be prevented. In fact, it appears in the negotiations had between the officers of the Central-West Publishing Co. and the American Press Association, looking to their consolidation, that the expectation was that in view of the great power thus acquired in disseminating information the united property could be disposed of at great profit to those interested in instilling certain economic ideas in the minds of the public...."[14]

In August 4, 1912 an article in the New York Times was headlined "NEWS TRUST CHECKED BY GOVERNMENT SUIT, AFFECTS 60,000,000 READERS---Government Saw Possibility of a Combination Which Would Be Used to Sway Public Opinion. The article stated:

"...the Federal Government to-day took an advanced step under the Sherman law to prevent what the Department of Justice regarded as the possibility of a combination to influence the thought of sixty million readers of rural newspapers.

"The proceedings in this anti-trust suit were terminated in record time. United States District Judge Kenesaw M. Landis entering the agreed decree immediately following the filing of the government's petition and the answers of the defendants.

"The suit was directed against the Central West Publishing Company (holding company of the Western Newspaper Union);...and the American Press Association.... Pointing out that an attempt was made in 1909 to bring about a consolidation of these interests, the Government petition says, "the expectation was that in view of the great power thus acquired (by W.N.U.'s absorption of the Association) in disseminating information the united property could be disposed of at great profit to those interested in instilling certain economic ideas in the minds of the public, and that it was the design that such a disposition of it should be made.

"The circulation from week to week of information and of articles dealing with questions of public importance is of itself inter-state commerce, and for one concern to acquire the power to distribute all such information and to deceive the public by its perversion is itself a serious and substantial restraint upon and a monopolizing of inter-state trade and commerce.

"...As the Western Newspaper Union has assets to the value of $6,500,000 and the American Press Association's assets are only $1,000,000 in value it is quite probable that the latter will be the one to succumb, leaving the Western Newspaper Union in control of the entire field."

In 1915 Joslyn and W.N.U. were again accused of illegally underselling competitors and issuing false reports about them in violation of the 1912 decree and were threatened with the charge of contempt of court.[15]

However, surprisingly, the government later stepped aside when, on September 15, 1917 W.N.U. bought out American Press for 500 thousand dollars (in deflated dollars, of course). W.N.U. took over the American Press Association's boilerplate and photographic business and the offices located in San Francisco, Portland, Buffalo, Columbus, and Philadelphia. American Press removed itself completely from the ready-print and boilerplate business, converting into an advertising agency. The road had reached the summit—the Western Newspaper Union and George Joslyn's ready-print trust finally had it all. The town press, on the other hand, was about to set out on a journey of its own.[16]

The options left to the American town press were diminished once again with the selling of the boilerplate business to the Western Newspaper Union. Increasingly, editors realized that their outside news source came from a monopoly supplier that lacked the restraints of free enterprise competition. The Federal law suits and national publicity were damaging over time to the W.N.U. The ready-print news monopoly, by its open zealousness in achieving its goal of driving all its competitors out of ready-print business, and grabbing the lion's share of the boilerplate, sowed the seeds of its own demise.

"A REAL CASE OF TAINTED NEWS"

The Federal Government was not finished. Investigators of a Senate Committee had uncovered incriminating evidence that revealed the company less innocent than it professed to be. Many believed that

Joslyn was taking money under the table in exchange for favorable news stories.

As noted before, a distinction can be made between the present day "news release"---such as those issued by the White House or some government or private organization—and the hidden propaganda in the ready-print. Unlike the turn of the century patent insides system, the newspaper of today can edit, criticize or ignore a press release.

Faced with a summons from the Senate, George Joslyn in 1914, left the turreted Joslyn Castle in Omaha, and testified in Washington, speaking quite frankly at times. While reminding his senate listeners that he technically had not been violating any laws then on the books (they were passed later). He had, indeed, been issuing hidden unaccredited propaganda, disguised as news, in exchange for payment. Some of the testimony went as follows:

> Sen. Overman: "I understand that any person...who desires to exploit their business and to create public opinion could pay you...to send it to the different papers.
> Mr. Joslyn: "Yes, sir.
> The Chairman: ..." without marking it 'advertisement'?
> Mr. Joslyn: "Yes, sir." A little later on Senator Overman made the point even more plain:
> The Chairman: "There is no way for the general public to know that it is paid for?
> Mr. Joslyn: No sir, there is no way for the general public to know that it was paid for. Today, there is a new law, I understand, with regard to that, which makes it necessary to have it marked in some manner to indicate that.

This kind of testimony was not as damaging to the ready-print service as one might expect, since Joslyn chose not to report it to his sixty million readers. However, *Colliers* magazine and the New York *Times* gave it much play.

Hidden propaganda is very difficult to spot by the average reader.

However, some sharp-eyed recipients complained from time to time about "banker's propaganda" disguised as news; even before the federal government stepped in to control the ready-print and boilerplate monopoly in 1912, warning of its potential for dangerous propaganda.

In 1914 *Colliers* magazine stated: "...the great majority of newspapers in small towns do not, and as a matter of economy cannot, set up the type of all their reading matter." The writers at Collier's, one of the nation's leading magazines at the time, were surprised to learn that ready-print existed; even though it had been in operation for 53 years. Their article was headed "A Real Case of Tainted News," and it included part of the Senate testimony.

The story stated: "The most serious example of 'accelerating' public opinion that has come to our notice for a long time was disclosed at the hearings of the United States Senate Judiciary Committee, commonly known as the Lobby Investigation."[17]

As it turned out it wasn't Russia or the European Socialists that were hiding in the stories in the the ready-print pages—it was Canada, our friendly neighbor to the north. A Senate hearing in 1915 brought out the story that Joslyn had accepted over three million dollars (30 million in 1988 terms) from Canada in exchange for a Canadian propaganda campaign that lured 600,000 American farmers to live in that underpopulated country. The increasingly wealthy Joslyn admitted conducting the campaign but said the amount was less, saying he only received 500 thousand dollars (five million, 1988).[18]

The committee was particularly upset over this revelation. The W.N.U. propaganda was believed by the senators to have caused hundreds of thousands of American farmers to abandon their homes in the U.S. and to move to that country causing economic disruption. The Congress took testimony from George A. Joslyn, the president of the Western Newspaper Union/Central-West Publishing Co. It revealed the extent that America had been propagandized for years. On the Canadian matter the testimony went as follows, as printed in *Colliers* magazine:

Senator Cummins---Do you put also put in plate matter that is furnished by people who desire to further a particular cause?

Mr. Joslyn—Yes Sir.

Senator Cummins (continuing)—Or the cause of a particular man, and distribute it to the newspapers?

Mr. Joslyn—We distribute it to the newspapers free. It is paid for by

The Family Farm, the nineteenth century American ideal.

the people who are interested.

The Chairman (Senator Overman of North Carolina)—I understand that any company, person, corporation, association or firm who desire to exploit themselves or exploit their business, and to create public opinion, could come to you and pay you a certain sum...and you would send out the matter they wanted you to send the different papers, which would print it?

Mr. Joslyn—Yes, sir.

The Chairman—And for that sum of money you would send it out to these papers -without marking it "Advertisement"?

Mr. Joslyn—Yes, sir.

A little later on Senator Overman made the point even more plain:+

The Chairman—There is no way for the general public, then, to know that it is paid for?

Mr. Joslyn—No, sir, there is no way for the general public to know that it is paid for....

The Collier's article also stated: "Senator Cummins expressed the belief that the emigration of some eight hundred thousand American farmers to Canada during the past few years was largely due to this paid propaganda in the guise of honest news. The Lobby Investigation revealed only one customer of the Western Newspaper Union. It would be interesting to know something about the other "persons, corporations, associations, or firms" who exploit themselves through the Western Newspaper Union." But no follow-up investigation was made as the politically powerful Joslyn was allowed to retire back into his castle in Omaha.[19]

Joslyn was followed to the witness stand by Courtland Smith of the small American Press Association, who testified that W.N.U. received large sums for the Canadian propaganda—and the American town publishers received absolutely nothing for running it in their paper. Smith testified that W.N.U. laundered the source of the money, to "hide their trail," as he put it. The articles succeeded in getting American farmers to emigrate. They painted the land in Canada as much better than that in America. They said there were more opportunities there than in the midwest or western parts of the United States. Americans in Canada were quoted as never wanting to return to their native country....the land in Canada was cheaper, more abundant, paid for itself with the first crop, etc.

One can get the message of the propaganda, disguised as a news story, from this portion of one of the articles that was re-printed in the Congressional Record. It had a headline over it saying: "Trip Through Western Canada." It claimed to be about the trip to Canada of a "prominent journalist," who was never identified:

> A prominent journalist from Chicago, some time ago, made a journey through Canada obtaining a thorough knowledge of the land and the people and of the "boundless possibilities" that Canada, the virgin land, affords. In an American Sunday newspaper he published after his return the interesting account which we print as follows. He writes:
>
> "Why did you emigrate from the United States?" I asked a farmer in western Canada.
>
> "I believe that for a poor man western Canada is the most favorable land," was the reply, "and I have found that it is the paradise of the poor."
>
> The Farmer, a pioneer of the west, had five years earlier left Iowa for Canada to secure a new home there. After traversing the country for some time, he started his home on the open prairie and with steady industry devoted himself to the working of the virgin soil. Now he is the well-to-do owner of that endless sea of waving wheat ears that goes on for miles before my eyes. His strong sunburned figure finds the best background in his farm itself, which is the outcome of his ceaseless activity—a pretty two-storied dwelling house, a clean stable, in the midst of a hamlet of barns, sheds, and outbuildings....

Senator Nelson stated during the questioning (the exact total of the emigrants changed from time to time during the testimony), "They have 600,000 of our people (ex-residents in America) up there." To which the witness, Courtland Smith, replied, "And you can not bring into our country 600,000 people from any place in the world to take the place of those people, because they are of the best type. Smith believed that the Canadian campaign also drew people from the South, as well as the Midwest, including 300 families he knew about from Tennessee that had emigrated. But Iowa and Minnesota were the worst hit.[20]

While the Canadian government was being charged with secret financing of propaganda in promotion of their farm lands, they also employed an open advertising campaign in American newspapers. Historian Lewis Atherton did not penetrate ready-print's disguise in the newspapers he researched to write his work "Main Street on the Middle Border." But he spotted the display advertisements that Canada also employed to lure settlers across the border from the United States. Atherton referred to the Hastings, Michigan newspaper's large advertisement, which offered to send, on request, a free pamphlet titled "Last Best West." The advertisement said that many farmers had paid for their land out of the first crop. The homesteads were offered without cost to settlers, were 160 acres in size, and the settler could purchase an additional 160 acres at three dollars an acre.[21]

The effect of the government investigation and resultant publicity caused the ready-print service to change some of its tactics. America was still being boilerplated, but boilerplate now was usually identified as a paid advertisement. McClure's magazine stated that Republican political boilerplate, which W.N.U. distributed, now contained no deception and articles were clearly identified as to source.

However, the advertisements for patent medicines often contained alcohol, opium or other dangerous drugs. Many of the ads were attacked by state press associations and various health organizations, but the degrading and disgusting quality of the advertisements continued. Until the mid-1930s the ads contained graphic discussions of female diseases and male impotence that resulted from syphilis and gonorrhea.

Despite its excesses, the ready-print and boilerplate business lived on into the mid-20th century. The Western Newspaper Union came under new owners and seemed to suffer very little, as ready-print customers fell away—forty percent had dropped the service by the mid-20s—they then signed up for the boilerplate service. In 1923 a company pamphlet, written by their writer Elmo Scott Watson, bragged that 14,273 newspapers were still customers, more than ever. The pamphlet was printed to look like an independent, scholarly study of the ready-print business—and unaccredited.

Watson later wrote a monograph entitled *A History of Newspaper Syndicates, 1865-1935*, using the earlier pamphlet as the basic material of his study, but with a more balanced appraisal of the ready-print scene. He summarized his view of the ready-print as follows: "The part which they have played in the swift increase in the number of papers and in the phenomenal increase in newspaper circulation is impossible to state exactly...the conclusion is inescapable that they must have had a tremendously important part in both."[22]

While its rural constituency remained, the competition of radio and television lured away the advertising dollars (to the very end still substantially patent medicine ads) and hastened its undoing. The last pre-printed newspaper appeared in 1953. Boilerplate still exists, but has diminished with the lithographic technological change in newspaper publishing that occurred in the 1960s.[23]

Still, the old ready-print type of story remained available in magazines like the *Readers Digest* (in its earliest editions an imitation of ready-print style), *National Geographic,* and *Good Housekeeping* But the impact on the reader was lessened as the eyes and ears of Americans were being hotly competed for.

Literacy events like the 1890s Indiana spelling matches have long since disappeared---no longer in vogue. America's children are absorbed with television, with uncertain prospects, it seems.

The ready-print was designed for its time, fitting into a nation filled with innovations, a land of innocents, a land being built, a land of "self-improving." Its part in the standardization and development of the American character and of the free press cannot be ignored.[24]

Notes

1. The entire quote of *McClure's* July, 1912 magazine was: "By 1911, a new thing had come into the world, a democracy of a hundred million people in America had passed through its fifth reader. Its reading was newspapers—and very little else."

2. *The United States and the Debate on the World Information Order,* p. 12.

3. *A. B. Paine, Thos. Nast, His Period and His Pictures* (New York, 1904) p. 129. from Innis, p. 173).

4. Lucy Maynard Salmon, *The Newspaper and the Historian* (New York: Oxford University Press, 1923.) pp. 134-135.

5. Uniquely in the United States the word "propaganda" has taken on a pejorative meaning; unlike Latin countries and the Vatican, which define the word as legitimate advertisements or information.

6. Neil M. Clark, "Patterson Helps to Edit Twelve Thousand Newspapers" *American Magazine,* Oct.,1927. p. 158.

7. In a competitive fight boilerplate did not have the impact of ready-print. In effect, the use of boilerplate gave the local editor the option of running or not running the stories sent from the service supplier. Ready-print, which was indelibly printed on the newspaper to begin with gave the ready-print supplier the added clout (political, financial, psychological) of being co-publisher of 6,000 newspapers and making the final decision on what editorial matter appeared on the pages. Therefore the American Press Association found itself facing W.N.U. competion.

8. Court Records, U.S.A. versus Western Newspaper Union and co-defendants, District Court of the United States for the Northern District of Illinois, statement of decree, 1912-1915, p. 13.

9. Ibid.

10. Please note the census figures on page 51 showing the preponderence of rural dwellers in the America of that time.

11. "We merely serve as an aid to newspaper publishers, and help to edit 12,000 newspapers," Republicans and Democrats, Protestants and Catholics," stated a typical W.N.U. press release in the 1920s.

12. From court proceedings.

13. District Court of the United States for the Northern District of Illinois; Summarized Statement of Pleadings and Decree, pp. 1-2.

14. United States of America v. Western Newspaper Union, American Press Association et, al., defendants. In the District Court of the United States for the Northern District of Illinois. Filed August 3, 1912. Records, U.S. District Court, North Dist. of Illinois.

15. "Accuse Newspaper Union," New York *Times,* June 8, 1915, p.9.

16. Watson, *History of Newspaper Syndicate* (Chicago:1936) p. 53.

17. "A Real Case of Tainted News," *Collier's Magazine,* June 6, 1914, p.16.

18. See Samuelson, p.271 (dollar figures are in current terms).

19. *Collier's Magazine,* op.cit. p.16. For a complete account see the Congressional Record, p.4645, 1914.

20. For comparison to other propaganda that caused southern Americans to emigrate from the United States, the reader may review the book *The Lost Colony of the Confederacy,* by Eugene C. Harter (Jackson, University Press of Mississippi, 1985) p. 13ff.

21. Lewis Atherton, *Main Street on the Middle Border* (Bloomington: Indiana University Press, 1954).

22. Watson, p. 83-84.

23. A variance in the number of newspapers appears in the sources. This is caused by their definition of "newspaper;" and the short life of some of the publications—many of them lasting little more than a year or two, therefore ignored in the various survey lists.

24. "The Hidden Newspaper" by Eugene C. Harter. Some of the material in this section is taken from the author's article in the *Lithopinion Quarterly,* Fall 1975, pp 40-47.

Chapter Nine

The Printers Spouted Shakespeare As They Swayed Before the Cases

> (Letter to Brander Matthews (July 22, 1911) referring to his love for Don Quixote: "Spain, where most of my boyhood was past while I was working at case in my father's printing-office in Ohio."
> —William Dean Howells[1]

> All the me in me is in a little Missouri village halfway around the world.
> —Mark Twain, speaking, late in life

Literary artists were created in the printing environment of mid-nineteenth century America. Time spent before a type case ("working at case") served writers well, many of whom came into the literary sphere directly from U.S. town newspapers. Since many of the stories set by them in their printing apprenticeship had to be thought up and typeset *simultaneously,* their dexterity with language was enhanced by the repetitious act of typesetting.

This act of typesetting at the case was a form of training, useful to writers of the time. It sharpened memory and vocabulary in a unique three-dimensional way. It also offered the ambience for daydreaming and creating the plots and characters of novels. Uniquely, the country editor-hand typesetter wrote directly in precise type to the final printed product; without the intrusive and distorting process of decoding handwriting.

Through the ages, writing for publication has been a procedure two or three steps removed from the printed page. It began with scribbling down the words by pencil or pen. Later, came the use of the typewriter, which approximated print in a rather crude form. The author passed his product on to the printer, who set the words into type and, then, printed the type onto paper.

The appearance of print conveys a subtly-altered message, not seen by the writer until he receives proofs back from the printers. Print displays absolutely precise ninety degree angles, proportionally-spaced letters, justified columns, neat edges and the artistic accouterments (spacing, borders, dashes and type design). Print is the clarifier. As examples of country editors and typesetters-turned literary masters in that time prior to the beginning of the twentieth century one finds a remarkably large and talented assortment: Mark Twain, Walt Whitman, Edward Eggleston, Bret Harte, Edgar Watson Howe, William Dean Howells, William Allen White, Horatio Alger, Hamlin Garland, Booth Tarkington, James Whitcomb Riley, David Graham Phillips, Jack London, Ambrose Pierce, Joel Chandler Harris, Frank Norris, Bayard Taylor, George Ade, Hart Crane and dozens of other authors. They were among the writers who, in their early life, earned their living as letterpress printers and country editors in the inland newspapers. They toiled in newspaper printing shops, gathering and setting the little type pieces by hand from identical "California" job cases (heavy pieces of furniture with drawers and individual bins for each letter in the alphabet). The use of the line casting machine, put into general use early in the twentieth century, of course, put an end to all this.

THE DEVELOPMENT OF WRITERS
"SCULPTORS" OF WORDS

The history of journalism and literature would have been different without the antiquated typesetting methods that existed. Typesetting was awkward; but its slowness had the advantage of training those printers with the proper talent to become skilled writers and subsequently to try their hand at the writing of books.

William Dean Howells was the dean of American letters in the 1880s and 1890s. One can picture him when he stood at the typecase of his father's newspaper, the Hamilton, Ohio, *Intelligencer*---endlessly crafting words and sentences out of little pieces of metal before him. Words so painstakingly created in type (contrasted with the simplicity of scribbling with pencil on paper) took on added value as they were sculpted in metal and were made three dimensional. As a psychological training method; words, sentences, paragraphs took on weight, literally. They could be turned around in the hand---a curious, but effective advantage to young writers burningly anxious to create.

*The upper case and the lower case,
another link between the language and the printing trade*

From Brook's *Howells: His Life and Works* we get a feeling for the print shop, town and countryside. Brooks wrote: "Here and elsewhere he evoked the forest of buckeye and chestnut, the herds of red cattle, the meadows dotted with stumps, and the odor of ink and dusty types in the country printing houses where he had learned to set type when he was six. The printers spouted Shakespeare as they swayed before the cases or flung themselves on the bar that made the impression, and Howells remembered his brother one day carting in a pig that had been accepted for a years subscription. The old-fashioned village paper was the staple of reading on this frontier and the elder Howells hoped to form the tastes and opinions of his farmer readers.[2]

The writer's brother was quoted: "Setting type as a little boy, the younger Howells, had altogether scarcely a year of schooling; yet he contrived to teach himself German, French and Spanish and even a little Latin before he grew up."

New York *Times* writer Hal Borland, whose father was a country editor in Colorado just after the turn of the century wrote a book about his experience in the country newspaper when he was a boy. He wrote: "I learned to set type (by hand) and in the learning I also learned about grammar, syllabication, punctuation and spelling, probably more than I ever learned in school. Father never finished the eighth grade in school...an avid and critical reader, he had an uncanny sense of words and a large vocabulary.... He got a basic education at the type case, broadened it with books and magazines, and was both articulate and informed. He gave me the rudiments of strength and clarity as a writer.[3]

City newspapers, on the other hand, offer a contrasting experience in the training of America's literary "stars" of that era. Country printers and editors pitched into all phases of their small sized newspapers and were less shackled to a fixed style of writing. In contrast the employees of the big city newspapers were made into specialists. They sometimes spent large portions of their working lives mechanically writing only obituaries, or police court news, or about accidents and fires. Such compartmentalization had its effect, added to the fact that large city newspapers would not allow the opinion of the lowly reporters to enter their stories.

On city papers the writing talent had to find other ways of training their minds to the ritual of literature and it is not difficult to discern a different, hard edged writing pattern in the works of city-trained ex-journalists not trained in typesetting such as Theodore Dreiser, Willa Cather, Ernest Hemingway and James L. Cain.

READING UPSIDE DOWN AND BACKWARDS

The letterpress, as compared to the lithographic, printing process requires efficient reading of inverted type (which reads not only upside down but backwards). Reading of it was a trick that took a while for a novice printer (including this author) to perfect. Even the most efficient high school or college Literature teacher could not now match the training of the mind offered by this tortuous and repeated setting into type.

Printers of that era came to know good writing from bad. Picture if you will: at one moment they would be setting an excerpt from a Charles Dickens novel, later, a note from a country correspondent, a windy presidential speech copied from another newspaper, or a sermon from a backwoods preacher.

Printers stood, poised hour after hour before their type cases, either reading from the copy or setting the story from their own imagination, replacing the letters in an upside down and backwards fashion onto the type stick.

The prime example of this training was that of printer Mark Twain. He was richly gifted, there may never be another like him; due to the link between his talent and the childhood typesetting training he received.

After the introduction of the line casting machine there never has reappeared another literary stylist even remotely similar, or as talented as Mark Twain. Hand typesetting, supported and perpetuated by the use of ready-print in country newspapers have had their impact.

Twain's genius materialized from what, from afar, seems barren literary ground. It sprung from the wilderness that was the midwest. He was not only a marvelous writer but also an exceptionally talented typesetter, much admired for his excellent, clean proofs. He set type not only for country newspapers, but also for America's leading book publishers and metropolitan newspapers. It was a talent he exploited to finance his travels and eventual entry into the world of full-time authorship.[4]

At age twelve,[5] after the death of his father, Twain was thrust into Hannibal, Missouri's town newspaper print shop. He was a printer for twelve years. A matter of survival became an education. Like many another frontier printer, he would stand for hours (occasionally sitting on a tall stool) before the case, lifting out the tiny, soot-smeared metal type, a letter at-a-time, adding spacers between the letters and words to make the lines come out even (justified) on both sides.

The country newspapers carried much literary matter at that time before ready-print and boilerplate---poems, essays, short stories, all swiped from other papers and the few books in the village. John Lauber, in his book *The Making of Mark Twain* wrote:

> The apprenticeship gave him a lifelong interest in the technology of writing;... it could provide a literary education.... Mark Twain would pride himself on his mastery of English grammar and punctuation; he was more likely to have acquired those abilities in the printing office than in the schoolroom...the printing office was said to be the poor boy's college.

But the work was hard and rough, with long hours. It instilled of burning lifelong desire in Twain to develop a better system of typesetting, exploring not only complicated line casting machines but also pioneer typewriters. Even into old age, the hunger for better typesetting was fixed his mind. He lost a fortune in futile attempts to design a practical type machine for the print shops of the world (we will cover this later in this work). The crudeness of printing and typesetting had a way of driving a man like Twain to distraction. Ready-print and boilerplate arrived at the right time to ease the burden but not to solve it.

THE LINE CASTING MACHINE ARRIVES

There were still around 1,500 newspapers using the ready-print when it went out of business in 1953. There were even some newspapers using the hand-set method to set their type as late as the middle 1970s.

Boilerplate, on the other hand, still exists in the form of camera-ready printed sheets, modem-received computer messages over telephone lines, and floppy disks mailed to newspapers. The reasons for the demise of ready-print can be laid to (a) The moving of America's population into the cities; (b) The Rural Free Delivery; (c). The arrival of radio and television; and (d) the increased popularity of lithography and its central printing plants. But the most important reason was the elimination of hand-set type by the use of the line casting machine even in the smaller newspapers. In an age of inventions, the development of the Linotype line casting machine, manned by a single compositor, was hailed far and near. It was in the cities that the dramatic new machine had its first impact as the swollen metropolitan newspapers, involved in ruinous competitive circulation battles, sought to cut costs.

In reality the Linotype line casting machine was, like its competitors, a ridiculous-looking device; with far too many moving parts, and far too difficult to operate. But it's grand reception into the printing and newspaper industries was a consequence of timing, good public relations by the manufacturer and long frustration---and, after all, it could do the labor of four hand typesetters. If it had arrived a few years later it would have been laughed out of existence. The public, the labor unions and social planners quickly took notice of this labor-saving device and its impact on the number of employees in the printing trade. In the big cities hundreds of hand typesetters suddenly found themselves without a trade as the big publishers gobbled up the early output of the Linotype factory. And across the country many

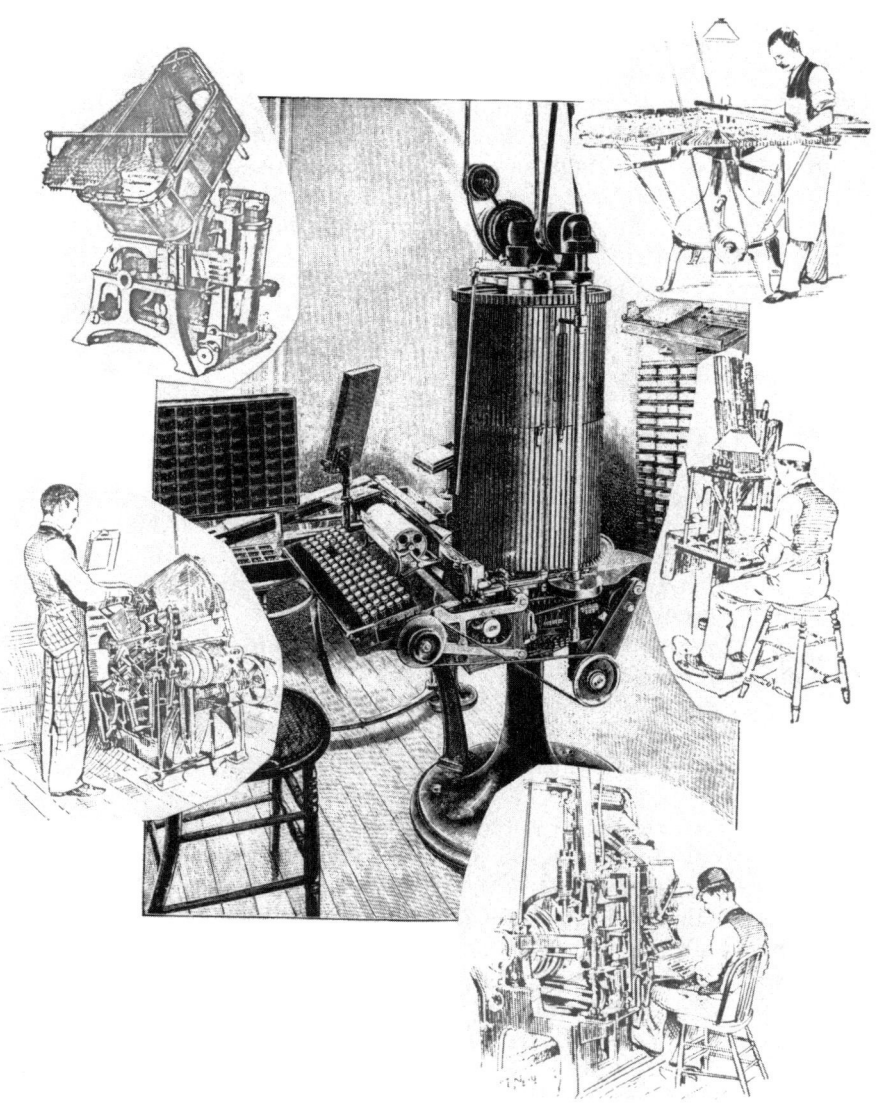

All types of machines were invented to set type automatically—few worked well.

thousands of hand-typesetters were put out of work by the machine. Like the Luddites of the eighteenth century, there was talk of strike and disruption---but little came of it because the number thrown out of work was relatively small in an economy that employed millions.

But the issue had its personal side, as many writers had earlier in their lives set type before the case. Charles M. Sheldon's best selling 1889 book charged that the device was an example of the unfairness of the economic system.[6]

He wove it's impact on the system into the philosophy of Social Christianity (called by its adherents "the Religion of Reason") with the following chronicle which became a parable in that time of U.S. labor upheaval and discontent. He summed it up in this scene:

> The entire congregation was startled by the sound of a man's voice. It came from the rear of the church, from one of the seats under the gallery. The next moment the figure of a man came out of the shadow there and walked down the middle aisle. Before the startled congregation fairly realized what was going on, the man had reached the open space in front of the pulpit and had turned about, facing the people.
>
> 'I've been wondering since I came in here.... I'm not drunk and I'm not crazy, and I'm perfectly harmless; but if I die, as there is every likelihood I shall in a few days, I want the satisfaction of thinking that I said my say in a place like this....
>
> I lost my job ten months ago. I am a printer by trade. The new Linotype machines are beautiful specimens of invention, but I know of six men who have killed themselves inside of the year just on account of those machines. Of course I don't blame the newspapers for getting the machines. Meanwhile, what can a man do?...
>
> I've tramped through this city for three days trying to find a job; and in all that time I've not had a word of sympathy or comfort except from your minister here, who said he was sorry for me and hoped that I would find a job somewhere. I suppose it is because you get so imposed on by the professional tramp that you have lost your interest in the other sort. I'm not blaming anybody, am I? Just stating facts. Of course I understand you can't go out of your way to hunt up jobs for people like me. I'm not asking you to, but what I feel puzzled about, what is meant by following Jesus? What do you mean when you sing 'I'll go with him, with him all the way?' Do you mean that you are suffering and denying yourselves

An early linecasting machine

Mark Twain's folly; granted a patent in 1895

and trying to save lost, suffering humanity just as I understand Jesus did?... I understand there are more than 500 men in this city in my case (put out of work by the Linotype). Most of them have families. My wife died four months ago. I'm glad she is out of trouble. My little girl is staying with a printer's family until I find a job. Somehow I get puzzled when I see so many Christians living in luxury and singing 'Jesus, I my cross have taken, all to leave and follow thee,' and remember how my wife died in a tenement...gasping for air and asking God to take the little girl, too.

Of course I don't expect you people can prevent everyone from dying of starvation, lack of proper nourishment and tenement air, but what does following Jesus mean?...What would Jesus do?'

GOODBY TO THE HAND-SETTING OF NEWS TYPE

Had the Linotype machine (patented in 1874) been put into use earlier, instead of 1890-1930, the ready-print charade would not have flowered, and spread across the land. Since ready-print was a system designed to fill blank spaces on a newspaper page, the new line casting machines would have, quickly, filled these "news holes" with locally-produced type and news gathered from a variety of sources: other newspapers, area news, the wire services.

Because of its slow acceptance (in part due to the excellent news service offered by the ready-print house), the line casters did not reach general use until the 1920s. By 1940 almost every single American rural paper had rustled up the money or credit to buy the devices, and it was imbedded as the "showpiece" item of equipment in the town newspapers. School children and court-house square loafers loved to drop into the press room and watch the marvelous device whir, hiss and spit out hot metal slugs the size of dominoes, automatically, right before their eyes.

Boilerplate, too, would have found a smaller market among America's publishers had the line casting machine been around earlier—as "news holes" would have decreased in size.

American newspapers, then, without ready-print, would have developed by the same tortuous route that European journals experienced. The number of newspapers would have been much fewer because line casters were very expensive. American newspapers would have grown at the pre-Civil War rate when the high cost of type and labor kept the newspaper growth quite limited. Newspapers would have continued to be elitist, more subject to government intimidation and control, but less subject to centrally-emanating propaganda of one sort or another.

Typesetting was in an arrested state of development from 1480 to 1890. Typesetters did their work in exactly the same manner as they did in Gutenberg's time: They reached into a box and with their fingers, pulled out the letter they needed and placed it into a small metal device called a "stick." It was painfully slow, monotonous work and hand typesetters were always in short supply. Presses, on the other hand, were improved dramatically in the period after the Civil War, but the larger, high speed designs were too expensive for the average ready-print newspaper. Until near the turn of the century many in the the rural press used the "wine press" design, crudely squeezing each sheet at the rate of 200 per hour. Papers that had acquired a solid economic footing in their towns purchased "Country" Campbell presses (the "flaying fingers" press that the author had in his Ohio newspaper).

At one time there were twenty two thousand newspaper publishers operating in America—and every one of them must have been praying that someone, somewhere, would invent a mechanical typesetting machine that would remove this dark cloud, this handicap from their lives. The speed of nineteenth century hand-setting of type could be compared to erecting large buildings by laying down tiny, one-eighth inch-wide bricks.

In that time, for a hundred years, the world's cloth fabric had been produced by machine, no longer on the fireside spinning wheel. Printing presses had been speeded up, 100 times faster; news was being sent instantaneously by telegraph wire and telephone; and locomotives had replaced horses. But still the mechanical typesetter had not arrived as the turn of the century (the Century of Progress, it was acclaimed) approached.

Inventors from Shanghai to Baltimore were trying their hand at inventing the perfect machine: capable of fitting into a small newspaper's press room, faster than hand set—and cheap enough to be purchased by even the smallest of the thousands of newspapers that were using ready-print and boilerplate.

The town press was the major part of the prospective typesetting machine market, as city newspapers had not yet predominated. Publishers were lured into frustration by repeated announcements of the "coming of the wonderful mechanized typesetter, marvel of the ages, etc." "Ready-print will die!" was the cry of the countryside press in anticipation of the invention of a typesetting machine, and secure in its predominant position in the national press. In the midst of the tremor of expectation of the Linotype, Edwin A. Start wrote in an 1889 issue of the *New England Magazine:*

> The hour of the country newspaper has come. The 'Patent Inside' is gradually passing into the limbo of things that have no right to exist, and the well-edited, well-printed newspaper, published in the county seat or business center of some small district, is taking its place. ...there will be successes as remarkable in their way as any achieved by a (New York) *Herald,* a *Tribune,* or a *World;* and when the great number on the one hand is considered, it is safe to predict that the record of aggregate results will put country journalism at the head of newspaper progress.[7]

MARK TWAIN'S OBSESSION

Among the small town editors who were driven mad by the absence of a typesetting machine was Mark Twain. His back was bent working over a type case in his youth and Twain was not able to put the experience out of his mind. In his later years his search for the elusive typesetting machine cost him his vast fortune, it may even have shortened his life.

This quixotic misadventure came about when Twain discovered what he believed to be the long needed machine---and he backed it's development from 1880 to 1894 with all of his large fortune.

But the timing was bad. An even better and cheaper (though still very complex) machine called the "Linotype," was patented by a German immigrant living in Baltimore." Richard O'Connor wrote about it:

> ...Pervasive...was the impact of the invention of an automatic typesetting machine, which revolutionized the newspaper industry and book publishing. For years, and at a cost of hundreds of thousands of dollars, it had shimmered dreamlike across the vision of Mark Twain, who might better have been occupied by his literary career. Twain backed a typesetting machine developed by James W. Paige, which supposedly was an improvement on an earlier device, the Pianotype, invented by Henry Bessemer, who also produced the iron converter on which the steel industry was based.

Into this crowded field came the newly arrived inventor named

Ottmar Mergenthaler. He was born in Wurttenberg, and migrated to the United States in 1872 at the age of eighteen. Apprenticed to a manufacturer of musical instruments in Baltimore, Mergenthaler began tinkering with the invention of a typesetting machine which wouldn't be so cumbersome (the earlier ones being the size of grand pianos) that they couldn't be accommodated in newspaper composing rooms.... Mergenthaler, though a late entry, worked night and day to perfect his machine.

...Compared to the machine backed by Twain, which had eighteen thousand different parts, Mergenthaler's was much more compact and simply constructed. It set a line of type from its own brass matrices, which were then redistributed automatically; the lead in which the lines were cast later was thrown back into the melting pot beneath the machine to be endlessly reused". O'Connor summed it up in describing the vastly superior Linotype machine: "Not the least of the Mergenthaler machine's contributions to mass culture was the fact that its success dissuaded Twain from his industrial ambitions and sent him back to the work at which he was superlative."

Twain had his obstinate and obsessive side which appeared in this period of his life. He wrote of the new Paige machine to his friend and fellow ex-printer William Dean Howells: "You and I have imagined that we knew how to set type—we shabby poor bunglers. Come and see the Master do it! Come and see this sublime magician of iron and steel work his enchantments." In a euphoric state, he also wrote his brother Orion in January 1889: "At 12:20 this afternoon a line of movable type was spaced and justified by machinery, for the first time in the history of the world!...All the other inventions of the human brain sink pretty nearly into commonplace contrasted with this awful mechanical miracle. Telephones, telegraphs, locomotives, cotton gins, sewing machines, Babbage calculators, Jacquard looms, perfecting presses, Arkwright's frames—all mere toys, simplicities! The Paige Compositor marches alone and far in the lead of human inventions. [8]

Were it not for our knowledge of Twain's experience as a twelve-year old child-typesetter, sitting, fidgeting before his typecase in that little Missouri village newspaper, we would find it even harder to understand why a practical man like Twain could become enamored of such a mechanical monster as the Paige machine. It was impossibly intricate with over 18,000 moving parts, and was oversized, weighing 5,000 pounds. It had 800 shaft bearings and thousands of springs, bolts and levers attached to it.

Probably the most obvious detriment to the Paige machine was its cost, $12,000. Mark Twain failed to consider the economics of country journalism and to bring cost into the equation. It was not the four or five millionaire city newspaper owners (perfectly capable of paying vast sums for ornate, expensive typesetting machines), but the little rural printers that were the prime market. Investors were much more willing to back the Mergenthaler Linotype machine because it was cheaper and could operate in country print shops that would be located far from repair facilities. The potential sales to rural newspapers was 27,000 machines (at an average of $3,000 per Linotype—$500 per year on a rental basis).

As for Mark Twain's typesetting machine, only a few were sold and the last surviving machine rests in the basement of his home, now a museum, in Hartford, Connecticut.

The Linotype contraption was a far from perfect machine but the mood of the newspaper trade was to accept any workable gimmick that would automate the typesetting. It also had many parts, was noisy, dangerous (it habitually spit hot, molten lead, sometimes onto the head of the author's bald linotypers) and took about a year to learn to operate successfully.

The machines in use, even in the 1980s, are basically the same as the 1872 model. Refinements have been added, but the basics (lead-spitting, etc.) remain much the same. But the Linotype was more efficient, setting type five times faster than by hand-typesetters. [9]

The Mergenthaler Linotype was the chosen one simply because the other machines did not work properly, were too large or expensive. Some required prodigious strength or agility, others produced pain, and even terror and violence as parts broke and flew, red hot, in several directions. Most of the other candidate machines fell by the wayside in the twenty years following the patenting of the Linotype. Some of the losers in the race included an early invention, the Simplex, which had a low cost, did not need molten metal, but broke too much type; and the Rogers Typograph, invented by J. R. Rogers of Cleveland, Ohio. The typograph was introduced into several of the midwest town newspapers, but the typesetters found that they could set faster than the machine. It had exposed wires which guided matrices down a chute, released by touching the keys. When a complete line was in place, a crank was turned three times to perform the casting operation. [10]

Then there was the W. Church machine (patented in 1820); the

Corsa, the Typotheter, the Low, the Hattersley—a mass of wires and pistons, patented in England in 1857; the Fraser, invented in Scotland, and was accused of causing hand paralysis; the Bracklesberg, operated by a foot treadle; and the St. John Typobar, invented by R. J. St. John of Cleveland (which failed during an important demonstration in Chicago).

The McMillan typesetting machine and its companion distributing device, both invented in 1884 by J. I. McMillan of Ilion, New York, were in the running for a while, but the device soon fell out of public favor. From 1820 till 1889 there were 120 typesetting machines patented, most of them manually operated with the exception of the McMillan and a few others, including the Intertypes, the Monotypes and the Ludlow.[11]

The Linotype (which used molten lead) made its appearance at a propitious time, as the Kellogg company was introducing lead-cast boilerplate to the country's newspapers. Thanks to the widespread publicity and promotion of the molten lead castings by the ready-print house, publishers looked on the radical Linotype as a workable method.

It's earlier appearance would have frightened them, especially when it would demonstrate it's lead-spurting propensities (the last machine that I purchased was in 1962 and it cost a horrendously large amount of money, $30,000).

With the introduction of faster typesetting the major ready-print houses prepared to do battle, upgraded their products, which they recognized were in competition with the new machines. New features appeared, new authors were put under contract, and cleaner typefaces and page design were introduced.

Notes:

1. William Dean Howells, *Life in Letters Vol.II,* p.301.

2. Brook's, *Howells: His Life and Works* (New York: E. P. Dutton, 1959, 4,5.)

3. Hal Borland, *Country Editor's Boy* (Philadelphia: Lippincott, 1970) pp. 56-57.

4. Margaret Sanborn, *Mark Twain, The Bachelor Years* (New York, Doubleday, 1990) p. 82-93.

5. His exact age at that time is a matter still debated by researchers.

6. Chas. M. Sheldon, *In His Steps,* (New York)pp. 8-14.

7. Paul Sharp, *Whoop-Up Country* (Univ. of Minn. Press, 1964) p. 331.

8. Mark Twain to Orion Clemens, January 5, 1889, Mark Twain Letters, Vol. II, p.506-508.

9. "Type-Composing Machines," a paper read before the Polytechnic Typographical Association by Thomas Fisher, November 1886, also printed in Trade Journals.

10. The Roger's Typograph, which failed commercially, had something that Mergenthaler's Linotype did not. It was able to "justify" the lines semi-automatically. Justifying, an act that seems to dress up printing, is the process that places type evenly at both sides of the column; and the separating of the type was done between the letters not only between the words. The patent on the device was owned by the Rogers company and the Linotype could not be considered a proper typecasting machine without the justifying capability. A deal was struck and Mergenthaler bought the patent from the Cleveland, Ohio company for over four million dollars (in 1990 dollar figures) allowing the finishing of the Linotype machine. Therefore, the linecasting machine could be more accurately described as a Mergenthaler-Rogers invention.

11. "The Contest of Composing Machines,"*Inland Printer* (1886) pp. 163-65.

Chapter Ten

Moving To The Cities, The Un-Europeans

If we could only learn to be small.
—Sherwood Anderson

Criticizing the provincial way of living has been a pastime of literati for hundreds of years, extending back to ancient Greece ---but the American literary pogrom against hamlet life was notably contentious and nasty. In a typical example, writing about the cultural barrenness of small towns and their boilerplate newspapers, The *New Republic* (April 11, 1923) proclaimed that boilerplate sanctified the generalities, upheld mediocrity and "aided the standardization of thought and custom...---a mock sophistication like that of a girl-child in her big sister's dress, flirting with a fat drummer on the depot platform.... Boilerplate feeds the quasi-sophistication to the bursting point."[1]

If the *New Republic* could sourly equate lack of sophistication with that which is "pitiful" and "grotesque"---and get away with it---then there must have been a strong current of resentment against the townspeople and agriculturists in that time. Irksome to the magazine was that this "quasi-sophistication" should be used so extensively in the boilerplate.

At that time it became customary to downgrade country life as the rift widened between the urban and a rural society where religious fundamentalism and the Anti-Saloon League prevailed. Americans were changing their attitudes as well as their calendars at the turn of the century. The countryside life was pronounced ugly and unpleasant, a green "slum," and more and more farmers and town dwellers moved to the exciting cities – about which they had been reading.

Three country newspapermen, E. W. Howe, Sherwood Anderson and

Mark Twain, without intending, set literature on its twentieth century course of questioning American rural values. Ironically it was Howe, who dearly loved village life, who was the first, writing in 1882 the classic *Story of a Country Town*.[2]

Twain followed with *Huckleberry Finn,* in which villages were painted as places of fear and doubt; and Sherwood Anderson came forth with his own masterpiece, a series of short stories of town isolation and lack of sophistication, published in book form as *Winesburg, Ohio*. However, Anderson was wary of caricature and his book contained passages that warned of the superficiality of city life, such as: "Although he had also been raised in an Ohio town, the instructor began to put on the airs of the city. He wanted to appear cosmopolitan... his voice sounded pompous and heavy."[3]

The impact of these works encouraged others who were at odds with the rural monopoly society of that time in America. They, too, wanted to put on airs of the city.

Borrowing heavily from Mark Twain, Sinclair Lewis drew on the village experiences of his boyhood to write *Main Street,* his best-known work. His novels about provincials were run-away best sellers. *Main Street* was a satirical jab at Sauk Center, Minnesota and all the other newly-formed inland towns in the U.S.A. Ernest Hemingway, Ring Lardner and Theodore Dreiser and many others joined in the literary attack.

Most visible and influential was trend-setting editor, book publisher and critic H. L. Mencken, who took editorial aim from his Baltimore *Sun* redoubt. Born to immigrant German parents, he was a promoter of wholesale importation of European culture and its arts, a grafting procedure unwelcome in the heartland, the still-forming sectors of the nation. Acting his role as social critic, he wowed the cityites by firing barbs at the countryside-dwelling national majority.

Mencken preached to the already-converted easterners. He was a skilled writer with remarkable command of the language, targeting the un-European cultural life in the towns, calling it the "village virus." He zeroed in on the easiest target and most radical part of the culture, the religious fanaticism. He lashed out at the inlanders, branding them "Boobus Americanus," "homo boobiens", "gaping primates" and the countryside he labeled a cultural desert, the "Sahara" of the "bozarts," in his haughty term. No insult was too harsh or too reckless in those days of city-building. Mencken's love affair with Europe was welcomed by many urbanites, admirers of his magazine, stimulating them to form

European-style symphony orchestras, and restaurants, buy European oil paintings and sculpture; attend European plays and the ritualistic operas.

City writers turned up the volume as countryside-induced Prohibition approached and World War I came to an end. The fight against the Constitutional Amendment reached the front pages of the big city papers while proponents of the liquor ban flooded the boilerplate and ready-print of rural journals. Using the ballot, the country folks, still in the majority and egged on by the newspaper editorials, the wilderness churches and the Women's Christian Temperance Union, rolled over the astonished opposition and shut off the liquor taps for the whole of America, city and countryside.

READY-PRINT, THE TROJAN HORSE OF TOWN JOURNALISM

Sherwood Anderson, when he was in his fifties, returned to town life. In his youth as an apprentice printer he worked for his hometown paper, the *Enterprise* in Clyde, Ohio. Early in life he learned to admire the town newspaper scene, incorporating many personalities he encountered into his books, most notably George Willard the small town newsman who was the main character in his *Winesburg, Ohio.*[4]

Anderson left the scene early in his manhood, not because he wanted to affect the airs of a city-dweller, but because he was full of the spirit of business enterprise, and possessed a talent for salesmanship. He had earlier founded a roofing materials company in his town in which he honed his literary skills by writing advertising copy. Anderson was never comfortable in the "sophisticated" city scene. Of the talented writers who questioned their midwest roots and ritually moved to New York and then to Paris, he, alone, had a change of heart about rural America, and returned. He saw through the affectation of city life. In this vein he wrote:

> The coming of industrialism, attended by all the roar and rattle of affairs, the shrill cries of millions of new voices that have come among us from over seas, the going and coming of trains, the growth of cities, the building of the interurban car lines that weave in and out of towns and past farm houses and now in these later days the coming of the automobiles has worked a tremendous change in the lives and in the habits of thought of our people of mid-America.

Books, badly imagined and written though they may be in the hurry of our times, are in every household, magazines circulate by the millions of copies, newspapers are everywhere. In our day a farmer standing by the stove in the store in his village has his mind filled to overflowing with the words of other men. The newspapers and the magazines have pumped him full. Much of the old brutal ignorance that had in it also a kind of beautiful childlike innocence is gone forever. The farmer by the stove is brother to the men of the cities and if you listen you will find him talking as glibly and as senselessly as the best city man of us all.

As an act of contrition and needing to earn a living during the 1920s in the latter part of his creative years, he decided that the small towns were okay, after all—not ideal, but better than the noisy city. He made a complete turn-about: pulled away from the boozy literary scene, separated from his writer friends and competitors—Ernest Hemingway, F. Scott Fitzgerald, Gertrude Stein, etc.---and began a period of regeneration as a country editor. He settled in Marion, Virginia, a small county seat village buried deep in the Allegheny mountains. He had distant cousins there—the area was where many Pennsylvania German and Scots-Irish settled in the early 1800s, splitting from their families who chose to move on to Ohio.

While there he bought the town's weekly newspapers, the Smyth County *News* and the Marion *Democrat*. He made Marion his permanent residence, living there in contentment for the rest of his life. The pleasure of small town living and being a country editor revived him. The paper helped draw his family together. He brought his son into the business, teaching him the trade and later stepping aside to let the young man assume the role as manager of the paper.

One of Sherwood Anderson's first acts upon buying the paper was to abolish the boilerplate and ready-print. Along with writing and editing the paper, he maintained a daily writing schedule resulting in several successful novels. He supervised the staff of linotypers, printers and reporters. He also sold advertisements and scribbled the news and editorials amid the clanking and hissing of the heavy line casters and presses. Thus he was able to become a midwest American (a real American, to his way of thinking) reliving his early small-town Ohio years---thinking and writing as a villager, casting off the gritty sophistication of city life. "A man has to begin over and over," he said.

Anderson wrote about many things while an editor. He covered sports and took sides on political issues. He sponsored a a new town park and in an ironic mood he named it "H.L. Mencken Park," after his friend and admirer, whose low opinion of provincials was not shared by Anderson.

A constant subject both in his paper and in articles for magazines was the analyses of his new trade, "country journalism." He criticized ready-print and boilerplate, pointing out that they were big-city products disguised with a provincial wrapper. He proved to be an aggressive foe of the W.N.U. output, disdaining to run the canned stuff from Chicago which, unlike the output at the turn of the century, had resorted to running second class novels and insipid feature material. Instead he overworked his linotyper, filling his newspaper with the classics— examples of fine writing by the world authors.

Believing that a major role of the grass roots newspaper was to act as the village educator, he opened up his office as the town's only public library. Rather than dole out the ready-print product to his readers, he broadened the scope to a multiplicity of subjects including the arts. As Ray Lewis White described it in his book about Anderson's return to the village life:

> Besides printing items of literature in the Smyth County *News,* Sherwood Anderson kept in his printshop nearly a thousand books which served as Marion's only public lending library. These books were usually donated to the author by various publishing firms and their arrival was announced and promoted in the paper. Townspeople dropped by to check them out. The shop itself became a social center for the town, rivaling the drug store and the courthouse steps as a popular meeting place. "There is a big stove in the center of the room," Anderson wrote, "and there are books here to be read and pictures on the walls. Nowadays you can get good colored prints of modern paintings at little cost. We have Van Goghs, Cezannes, Marins, Gauguins, Renoirs. People come in and stare at these paintings but they are interested...There are political discussions, stories told, news of the county is brought in. I swear you'd be surprised. There is a workman's wife here who reads Dostoyevsky."[5]

Like the thousands of editors who came to the business at the height of the ready-print newspaper "revolution," Anderson had the realization that he was doing something he enjoyed. He became a permanent transplant, never to move away. Once in responding to an offer to buy his newspaper he wrote: "I have an occupation here, something to do, I like the smell of the shop, the business, the uncertainty, the position it has given me in the community...I must have a job and I never have had another job that gave me half so much pleasure. A man has to work. He cannot be just a teller of tales. He has to find somewhere a place into which he fits.[6]

His town life reincarnation did not exempt parts of America from having their small-town bad habits criticized by Sherwood Anderson. He took aim at fellow rural editors who used ready-print and boilerplate. He wrote, "A profound mental laziness has become characteristic of America...Canned stuff is sent out from Chicago to weeklies like ours and sold to editors at $1.00 to $1.30 a page.... They send it in all ready to drop into the paper.... We are all for the country weeklies and their possibilities,...a country weekly can also be easily enough as lazy and insipid and no-account as anything we know of in this world."

Anderson also criticized the big city papers: "Buy an American newspaper in a city of Louisiana, in Maine, in California, and they are all pretty much alike (as well), pretty much in the same tone. They have really become big commercial ventures. Businessmen own and run most of them."

Unlike most town editors in the '20s, Anderson was willing to stand his ground and put forth opinions---he had, after all sharpened his vision and had been trained by his world travels, not by the boilerplaters and ready-printers that had dominated, and earlier even controlled, the country press.

Ready-print and boilerplate could not stand much of this kind of criticism within the trade, as leveled by Anderson, coming on the heels of the Congressional and Justice Department investigations. Many of Anderson's ideas were repeated and his newspaper articles were widely read around the country and ready-print/boilerplate fell even lower in esteem.

A WORD ABOUT NEWSPAPER "UNIONS"

Ready-print history might have taken a different course had it been formed within a social co-operative (or Union) of newspapers. However, wide swinging free enterprise triumphed. Commercial suppliers, especially Ansel Kellogg and George A. Joslyn, did the providing of ready-print sheets rather than state press associations or groups of newspapers. Almost from the very beginning of ready-print in America publishers would complain about the propaganda in the ready-print (which they sometimes referred to as "advertising" revenue) and the lack of editorial control. But complaining seldom went beyond talk.

Criticism of ready-print and boilerplate was muted but constant. Publishers seemed to resent it, but at the same time were mesmerized by its profit potential. Their own trade publication, the *Journalist,* commented in 1889: "The ready-print is a fraud on the reader and ultimately proves to be a fraud on the publishers as well. It served a purpose when printers were scarce, presses dear, and news hard to get. But there is no longer any reason why the ready-print should exist at all, even in the remotest districts."

American cultural tradition works against newspapers participating in groups. Town and city editors are decided individualists, seldom capitalizing on the familiarity of association and working in concert. In 1862 T.L. Terry, editor of the *Courant* of Berlin, Wisconsin attempted to draw neighboring publishers into a union or co-operative. The idea came to him soon after he noted the action of his neighbor Ansel Kellogg, who had begun his early ready-print experiments.

Elmo Watson, who was an employee of W.N.U., in his pamphlet "A History of Newspaper Syndicates," told about Terry's plan for an association of publishers.[8] His aim was to establish a central office for printing inside sheets containing news and feature material. A heavy snowstorm came up, however, and only four editors were able to make the trip. Apparently sensing that the editors would probably not join the venture he abandoned it.

Like growing children, striving to move away from the domination of their parents, town newspapers through the years made attempts to break from the privately-owned ready-print companies. Some small groups of newspapers were eventually able to form co-operatives; but never faced up to the challenge of the skilled merchandisers like Western Newspaper Union, Inc. (also known as the Central-West Publishing Company, Inc.), whose sales practices grabbed off and held the newspaper-customers.

In one attempt to take back control of their news columns and advertising, Illinois newspapers met in 1895—buoyed by the expectation that the invention of the Mergenthaler line casting machine would eventually lead to the elimination of the ready-print. The Illinois newspapers, however, again demonstrated that newspapermen always work alone and find it difficult to organize into effective concerted groups. The commercial ready-print companies proved too tough an opponent and no action was taken.

At the meeting a paper was read by R.D. Parker, editor of the Downer's Grove newspaper which detailed the plans of the revolt. The battle plan called for the town newspapers to (a). Set a uniform price with the ready-print companies; (b). Join all of the 748 Illinois newspapers using ready-print into a single organization to pressure the ready-print companies; (c). Hire their own representatives to sell advertising in the cities for our ready-print pages; and (d). Abandon the big ready-print companies and form their own co-operative organization. None of the propositions were ever put in place and the effort died out.[7]

A middle-of-the-road stance was taken by a new ready-print seller in 1898. It was called the Country Publishers Company of Omaha, Nebraska, which advertised that "it was the only Ready-Print house west of the Mississippi not controlled by a trust, furnishing ready-prints at a price agreed on by a committee of publishers."

Another, the Central Newspaper Union of La Crosse, Wisconsin and Davenport, Iowa announced at its formation in 1901 that it would divide its profits with the publishers. Its motto was "They are With You! Are You With Them?

Ready-print and boilerplate companies were, early on, made aware of the strivings for independent co-operative effort by the newspapers. Their domination of the nation's news output gave them the feeling that they were not exactly an outside commercial service but actually an integral part of the press system---like the heart or lungs. And they sort of invited themselves in, appropriating pompous names like the American Press Association, Pacific Newspaper Union, Chicago Newspaper Union, Western Newspaper Union, the Indiana Newspaper Union, etc. The holding company for many of these was the Central-West Publishing Co. of New York.

CONGRESS AND ALL-HOME-PRINT FIGHT READY-PRINT

Town newspapers had all become customers in one way or another. They either bought ready-print or boilerplate. After the turn of the century less than two percent of America's newspapers disdained the use of one or the other and its use in the town and small city weeklies and dailies became commonplace. The criticism began soon after the

MOVING TO THE CITIES

They Are	**CENTRAL**	*Are You*
With You!	**NEWSPAPER**	*With Them?*
	UNION	

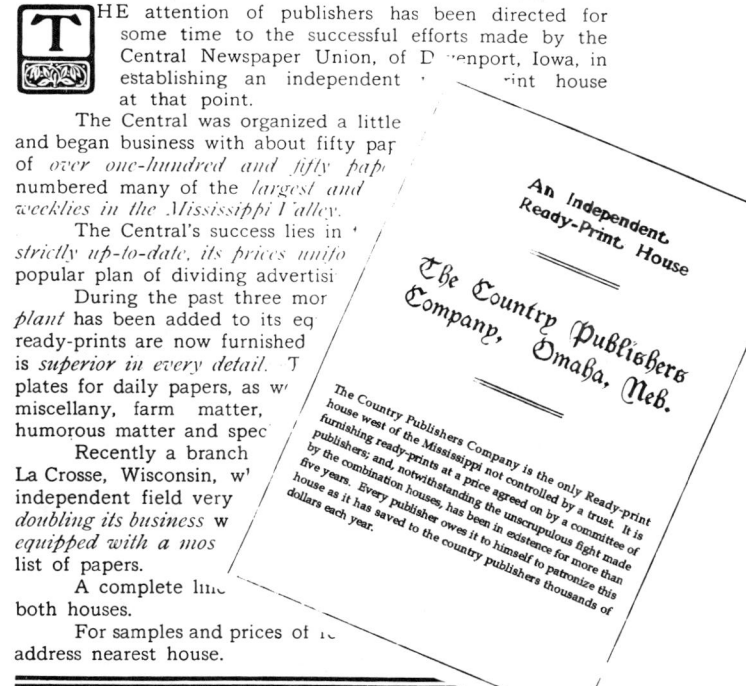

THE attention of publishers has been directed for some time to the successful efforts made by the Central Newspaper Union, of D‑venport, Iowa, in establishing an independent ‑int house at that point.

The Central was organized a little and began business with about fifty pap of *over one-hundred and fifty pap* numbered many of the *largest and weeklies in the Mississippi Valley.*

The Central's success lies in *strictly up-to-date, its prices unifo* popular plan of dividing advertisi

During the past three mor *plant* has been added to its eq ready-prints are now furnished is *superior in every detail.* T plates for daily papers, as w miscellany, farm matter, humorous matter and spec

Recently a branch La Crosse, Wisconsin, w independent field very *doubling its business w equipped with a mos* list of papers.

A complete lin both houses.

For samples and prices of address nearest house.

CENTRAL NEWSPAPER UNION

An Independent Ready-Print House

The Country Publishers Company, Omaha, Neb.

The Country Publishers Company is the only Ready-Print house west of the Mississippi not controlled by a trust. It is furnishing ready-prints at a price agreed on by a committee of publishers; and, notwithstanding the unscrupulous fight made by the combination houses, has been in existence for more than five years. Every publisher owes it to himself to patronize this house as it has saved to the country publishers thousands of dollars each year.

Several companies attempted to compete with the Western Newspaper Union but failed. Two examples are shown here.

ready-print came into general use. In the mid-1860s, at the birth of the pre-printed page idea, some publishers, egged on by their employees who were concerned about losing their jobs, rose to attack the idea of ready-print. They voiced their objection to the idea of an almighty, omnipotent, un-editable single source of news and opinion for the whole area. One wrote: "If this practice is to become general, a score of journeymen printers will be sufficient for the whole state. The idea would be worthy of a "rattling" (bankrupt) publisher or a strapped printer, but we can hardly consider it a legitimate business. The plan, if universally adopted, could give almost absolute control of state affairs to the editors who could be employed to do all the thinking for the papers in the state."[7]

But as I have stated, ready-print grew from an area enterprise to a service covering entire sections then the entire nation by 1880.

One of the critics of ready-print was Captain Henry King, one of America's best-known journalists, who in his career served with distinction as editor of the St. Louis Globe-Democrat. On October 25, 1871 he was the featured speaker at the annual meeting of the Kansas Editors and Publishers convention, a group with a membership of all the newspapers in that state. An advocate of personal journalism and investigative reporting King was quite properly incensed by the inability of editors to control the stories that appeared on the ready-print side of their own newspaper. He lashed out: "The whole paper should be 'set up' and printed in the office from which it purports to come. Ready-print is a fraud and an abomination: a half a paper is little, if any, better than no paper at all. Selection of news stories should be made with great care, preference always being given to that which will enlighten as well as entertain."[9]

Early in the development of the ready-print network, members of Congress viewed the practice with skepticism. In 1873 a postal bill aimed directly at the ready-print was passed making newspapers who used ready-print ineligible for the favorable postal rates given liberally to America's newspapers. The passage read: "Weekly newspapers within the respective counties where the same are actually and wholly printed and published, none other, may pass through the mails free of postage..."

Congress had apparently waited too long to act. The 1,300 newspapers already using the service rose as one to fight, attacking Representative Farnsworth of Illinois, chairman of the postal committee that had framed the bill. Protests in the form of letters and petitions flooded into Washington. Their special-interest tactics worked and the law was repealed in 1874.

Within the trade, the steady drumbeat of criticism against the ready-print never diminished. Editors in the northeastern part of the country were the most critical. The Digby, Massachusetts[10] paper ran this notice in every issue:

> No Boilerplate or Foreign Sterotype Metal
> Is Permitted Appear in this Sheet.
> No Foreign Importations Ever!

Several Minnesota editors went so far as to organize the All-Home-Print Association in order to fight it.[11] At the 1877 annual convention of the New York State Press Association the gathering adopted, after a vote, the resolution to "Discourage the use of patent insides and outsides, with a view to their abolition." They also passed another resolution to abandon the use of boilerplate. The vote had little effect on the state's town press, however, as the number of users of the companion systems increased steadily every year.

In the 1920s, magazines would occasionally comment on the ready-print. Typical is the following which appeared in a 1923 edition of the New Republic magazine: "Significantly large numbers of country newspapers are today like the appendix—an organ without a purpose. Their readers are ailing with boilerplate appendicitis. This disease brings about many complications in the afflicted community. It helps further to sanctify the sacred generalities. It upholds mediocrity as the relief from reality. It aids in the standardization of thought and custom. It provides a better breeding place for propaganda of one sort or another."[12]

Criticism never diminished the growth in the earlier days, however, as most of the publishers joined the ready-print and boilerplate bandwagon. By 1910 over 90% were taking either ready-print or boilerplate and therefore controlled only part of their local papers. The continued criticism seemed to come mostly from the local publisher's employees, the printers and typesetters whose jobs were threatened by the labor-saving practice.

Some publishers, a small minority, resisted the use of ready-print and boilerplate. Grass roots journalists always seemed uncomfortable around it. In press associations a running debate ensued, centering around the premise that one man (or even several men) should not be given the power to do the thinking for all Americans. But moral discussion and hints that it was a deceptive practice and unhealthy for the national psyche, were pushed aside by the discovery that it was profitable.

CONTRASTING VIEWS OF READY-PRINT

However to editors who were less renowned than Sherwood Anderson, but who had seen the contributions of the ready-print before the turn of the century, a different, more positive view still prevailed: In a February 25, 1928 article in Inland Press, Frank Stockbridge wrote admiringly about the American town newspapers and their patent insides. He described the system as a "stand-by in country newspaper shops," and made a plea that the practice be allowed to live on. At the time of Stockbridge's article there were between four and five thousand newspapers still using it. He wrote: "Such cooperative services make it easier than ever for the ambitious young man to establish a creditable country paper on small capital."

Of an earlier time, writing about the West, one historian looked back almost reverently at the contribution of the newspapers. Edwin Emery, in "The Press in America," stated: "Indeed the press was more and more counted upon to supply the information, inspiration, agitation and education of a society often unable to keep up with its need for schools. In many communities, newspapers were the only literature available for the bulk of the citizenry. They served as the main educational device until the other cultural institutions could take up the slack caused by rapid migrations."[13]

The editorial mass of the ready-print services was always remarkably large. The typical issue was eight pages in size, small type, either six or eight columns wide, 21 inches deep. Bought by the reader for only two cents per copy, the amount of literature and number of articles offered was quite large, frequently the equivalent of a small book.

In writing about the rise of Southern newspapers after the War Between the States, Southern historian Thomas D. Clark, who at one time in his youth had been a weekly newspaperman, stated: "The syndicates sinned unforgivably by permitting the proprietary medicine companies to prostitute their advertising columns with repulsive and fallacious claims. On the credit side, many Southern towns and counties enjoyed the benefits of a local press only because of the availability of ready-print and boiler plate.[14]

Clark commented: "Whatever the sins of the syndicates might have been, their material was well edited, and within a narrow framework of operation they gave their readers fairly accurate news coverage. The patent pages were well printed and reasonably well illustrated. They brought into empty rural lives reading material which could never have reached them otherwise. Many Southerners learned to read novels in the syndicate pages. When pious mothers and fathers objected to their sons and daughters reading novels in book form, they may not have realized that the banned literature was in the weekly newspaper.

CUTTING CORNERS:
EDITORS WHO AIMED TO JUST "GET BY"

Even in the quiet small village, with little crime or accidents, changes in the printing forms did not merit setting the type. The author recalls on one occasion, probably the only time when a death occurred from something other than old age in that town, a telephone lineman touched the wrong wire right in front of the newspaper office and was electrocuted, hanging there within sight of the entire staff of the paper. The accident happened just before press time for the once-a-week paper, but the publisher would not re-make up his front page, forcing his readers to wait a week to learn about the dramatic event.

There were (and still are) many country editors who just aimed to get by, seeking a profit, avoiding the expense of an editorial staff. Using the ready-print/boilerplate system, almost anyone could operate as an editor. However, some of the more inarticulate editors carried editorial mass-production, even into their own writing.

Some used a method of pre-fabricating stories for much of their news output. A "form" was devised with blank spaces for name, date of death, cause of death, place of funeral, etc. Retirement stories were composed the same way—as were school graduations, weddings, births, illnesses, and a multitude of other community events.

The type was kept standing for these stories and type slugs with the new names, dates, etc. were dropped in the blank spaces. This type of journalism demonstrated a certain ingenuity, but also contributed to the repetitious form of town coverage in a society that shunned individual distinction, putting on airs; people who act alike to an unusual degree.

Headlines, also, could be used over and over again in many of the papers. Town journals used long-running heads such as: "Society News," "Births," "Deaths of the Week," "Sports Scores," etc. Journalist Robert St. John tells about one stubborn Vermont weekly refused to change its standing head even though it had unintended comic meanings. Therefore the readers were treated to the long-running "Social News by Miss Rosey Bottom, the Social Correspondent."

A way of cutting cost was to use old material that had lain about, sometimes for years. When enough local news and ads were not available, the editor would reach into a drawer and abring forth a boilerplate casting, just the right size of the "news hole."

Another inexpensive source of news material are the "exchanges." In an act of quid pro quo, town newspapers across the country give each other free subscriptions knowing that the stories will be copied to fill up their issues. Proper size is at least as important as content.

My friend, the publisher who never would run commas in his paper, claimed that he could save about $150 in typesetting costs a year in typesetting costs by eliminating these thousands of little grammatical fly specks from his paper. He claimed that not one of the readers ever complained or commented on it, therefore he saw no reason for them.

Notes

1. *The New Republic* (April 11, 1923).
2. Edgar W. Howe, *The Story of a Country Town* (New York: Dodd, Mead & Co., 1927.
3. Sherwood Anderson, *Winesburg, Ohio* (New York: Random House, 1919) pp.292-293.
4. Milt Townsend, *Sherwood Anderson* (New York, Houghton, Mifflin, 1987) p.14.
5. Sherwood Anderson, edited by R. L. White, *Return to Winesburg,* (Chapel Hill, Univ. of No. Carolina Press, 1967)pp.15, 195.
6. Sherwood Anderson, "I Will Not Sell My Papers," *Outlook Magazine* (Dec. 5, 1928), p.1287.
7. "Ready-prints," *National Printer-Journalist,* 1885, pp.191.
8. Elmo S. Watson, *History of Newspaper Syndicates* (Chicago: self-published, 1936) p.8.

9. Henry King, *American Journalism,* (New York: Arno Press, Inc. 1970), p.9.

10. The *Journalist Magazine,* year unknown, author's collection.

11. "All-Home-Print Association," *National Printer-Journalist,* May, 1904, p.266.

12. Lynn Montross, "Boilerplate Appendicitis," *The New Republic* (April 11, 1923) pp.189-90.

13. Edwin Emery, *The Press and America* (New York: Prentice Hall, Inc. 1954) p.192.

14. Thomas D. Clark, *The Southern Country Editor,* (New York: The Bobbs-Merrill Co. 1948) p.65.

Chapter Eleven

What is News?

Ready-print, realizing that business was declining, resorted to a new policy of operating in the open. In October, 1927, after over a decade of law suits, Senate hearings and rumors of propagandizing, this new open attitude was demonstrated when avuncular Wright Patterson allowed himself to be interviewed by American magazine. In the article he freely admitted that he was the behind-the-scenes news editor of over 12,000 U.S. newspapers, weekly, semi-weekly and daily. Exhibiting candor and folksiness, he spoke convincingly of the advantages of his ready-print, its honesty and educational advantages. He answered the magazine's questions very carefully, however, never revealing why he had remained hidden for so long.

This disclosure must have come as a surprise to the newspaper readers thoughtful enough to care about the source of their printed diet of opinion and news entertainment. Simultaneous with the American Magazine article, the Western Newspaper Union began identifying articles on its pages with "WNU Service" and "Released by WNU" in barely visible, tiny agate-size type.

The effect of this disclosure would be hard to measure, but the reason for it was not difficult to fathom. Participating newspapers began to drop away from W.N.U. following the initial revelations in 1912 in the New York Times article. By the mid-1920s member-newspapers pulled away from both ready-print and boilerplate by the thousands.

Simultaneously a diminution in number of newspapers began, with many consolidations between publications as weaker papers sold out to stronger rivals, leaving one paper per town. The one-paper town was a different type of species, invariably becoming more conservative and less watchful of politicians, avoiding anything that would result in controversy and, cause another paper to be founded in opposition.

This new W.N.U. openness did not stop the slide away from using the service—in fact it may have hastened it. Many of the town editors (unlike their city counterparts) seemed embarrassed by the obvious inclusion of "outside" material in their newspapers. Anything noted to be from "out-of-town" was frowned on editorially in the smaller hamlets of America—as newspapers sought to support local advertisers, who struggled to keep shoppers buying at home despite the growth of smooth highways leading to shopping centers in nearby cities.

After the *American* magazine article of 1927 the ready-print continued in the country press, still hidden both by its method of camouflaging its type but also it was lost from sight by an increased lack of interest in "small town events" in American media. Thus, ready-print was destined to be breathlessly re-discovered periodically. One of those occasions was the revelation and attack by Morris L. Ernst in his book *The First Freedom*.

Ernst devoted several lines in his book to lambasting ready-print, boilerplate, and the Western Newspaper Union. He stated about ready-print: "...we have block booking of content and ads, probably one of the most insidious and disastrous marriages in our entire economy, doubly pernicious because the dual deal is not disclosed to the readers....most of the readers assume that this is the product of their own editor. Again there is no honest full disclosure to the reading public....That they are undisclosed and concealed from the public augments the evil."

Ernst wove the ready-print and boilerplate revelation into his book which was a hortatory essay on the preservation of press freedom. He has been one of the few writers to consider the significance of the country editor and his press. He wrote: "...it is important that the Big City folk stop disparaging the country press because of its defects. Some critics feel that because of gaucheries and occasional poor craftmanship, as well as near-bankruptcy, the country press is not worth worrying about. Rather do I say, 'This is our press for good or bad. We can make it better. And for the survival of our way of life we must make it last.' The surest path toward increased concentration of power in our national government is along the road of destruction of local newspapers and removal of local media of expression. A strong and free country press is the backbone of our democracy."[1]

But monopoly seemed on the media's mind, both in the big city and small community. To be outspoken was to invite a competitive paper to start up against you. "Don't make waves," became the editorial cry across the land.

The effect of these events was noted by Mott in 1960, writing about his father's weekly newspaper of the 1890s. He bemoaned the effect in the wake of these changes, the loss of the editorials and outspokenness prominent in that golden age. The change produced a lessening respect for the rural press, as editors kept things quiet and politicians could operate with a freer hand, unwatched:

"Most country editors provided a column or two of "editorials." These were usually written with care and read with respect. Later consolidations, which have commonly left only one paper in a town, have had a tendency to prevent participation in controversies; but sixty years ago, when every town worth its salt had at least two newspapers, sides were always vigorously taken. The rival editors often engaged in bitter quarrels. Those battles in type were frequently carried too far and were filled with personal attacks, invective and intemperance, but they stimulated reader-interest in editorial columns and sharper thinking about issues.

U. S. COUNTRY EDITORS
RUN ONLY LOCAL NEWS

It has always been believed in the trade that it was the threat of invasion by the metropolitan press that caused town editors to increase their coverage of local news---a news beat that the cities could not possibly cover adequately. But that may have been only part of the story.

The American free press system was an achievement by the country editors at the time they were dominant, their numbers commanding power. But now the USA has changed, no longer do we have only a few large cities, we now have dozens. But towns still remain and they are growing, and their newspapers still command a wide and important audience. The country editor has changed also. The surviving towns and their newspapers have retreated en masse from their role as informal educators and editorialists. They now look like "shoppers" filled mainly with advertisements. The result has been a decline of

---

1. Morris Ernst, *The First Freedom* (New York: McMillan, 1946) pp-90, 108-111.

their influence over the past 60 years. Nothing has filled this gap in American democracy and communication---and, sadly, commercial television, which claims to be part of the nations press system, has added only a glitzy, nervous and illiterate element to the scene.

In the Victorian, ready-print days the hidden Chicago editors covered news of the world. The town editor was left only local events to write about. Ready-print's decline in the twenties (with the surge of magazines, the threat of radio and other communication technology) and ultimate death in the early 1950s, caused America's town newspapers to face a decision. Should they employ news writers and sign up for news wire services---or should they ignore the outside world and cover only local events?

By the 1920s the country editors had made their decision: they turned to exclusively local news coverage, shunning events outside of their counties. Some readers, to learn more of the world, subscribed to outside reading matter to stay in contact. The others, a large percentage no longer received the outside news, encountering events almost by accident on a nearby radio and, later, television.

The decision was unanimous. Newspapers would not take on the responsibility of writing "out-of-town" (worldwide) stories. The expression "local coverage" took on a saintly cast as paper after paper proclaimed the wonders of the ol' home town. Boosterism flourished as isolationism and dullness increased.

It was the profit and loss column that dictated the change, and country editors decided that they could not afford to hire writers to do the job. No longer was their newsprint sent from the Chicago ready-print house, almost free of charge.

The eliminating of the wider coverage fell like a dark, protective cloud across the countryside. Town newspapers have stubbornly remained strictly-local to this day despite America's later turnabout in international affairs in discarding its isolationist tendencies. Even the arrival of the atomic bomb was not enough. America's 9,000 or so town editors locked themselves in, and restricted coverage to their line of sight. The city dailies have not filled the vacuum, nothing has.

To town newspapers it seemed as if the world were flat and ended at the county border. The editorial abdication further loosened cultural bindings of community---as increasing numbers, mostly the youth, moved to metropolitan areas. Eliminated was an information link to the outside world and forever diminished was the importance of the country editor's newspaper.

Chapter Twelve

Goodby Gutenberg!

Independent journalism! that is the watchword of
the future in the profession
    Scribner's Monthly, June, 1872.[1]

You can note how times have changed when Harold A. Innis wrote in 1950: "Mechanization has emphasized complexity and confusion; it has been responsible for monopolies in the field of knowledge; and it becomes extremely important to any civilization, if it is not to succumb to the influence of this monopoly of knowledge, to make some critical survey and report. The conditions of freedom of thought are in danger of being destroyed by science, technology, and the mechanization of knowledge, and with them, Western civilization."[2]

But Innis' gloomy comment preceded the introduction of new technology that made the publishing of newspapers available to almost anyone who cared to enter the profession. It began in the early 1960s. Just when high costs were forcing thousands more newspapers out of business, lithography arrived on the scene. Like a descending angel, litho came to newspapers and the typesetting problem in printing was finally conquered. Type could now be produced inexpensively and with little training.

Goodby Gutenberg! Mark Twain can now rest easily in his grave! The solution was drastic, and clear cut. Printing would have to start over. Complete change was called for, throwing out all the equipment and printing ideas then in use, and moving onto a new method.

It suddenly became apparent to country editors that linecasting

Like Ansel Kellogg in Baraboo, Wisconsin during the Civil War, this country editor operated all the equipment himself. He no longer had the ready-print to rely on since it no longer existed. It had expired in 1953 and this was 1959. Instead, W.N.U. boilerplate and an unreliable Linotype machine were pressed into service to take up the slack.

Lacking time, this country editor was unable to write the news adequately and readership had dropped off to 300 subscribers. He was like thousands of other small American newspapers, damaged by ready-print's demise.

While many other papers folded, this country editor held on with his low cost, one-man operation. He would get up at five a.m. every morning, write news copy directly on the Linotype—call the advertisers from a phone next to the smoky device, set more type, call more advertisers—impelled by the mystique of journalism and the need to make a living.

But age and health problems had caught up with him and he had decided to sell. I drove up to look over his plant. He accepted $2,500 for the business, which consisted of little more than the "good will" and second class postal permit. The printing equipment was retained by him, but that didn't matter to me because I was intent on modernizing the back shop.

Earlier I had discovered that several southern country editors were experimenting with the lithographic process for their printing. I visited their plants and was convinced that this method was the only way to publish.[4]

So, I arranged for our newly purchased Mundelein paper to be printed at a nearby printing company's web offset lithographic press. After some experimentation we decided to set the news copy on an office typewriter and the typed sheet photographed ("burned") directly onto a printing plate.[5]

The final product was not a pretty sight, but we were pioneers, experimenters, and confident that a typewriter with proper type face was just around the corner. After several months of operating the newspaper, and itching to tell other publishers about the new method, I accepted an offer by a major press manufacturing company. The company, manufacturers of massive multimillion dollar presses for magazine publishers, saw a market developing for a scaled down litho press for the small newspapers.

The job entailed contacting the small and middle-size newspapers adrift and ailing in America, still trying to cope with Gutenberg's letterpress. The big litho press manufacturer needed to be introduced to America's small town press but didn't know the language of the country editor. My role was to act as a salesman-translator, to establish communications between these two dissimilar, city and town, elements, and this I did for two years.

The press being offered by the large manufacturer was designed and manufactured by Grant Ghormley of Kennedale, Texas and it seemed just the ticket for printing newspapers. It was small enough to fit into the country newspaper printing shops, it was fast (20,000 newspaper copies per hour), and it was inexpensive, costing a fraction as much as the web litho presses then being manufactured.

In 1960-62 I criss-crossed the country many times by plane, talking to hundreds of fellow editors of suburban papers, county seat dailies and weeklies. I lectured at press associations and surveyed many antiquated town printing plants.

In a short time twenty four publishers signed up with me for the new press. The press manufacturer, my employer, had almost hesitated too long as competitive firms quickly decided to get into the act and built their own similar presses.[6]

Grant Ghormley's country newspaper press was as revolutionary to the industry as Ansel Nash Kellogg's ready-print. It printed on newsprint remarkably well. The printed papers fairly flew out of them, delivered folded and dry. Ghormley was not encumbered by the cultural baggage of the mainline press manufacturers. His press was a stripped-down model without expensive ink dryer ovens, flying pasters or over-complicated folders.

Applying pioneer Texan ingenuity, he removed all the heavy stuff; linking the lightweight units with a motorcycle chain after removing the pounding heavy gears—cutting cost dramatically without sacrificing quality. Quiet, smooth running, it was more akin to a watch than a locomotive. It contrasted mightily with the established, over-engineered presses of the time, that were needlessly heavy and setting one in a printing plant was like lifting and installing Mount Rushmore. The two-unit Ghormley press, capable of printing and automatically cutting and folding a (16 page tabloid or 8 page full size) newspaper, cost only $38 thousand dollars—the price of a linesetting machine like a Linotype. In contrast, the larger litho presses, the clattering "iron monster" magazine presses, cost well over one million dollars each.[7]

For me it was an interesting experience, bringing me in contact with hundreds of country editors. But two years of daily flying about in propeller-driven plans and landing on small town airstrips were quite enough for one accustomed to having his legs solidly on the ground, preferably in a scrappy country newspaper. Late in 1962 I returned to my normal condition as country editor-publisher, settling in a town of 10,000 lost in the hills of Kentucky. There, removed I saw from afar the

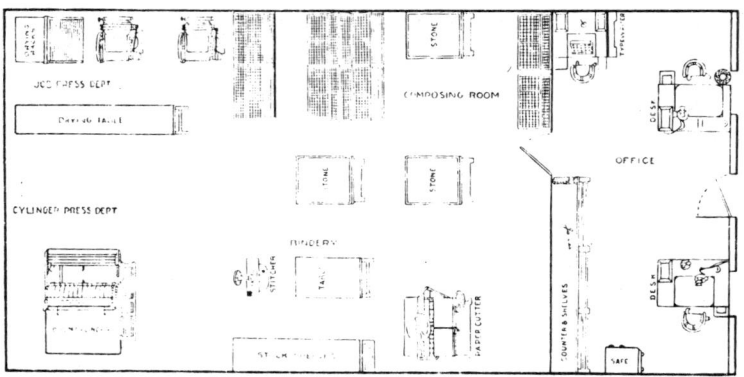

Unchanged since the Civil War, offset revolutionized the country press layout

switch to lithography roll over the land, engulfing almost all of the smaller, then the larger newspapers. In 1963 I purchased my own three-color web offset press, and linked it to the authomated typewriter, the Justo-writer. We then, proudly, announed on our masthead that we were the most modern newspaper in Kentucky.

THE CENTRAL PRINTING PLANT

The joining of the reasonably-priced web offset press with a mass-producing major manufacturer made it available at low cost to the beleaguered town newspapers across the country. The country editor could either choose to buy one and squeeze it into his tiny back shop, or he could patronize a nearby central printer who leased his services. The central printer concept, as it has been employed since 1960, features the use of a central web offset press to print newspapers from the surrounding towns. This new concept was readily adopted, and many new newspapers came into being as overall publishing costs dropped dramatically. It became possible to start a newspaper for as little as ten percent of what it cost 35 years previously. Papers are able to set their own type on a variety of typewriter-like devices that made the Linotype an anachronism.

In the face of this change, the line casting typesetter did not survive. Many, along with their companion letterpresses are being put into museums for preservation.

Georgia was a typical state in converting to litho offset printing. Here is a chart showing the speed with which the editors switched to the new process when four or five web offset presses were set up in the state, acting as central printing plants.

THE SWITCH TO OFFSET (LITHOGRAPHY)

Country and Suburban Weekly Newspapers in Georgia

Year	Number of Newspapers	Litho (Offset) Newspapers
1960	192	2
1961	194	7
1962	198	20
1963	197	27
1964	196	32
1965	189	50
1966	189	64
1967	189	86
1968	186	100
1969	184	109
1970	185	134
1971	186	152

By 1977 the changeover was complete. Only two weeklies still used the "hot metal" method) [7]

Communication technology improved steadily in the late 1980s. Pivotal was the invention of the laser printer for the inexpensive desktop computer, allowing the computer to be used as a typesetter for newspapers.

The complex typesetting portion of printing can now be done by almost anyone. But most importantly the laser printer placed a professional-quality proof press in the hands of that uncommon, common man, the country editor—the better of whom are editorialists, government watchdogs and town anthropologists.

A writer for the New York Times News Service stated, in describing laser printers: "Just as the development of the automobile returned the control of travel to the individual from railroad timetables, developments in technology are now giving the individual new freedom of choice. Rather than being controlled by the products of high technology, the individual is beginning to exercise new power over the machines.[8]

For the past thirty years, along with lamenting the existence of the monopolist press, it has been the conventional wisdom for futurists, amateur and professional, to predict the death of the newspaper, especially the small ones. Some have predicted the death of printing as well.[9]

There was, for example, a documentary produced in 1963 entitled "The Dying Breed," which consisted of, in the main, an interview with a Kentucky newspaperman who was struggling to stay in business. Profit-oriented corporate mergers of big city newspapers have been systematically reported on television as the press "dying."

Science fiction books and movies thumbed their noses at printing. The television actors, crewmen of the "Starship Enterprise" were never pictured huddled in a corner of their craft reading a book or newspaper.

I can remember a drawing in a 1930s magazine of an overstuffed chair in which the picture tube rose up out of the arm, the caption saying that this device would replace the newspaper.

But the related institutions of printing and newspapers have refused to roll over and expire. For better or worse, and barring the invention of something better, mankind still needs his alphabet to simplify, code, transmit and store his thoughts.

The TV screen-monitor (also known as the cathode ray tube) has been in wide use for 60 years, yet has not found acceptance as a reading surface. It is yet unable to offer portability and is uncomfortable, often irritating to the eyes.

So, an escape mechanism has been devised to allow a graceful retreat from the electronic tube so many thought would supplant paper. The people who have consigned the printing press to oblivion need only peek under (or beside) their computers. There they would find a miniature printing press, a version of the country editor's newspaper press of a bygone day.[10]

These low-cost printers, even the bottom-of-the-line $495 ink jet, or laser models, provide excellent, sharp-edged camera-ready proofs for the lithographic web presses.

Surprisingly, there is even a computer-linked "boilerplate" providing features, recipes and columns on a variety of subjects for the country editor too busy to write or too penny-pinching to hire reporters.

Desktop publishing with a computer, linked to litho printing, allows one to perform typesetting tasks previously possible only with old, traditional methods. Pages of type can be produced that look exactly like the finest metropolitan newspapers now existing. This new equipment is inexpensive (as little as $1,500, total), and most people can train themselves in its operation.

As in the days of ready-print, newspapers (city or rural) can open up with a minimum of investment and surprisingly little technical knowledge. A few hundred dollars can buy a desk top computer and its attached printer, with a disk memory system. It can be powered by a $59 dollar desk-top publishing program. The equipment and service is readily available, by lease or purchase, from your corner computer store. After the page is typeset it can be taken to a web press central plant for printing and collating; or the publisher can set up his own small printing press. The final step is to deliver it to your readers.

DEMOCRACY, NO EXPERIENCE NEEDED!

The unique quality of ready-print was its ability to allow the willing and able amateur to become editor of his own newspaper—to compete with the elitist and the press monopolist and thus build a free press in America.

How ironic it is that the most recent breakthroughs to easier printing came just as millions focused, hypnotically, to the television screens in their parlors. They imperiled their literacy to watch easily manipulated images, transmitted to them by a limited number of network and government sources.

The wonder is how political dictators have survived so long around the world. Printing and the newer communications technology played a large part in the rush to a more democratic government in the Soviet Union. Technology led to the overthrow of dictators in Eastern Europe and the movement for democracy in China---not to mention the nearer-to-home military dictatorships in Brazil and Chile. National borders no longer seemed like walls to imprison citizens. Facing the use of modems hooked to telephones, computers, laser printers, and small presses, even the most entrenched political organization finds it difficult to stay in power forever. Television and radio remained under state control right to the very day of toppling the Eastern European dictatorships. The words and ideas of freedom were, instead, delivered by underground newspapers.

America and Europe are now routinely accepting the use of desk-top publishing computers in producing their publications. These little computers were brought into the mainstream in 1986 and are bringing about more and more news and business journals.

It is encouraging that in the United States the technological revolution has caused a profound effect on the numbers: Gale's Directory shows an almost 30 percent increase in the number of American newspapers from 1987 to 1990, brought on in the wake of these technological inventions. These new newspapers are mostly small publications (many composed of family groups or just man and wife operations) appearing once or twice a week.

At the same time, there has been an increased criticism of "media." Is this a kind of shorthand? Do they mean that they want a more active, more skillful free press? The source and reason for the outcry is hard to pin down, but it seems to be coming mostly from the inland regions. The word "media" now has gained a negative connotation, and many politicians have been quick to pick up on it, giving it currency. Americans reputedly ever mindful of their freedoms should know that this kind of talk can be dangerous to their democracy. The link between this "media-bashing" and the national perception of a lack of competition between newspapers bears study.

Americans apparently are calling for a return to the old, non-monopolizing, free enterprise news system. One-newspaper towns and cities are now the norm in the U.S.A., but the trend away from that may be coming. Writing, sales, administrative talent, not only experience, is needed! Many can now be proprietors of newspapers, country editors, wherever you are in the world! If needed, borrow the money to buy the equipment—even throw in some of this new-fangled computerized boilerplate to ease your burden—but please publish!

PROGRESS REPORT

In the 1950s things were quite different from today. Without ready-print one could not start a newspaper. The only option was to buy an established one—and in those days the word "computer" was seen mainly in the futurist Flash Gordon comic strip. It is now 1990 and we are still seeking that special, spiritual editorial home in a perfect small town, mentioned in the first chapter. The search has been long, covering over a dozen countries. However, in 1959 we came close to buying the ideal country newspaper. This is how I remember it:

> The Gazette, the weekly newspaper in Galena, Illinois was for sale. Clint Youle, the congenial owner who was also a television weatherman in Chicago, had approached me to buy it. The property, as he described it, included a sturdy three story business building. It was early spring and we needed a sunny outing. We had cabin fever, brought on by a stinging winter in "Windy City" (a nickname Chicago has well earned). Dorothy and I put the sleepy children in the back seat, and drove west across the state to take a look, arriving early in the morning.
> The Gazette was on Galena's picturesque, curving main street, in one of its most imposing buildings. American history lay all about us. All the buildings pre-dated the Civil War. Neat, midwest, carpenter-gothic frame houses sprinkled the town.
> The dry goods store building once owned by Ulysses S. Grant was there, near the newspaper building. The Mississippi river, covered in haze, lay at the foot of the street, flowing by the wharf where Mark Twain tied up his steamboat. Friendly Victorian ghosts could be sensed all around.
> First we walked about, talking to the town businessmen and shoppers. In true midwest fashion, they were friendly and seemed eager to exchange words. We walked the curving street to the Gazette. Looking inside the building, we noted that nothing seemed to have been disturbed since the nineteenth century. On the first two floors were offices. The editor's was at the back, its decor centered around an upright Remington typewriter and a wall calendar advertising an ink company. The locomotive-size 1887 Goss Perfecting press (the more prosperous weekly papers had perfecting presses---machines that printed on both sides simultaneously) and the almost-as-old Linotype crouched as though waiting for the editor to signal them into action.
> On the third floor, which was sealed off, lay row after row of typesetting job cases made obsolete by the line casting machine. They were filled with clean type.
> We stood and looked, and could feel the past around us, sense the type setters swaying at their cases, clicking the type, setting the home side of their ready-print newspaper.

But no one was there on that floor and, obviously, no one had used the room in 40 years. There was space for about ten typesetters to stand at their cases—perhaps mother, father, aunts and uncles and some of the larger children in the country editor's family.

The windows were large, admitting daylight from four sides. The hell box, the quoin key, the pounding block and hammer and the cuspidor were still there, waiting, at the end of the row of type cases. It was at that moment, in that light, that I felt the urge to buy the *Gazette*, not for its business potential, not for its large subscription list, but as a way of bringing back a lost way of life.

But I let the moment pass, realizing that I had reached the end of the ready-print trail and more modern ways were beckoning.

NOTES

1. *Scribner's Monthly,* June, 1872, Bol. IV, p. 204.
2. Harold A. Innis, *The Bias of Communication* (Toronto: University of Toronto Press, 1951) p. 190.
3. John W. Moore, *Historical Notes on Printers and Printing 1420 to 1886* (New York, Burt Franklin Co., 1968) p. 86.
4. Printers and editors have a reputation for "crankyness" in those days, lead poisoning may have been part of the problem.
5. Staley McBrayer, publisher of several Texas newspapers, was a pivotal force in promoting this lithography and central printing plant idea. He was an associate and partner of the press designer Grant Ghormley. McBrayer used his newspaper to demonstrate the web lithographic press to many editors. *Editor and Publisher* magazine called McBrayer the "founder" of newspaper offset (litho).
6. Heavy presses react negatively to heavy pounding as illustrated in the author's "Printing Under Fire" by Eugene C. Harter, *Graphic Arts Monthly,* February 1985, p. 41.

7. Millard B. Grimes, *The Last Linotype* (Macon, Ga.: Mercer University Press, 1985) p. 65. Fig. numbers prepared by Dan Kitchens, Univ. of Georgia, 1981.

8. Erik Sandberg-Diment, "Laser Gives Individual Control Over Printing," Baltimore *Sun,* Sept. 4, 1985.

9. It should be noted that the number of American newspapers rose from 9,943 in 1987; to 11,077 in 1988; to 11,520 in 1989, and to 12,861 in 1990 (Ayer/Gale's Directory). Most of the new papers were town and suburban, and almost all of them were litho, computer, cold-type operations. It begins to look like once again technology will to the assist of a larger, freer press.

10. Alternately, a facsimile machine might also be around in the future if the information is sent over a distance. Currently some newspapers are trying once again to circumvent their costly distribution methods by offering "fax" news service to paying customers—home or office. This method of distributing miniature newspapers has been around since the 1940s, but who knows, like litho, maybe it will suddenly find new life.

Epilogue

The American political establishment gave its consent to a "free press" in the United States when it incorporated into the Constitution a Bill of Rights in 1791. But many decades were to pass before anyone could say with a straight face that the American press was in fact "free."
                                                                                Richard Harwood, Washington Post[1]

LEGAL VERSUS ASSUMED PRESS FREEDOM!

Three hundred years is a long time. Few nations and some religions have not been around that long. The first newspaper was successfully published in America in 1689. It was a single sheet printed on one side and called *The Present State of New English Affairs.* It was published by Samuel Green in Cambridge, Massachusetts, and proclaimed on its masthead: "to prevent false reports".[2]

Today at the close of the twentieth century there are several editorial vehicles available to the free press, such as computers, radio or television. There no doubt will be others, and each will face its own special trials. Newspapers have been put through the testing period, however, and have survived.[3]

This book was written in Chestertown, Maryland, a community where 200 year old buildings are found preserved on almost every block. This historic colonial town was once the home of John Peter Zenger, America's first hero in the cause of press freedom.

Zenger, whose story is known to all journalism students, was born in Germany. He emigrated to America, arriving in 1710. In 1733 in New York, where he had moved from Chestertown, he challenged the restrictive press laws by starting a newspaper that spoke out against the corrupt Colonial administration of that time. For this he was imprisoned for a year by the colonial governor. His acquittal of the charge of seditious libel was the first step on the long road to the press system in the United States.

Zenger did not serve as a precedent for the framers of the Constitution. As Leonard W. Levy pointed out in his Original Intent —not one of the members of the Constitutional Convention showed any serious concern for the guarantee of a free press. Not one endorsed the principles of the Zenger case and America has since allowed an all-too-vulnerable press to be subject to both criminal and seditious libel laws, a menacing weapon in the hands of a future despotic leader of this country. It matters little that current draconian libel laws have not been frequently applied, what matters is that the laws exist at all.[4]

Chestertown was the scene of another event in history. In one of the examples where draconian laws were instituted in America, the country's president, Abraham Lincoln, set about to insure his re-election in 1864 by jailing his political opposition, those residing in the northern states. In the midst of the presidential election campaign, the outspoken Democratic editor of the Kent News was taken from his home by Union troops and jailed without charge (his house, owned now by the Meredith family, still stands next door not 50 feet from where I sit). The incident was not an isolated one, as the editor, W. B. Usilton, was one of 40,000 Americans (newspapermen, attorneys, farmers, businessmen, mostly of the opposition Democratic party) held without trial by the North by order of Lincoln.

President Woodrow Wilson, on the other hand, utilized peacetime laws already on the books to limit press freedom. Influenced by the threats imposed by the war against Germany, he gave support to a law restricting press liberty far beyond that necessary for the perceived emergency. Action against free speech and a free press in the first World War was drastic, especially as it involved, as one writer phrased it: "small-town editors...foreign language publications or little far-western publications."[5]

Politicians are not the only ones to exercise their powers, courts do so as well. National paranoia and vigilantism exibited during the periodic Red Scares are not proud times in the American history of free speech. Editors shudder when thinking about them, knowing that another McCarthy Period may be just around the corner energizing another president, court or Congressional committee to freshly reinterpret laws restricting press freedom. A peculiar legacy of the French Revolution, the Red Scare phenomena in America rises and falls like lunar tides.

The problem is at the local and state level as well as national. Legal threats to American free press come just as frequently from county and state judges, mayors and police in many a town, large and small. The records of the International Conference of Weekly Newspaper Editors Association and *Editor and Publisher* magazine contain many accounts of limiting of press freedom by government agents – state, national or local. Scores of these incidents never reach the eye of the reader, some editors preferring to be publicly non-controversial in combating restrictions to press freedom. However, most American newspapers, especially those economically-vulnerable small town journals are wary of the threat to their freedom of speech, a freedom that they, themselves created, and only they can maintain.

CROSS-CULTURAL PROBLEMS

In writing about the syndication of ready-print and boilerplate in America it would be useful to gauge the effect of the news services on American values and culture. In the U.S. the news appears to pass from sender (the journalist) to receiver (the reader) with little apparent disruption, a natural flow. But to understand the impact of the single (or limited)-source news emanation of ready-print and boilerplate, it might be useful to turn the picture around and look at the recent experience of America's news services in sending its words overseas to a foreign audience.

The syndication of news in America had been accomplished with relatively little cultural disruption; granted, though, many cultural influences were painlessly formed. But when America's press services such as the Associated Press and United Press International expanded their overseas distribution in the mid and latter twentieth century they collided with much of the world over the interpretation of "what is news?" and, indeed, the definition of a free press.

Third World countries (many of them with a press that is government controlled) did not agree with our definition of news, nor had they the experience of a commercially competitive free press, as in America. Historically the U.S. ready-print editors and the metropolitan press had long trained Americans that much that is "bad" is news: tragic ferry boat accidents and earthquakes were staples for the ready-printers; while political scandals, murder, the morbid and aberrational were the constant topics of the metropolitan press and the "non-Chicago" side of the town press.

But foreigners did not all receive this kind of news indoctrination without protest. Unlike the unaccredited Chicago ready-print spread across the U.S., the accredited American news service dispatches were identified immediately by the receiving foreign countries, causing predictable back-lash.[6]

Some of the outside cultures displayed deep resentment at this type of "news," and were becoming accutely aware of the cultural influence of the flood of news coming from the United States and its press services, expanding around the world. News items, emanating from a concentrated source such as America's Associated Press, alarmed many countries, who noted that their cultures were being affected by American values and propaganda. Their complaints were similar to the ones emanating from some town editors when Kellogg introduced ready-print following the U.S. Civil War.

Many Americans have been rightfully proud of their free press system and many of the complaints from overseas were brushed off (with some justification) as the bleats of military dictators. Many spokesmen attempted to analyze the situation which had become very abrasive, especially in the halls of UNESCO (the United Nations Educational, Scientific and Cultural Organization). A Tunisian official commented about "the near-monopoly of world publicity" by the American news agencies: "...which earn their incomes by serving the interests of the transnational industrial and commercial corporations which dominate the world of business.[7]

Others charged that the messages offended the morality of the receiving nations. Still others protested that American beliefs in upward mobility and efficiency spurred frustration and discontent in foreign countries.

MYTH AND FREE ENTERPRISE ECONOMICS JOIN FORCES

Despite the new winds in favor of press freedom stirring around the globe, the debate with the world governments (not necessarily with the world's people) is still bitter in defining the meaning of "freedom of the press." Americans in the United Nations resented the charge that our system would not work in most societies of the world. Though the role model of the free-swinging, freedom-gathering U.S. editors should have been on their minds, the U.S. diplomats in the U.N. fell back on the myth of the ambiguous First Amendment. Rather than note the complex development of the U.S. free press and the similarity of development in countries everywhere, the American diplomats chose to emphasize our poetic First Amendment rights. In the debate they advocated a world-wide free press based on the American free enterprise model.

It fell to the Washington Post to summarize the American case against much of the world. The paper, like the diplomats, joined in the general myth-making by emphazing that, alone, the U.S. Constitution was the reason for the uniquely free "free press" and also emphasizing the press' commercial self-interest. The paper's views ran as an editorial, stating:

> Now, this newspaper, which offers its news product for foreign sale, has an undeniable self-interest in nourishing an international climate in which the commercial opportunities for Western media are maintained. But this, of course, is no different from the vested interest that the American media---being free, competitive institutions---have in maintaining the same commercial opportunities at home. It is a simple matter of principle coinciding with commercial self-interest, and the principle involved here, of course, was set forth at a rather early stage in our history, in the First Amendment to the Constitution. And if it is a sound principle for us in this country, it follows, or so it seems to us, that it is also a good rule to apply to the communication of ideas abroad....[8]

The debate---really an argument between radically different cultures---continues to this day. As with most cross-cultural conflicts, solutions are hard to find. Compromise among established tribal ideas is exceedingly difficult. Narcissism prevails as nations instinctively guard their cultural uniqueness.

The cultural ready-printing and boilerplating of America was a similar experience, with a minimum number of sources passing on information to the majority of the U.S. population in the post-Civil War Period, well into the beginning of the twentieth century. Its impact must have been overwhelming to the eager readers who received it packaged in their local newspapers.

THE HISTORY OF THE U.S. NEWSPAPER SYNDICATES

Foreigners were quick to point out the parallel between their concerns about receiving their news from limited foreign sources and the development of the U.S. press syndicate system into which ready-print and boilerplate are historically categorized.

Americans, themselves, in their period of development following the Civil War, had frequently complained about the single-source, quality and bias of news coming from Europe since most of the European news of the time was brought into America through the Associated Press monopoly relationship with Reuters. Reuters, foreign-owned, controlled all foreign news sent into the U.S. and all news sent out of the U.S. to the rest of the globe. In their gate-keeper role, Reuters sought out the sensational news from America to send to foreign newspapers: the Indian massacres, the sordid crimes in the cities, and the lynchings in the South, for example. Americans complained loudly, but to no avail.

In addition, Reuters had the monopoly on news entering America through its Associated Press connection in New York. The A.P., in turn, fed the wire reports into the Chicago ready-printers. The cultural consequences can still be noticed from this influx of European news. One author wrote: "Their countries were always glorified. This was done by reporting great advances at home in English and French civilizations, the benefits of which would, of course, be bestowed on the world. Figuratively speaking, in the United States, according to Reuters, it wasn't safe to travel on account of the Indians."

The writer, Kent Cooper, who at one time headed the Associated Press, stated: "With Julius Reuter at the head of its world news division, England strove for world trade. It is not difficult to see that, holding control of world news communications and with the genius of Reuter, it had the means for success."[9]

NEWSPAPERMEN, NOT THE CONSTITUTION, CREATED THE FREE PRESS

Even countries with dictatorships have elaborate and stirring Constitutions, rich in philosophic resonance—suitable for framing. The difference lies in how the words are applied over time, forming a legal tradition. Alexis de Tocqueville in his *Democracy in America* warned: "I should put no trust in great political assemblies, parliamentary prerogatives, or the proclamation of the sovereignty of the people to secure personal independence. All such things can, to some extent, be reconciled with personal servitude. But such servitude cannot be complete if the press is free. The press is, par excellence, the democratic weapon of freedom."

American journalists are surprisingly naive, or hate to "put on airs." Rather than take the credit they deserve for the Free Press system in America, they invariably cite a protective higher power, the Constitution's oft-quoted, ambiguous, First Amendment. However, the phrasing of that document and the subsequent laws pertaining to the press should give them cause to wonder whether the freedoms are as protected as prevailing wisdom would have it.

EPILOGUE

The problem of "legal" press freedom versus "assumed" press freedom continues unto the present time. Outspoken editors, aided by their talent, their numbers and their independent viewpoints, have always been the barrier that stood in the way of full and enthusiastic enforcement of the "seditious libel" laws incorporated in the Sedition Act of 1798, the Sedition Act of 1918 and the Smith Act of 1940 and various and sundry other federal, state and local laws.

Legal historian Leonard W. Levy, in his work on the origins of America's most cherished freedoms, states that "so long as the press may be subject to government control, whether or not that control is exercised, the press cannot be free—or is not as free as it should be."

He also argues that "we do not know what the First Amendment's freedom of speech and press clause meant to the men who drafted and ratified it at the time they did so...the security of the state against libelous advocacy or attack was always regarded as outweighing any social interest in open expression, at least through the period of the adoption of the First Amendment."[10]

To learn about the quicksand that editors and journalists ---and indeed all Americans---stand, it is suggested that readers scan the literature on the subject. For example: Harry Kalven, Jr., writing about the seditious libel laws that remain in U.S. federal and state government, stated: "It is the hallmark of closed societies throughout the world. Under it criticism of government is viewed as defamation and punished as a crime.

The treatment of such speech as criminal is based on an accurate perception of the dangers in it; it is likely to undermine confidence in government policies and in the use of its powers and its courts to silence its critics. In my view, the presence or absence in the law of the concept of seditious libel defines the society. A society may or may not treat obscenity or contempt by publication as legal offenses without altering its basic nature. If, however, it makes seditious libel an offense, it is not a free society no matter what its other characteristics."[11]

There have been so few trials for seditious libel in the United States, especially in peacetime, that observers have been distracted into a feeling of security.[12]

Levy, who has written the standard work on the subject of free press and despite his mastery of law frankly admits to confusion. In his book, *Emergence of a Free Press,* after years of studying the constitution and noting the probable intent of the framers to construct a controlled, not a free, press in America, says "I am puzzled by the paradox...of nearly unfettered press practices in a system characterized by legal fetters and the absence of a theory of political expression that justifies those practices."[13]

Levy cites John Roche's criticism of historians for artificially adding symmetry to confused historical conditions "by giving present convictions a patriotic lineage and tradition."[14]

And Levy, himself, comes to the conclusion that "rights that should exist are established on the fictitious pretense that they have always existed, and arguments are concocted to give the appearance of both reality and legality.

But the issue of Freedom of the Press is not only the province of law scholars. Perhaps journalists and journalism historians can help remove some of the admitted puzzlement of the legal historians by noting that it was not only the basic laws, but the mechanical and economic inventiveness as well as the courage and editorial anarchy of American journalists that gave us our press freedom.

Historically, journalists and their multitude of independent newspapers have brightened the light of disclosure. Therefore we come up with a press that seems to operate in the freest of fashion—criticizing and investigating government and the marketplace. But, of late, it is apparent that the press is overmatched by the forces within the government.

The American citizen has been able to hold off most of the press-restraining legal maneuvers by political office holders (national and local) against free expression. But can willpower alone serve to maintain press freedom in this country?

In addition to the legal restraints against the press resting in U.S. law, the American citizen faces the burden of having public information hidden from him. What good is editorial boldness when we are faced with conditions in which our media is pitted against clever political public relations psycho-technicians who control access to information that is rightfully the property of the American citizen?

In America's non-parliamentary system the legislative sector is not permitted to confront the president, to question his actions to his face. Who, then, can ask the hard questions if the press is excluded? Presidents get a free ride—and they take unfair advantage of it.

It is impossible to believe that research on the effect of the American Constitution can be made in a legal ivory tower. It is necessary to move out into a real-life context. To widen the historical scope, legal research should include study of journalism history---how the mechanics and idea of the press developed, spawning great numbers of editors, some of them healthily outspoken and investigative.

America's democracy depends on numerous media outlets with differing points of view, editors with backbone, too many newspapers for government to suppress, even with harsh laws or clever public relations departments (the "spin doctors"). The more newspapers and other media there are, the less the information is controlled---for America is a country protected as much by a *tradition* of free speech as by the law.

Notes

1. Richard Harwood, *Washington Post,* September 18, 1988, p. C-6.

2. Isaiah Thomas, *The History of Printing in America* (New York: Thomas, 1808).

3. The first "daily" newspaper was the *Pennsylvania Packet and Daily Advertiser,* published by David C. Claypoole and John Dunlap in Philadelphia, which appeared in September 21, 1784. Originally it had been founded as a weekly in 1771. From: Isaiah Thomas —*History of Printing in America.*

4. Leonard W. Levy, *Original Intent* (New York: McMillan, 1988) p.196.

5. Page Smith, *The Rise of Industrial America* (New York: McGraw-Hill, 1984) p.542.

6. However, Patterson's column which began during World War II, entitled "Grassroots," was identified on the page as a Patterson-WNU product).

7. Mustapha Masmoudi, "The United States and the Debate on the World "Information Order," (pub. U.S.I.C.A.) paper presented at UNESCO Conference, July 10, 1978, p.7.

8. "UNESCO's Assault on News," *The Washington Post,* July 30, 1976, Sec. A, p.22.

9. Kent Cooper, *Barriers Down* (New York: Farrar & Rinehart, Inc., 1942), p.12.

10. Leonard W. Levy, *Legacy of Expression* (Cambridge: Harvard University Press, 1964) p.237.

11. Harry Kalven, Jr., *A Worthy Tradition* (New York: Harper & Row,

1988) p. 63.

12. Frank Luther Mott, *American Journalism* (New York: The Macmillan Co., 1960) p. 152.

13. Leonard W. Levy, *Emergence of a Free Press* (New York: Oxford University Press, 1985) Preface xvii.

14. John P. Roche, *Aspects of Liberty* (Ithaca: Cornell University Press, 1958) p. 130.

APPENDIX

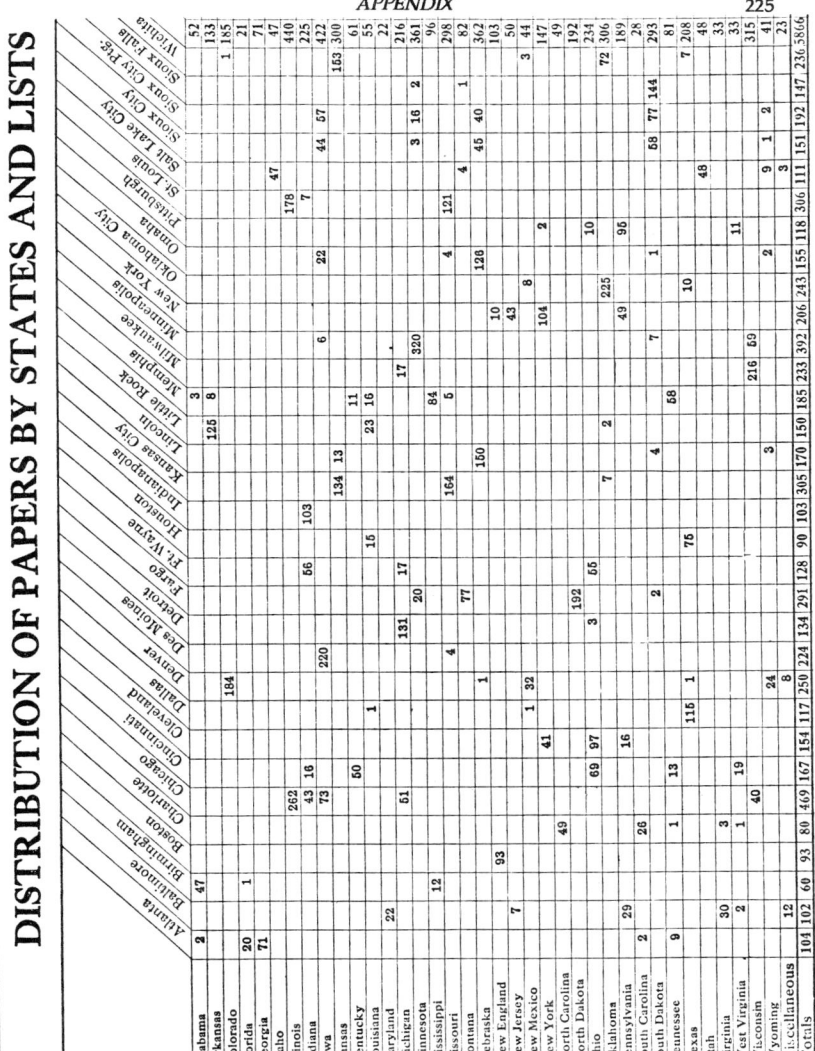

Shown is WNU's 1915 list of ready-print newspapers. In addition there were approximately 12,000 more newspapers that took the boilerplate.

Index

Ade, George, 166
Agriculture, isolation, 79
All-Home-Print Association, 191
Allbee, Burton, 49
Alger, Horatio, 166
American Press Association, 148, 156
Anderson, Sherwood, 7, 183-86; Clyde, Ohio, 183; Marion, Virginia, 184
Andrews, Alexander, 82
Ansonia, Ohio, Times, 1
Anti-trust law, 147, 150
Appomatox, 124
Arnold, Mathew, 66
Arp, Bill, 124, 126
Atherton, Lewis, 65, 161
Atlantic Monthly, 138
A & P Company, 6
Auburn, Indiana, 6
Avery, Frank L., 102

Baseball, 151
Berger, Victor L., 119
Bible Belt, 129
Bird, George, 63
Boilerplate, 32-35
Boorstin, Daniel, 60
Borland, Hal, 50, 167-168
"Boss" Tweed Ring, 146
Bribery, 145,146
Bottom, Rosey, 194
Brazil, 4
Britain, 81-83
Bryan, William J., 38; *The Commoner* newspaper, 38
Bryce, Lord James, 38, 60, 64, 138
Byers, William, 110

Campbellsville, Ky., *News-Journal,* 7
Cain, James L., 168
Canada, 158-161
Carpetbagger, 123
Carter, Hodding, Sr., 108
Cather, Willa, 168
Census, U.S., number of editors, 38
Central West Printing Co., 151-156
Central Newspaper Union, 189
Central printing plant, 206

Chestertown, Maryland, 215
Chicago, 30, fire, 30, 81
Church, W., 178
Civil War, 22, 62
Clark, Thos. D, 116, 124, 126; patent medicines, 192-93
Collier' magazine, 148, 157-158
Commager, Henry Steele, 127
Communists, 2
Copper, O. Byron, 108
Country Campbell press, 8, 74, 97
Country Publisher's Company, 189
Cramer, John F., 89
Crane, Hart, 166
Cummins, Senator, 158-159
Current, Richard, 128

Darwinians, 120
Democracy, China, Brazil, Chile, 209
Department of Justice, 150-156
DesPlaines, Illinois, 6
Dickens, Charles, 168
Dohan, Mary Helen, 139
Douglas, Harlan, 71
Dreiser, Theodore, 168

Edison, Thos., 202
Editorials, 4
Eggleston, Edward, 72, 166
Emerson, Ralph Waldo, 66
Emigration, 158-161
English, language, 13
Enquirer, Kentucky, 25
Ernst, Morris, 26, 198

Farnsworth, C. L., 96
Federal Reserve Board, 147
First Amendment to the U. S. Constitution, 102, 220-223
Fish, H.H., 96
Ford Foundation and International Communication Agency, 145
Franchising, 39
Franklin, Benjamin, 60
Free Press, 41, 99
Freud, Sigmund 73
Fulton, T.P., 113

Galena, *Gazette,* 211
Garland, Hamlin, 166
Garrett, Indiana, 6; *The Clipper,* 75-77
Ghormley, Grant, designer of litho press, 205
Greenville, Ohio, 4
Guest, Edgar A., 141
Gutenberg, 12-15; "goodby", 201

Hadacol, 4
Harding, Warren G., 106
Harger, Chas., 112
Harris, Joel Chandler, 166
Harte, Bret, 130
Harter, Dorothy, 5
Harter, Eugene, 1-5,
Hemingway, Ernest, 168
Hoe press, 66
Howe, Edgar Watson, 137, 166
Howells, William Dean, 165-167
Huntsville, Missouri, *Herald,* 25

International Conference of Weekly Newspaper Editors, 216
Iowa, 161
Iszvestia, Russian, 28

Jaycees, 4
Joslyn Castle, 157
Joslyn, George, 86, 90-96, his "castle," 88-90, 120, 129, 148, 149, 150-162
Journalist, The, 31

Kalvin, Harry, 221
Keillor, Garrison, 37
Kellogg, Ansel, The Baraboo *Republic,* 17
Kellogg Company, 24-30
King, Henry, 190
Kentucky newspaper, 105, civil rights act, 108, bought newspaper, 203
Kiwanis, 4
Knight, Charles, 82
Korea, 4, 8

LaFollette, Robert, 119
Landis, Kennesaw Mountain, 150-156
Latin America, 8-9
Laser printing, 207

Lauber, John, 169
Lewis, A. H., 118
Lewis, Sinclair, 123
Levy, Leonard, 221-23
Liberty Bonds, 147
Lincoln, Abraham, 216
Linecasting machines, 171
Linotype, 170
Lithographic printing, 168, 202-04; switch to, 207
London, Jack, 166
London *Times,* 28
Lupton, M. F., 14
Lynds, 52, 138

McClure's magazine, 106, 114, 145, 148, 161
McGill, Ralph, 108
McGuffey Readers, 40
McMillan, J. I., 179
Main Street, 87, 123
MacKellar, Thomas, 101
Mencken, H. L., 182-83
Merwin, Frederick, 63
Middle Border, 5
Minnesota, 161
Michigan, Hastings newspaper 161
Montrose, Lynn, 37
Moog, Vianna, 128
Moore, John W., 203
Mott, Frank Luther, 73
Mundelein, Illinois, 6
Mergenthaler, Ottmar, 177
Missouri, Hannibal, 169

Navy, U.S., 4
Nasby, Petroleum V., 139
National character, 54; conformity, 55
National Printer-Journalist, 46
New England, 128
New Republic, 181
Newspapers, 51; numbers of, 51; distribution in the countryside, 52-54; courageous and faint hearted, 108; battle between country and city, 68-70; headlines, 113-114; southern editors, 124; "unions;" diminishing in

INDEX

importance, 200; layout, 206; a dying breed, 208; start your own, 210-212; *The Present State of New English Affairs,* 215; Third World, 217
New York Newspaper Union, 148
New York *Times,* 28, 155, 157
Norris, Frank, 166

Oliveira, Carlos, 55
Omaha, Nebraska, 157
Ong, Walter J., 54
Overman, Senator, 157-161
Parker, R. D., 188
Patent Medicine advertising, 116, 129, 130, 161
Patent Insides, 116
Patterson, Wright, 83, 117, 119-120, 129, 134, 136, 141, 147, 148
Peruna, 4
Phillips, David Graham, 166
Pickett, Calder, 137
Pierce, Ambrose, 166
Pierce, Arthur E., 110
Population, U.S., 61
Presidents, U.S., 5
Press barons, 47-49
Prohibition, 89, 117-118, 130

Ramage press, 20
Ready-print, 4, 17-22, 26-28, 114, 149; late, 29-31, examples, 85, 95, 129, 130, 135, 136; contributors, 85-86, 116, 128; socialist, 119; novels, 128, 129, 130, 136; poems, 129, 141; American Language, 139, 141
Red Bird, Arkansas, 42
Religions, 89, 117, 131, 132, 133, 134, 136, 137
Republican, 4
Reuters, 219
Richmond, Indiana, 4
Riley, James Whitcomb, 166
Roche, John, 222
Rockwell, Norman, 5
Rogers, J.R., 178
Roosevelt, Theodore, 89-90, 119-120, 148
Rotary Clubs, 5
Royal Baking Powder, 4
Russia, 158

Propaganda, 147, 156-162
Rural Free Delivery, 67; routes, 71; dailies, 127
Russell, Bertrand, 120

Saunders, W. O., 110-112
Salmon, Lucy Maynard, 146-147
Schudson, Michael, 56
Sears and Roebuck, 72
Sennefelder, Alois, 203
Sharp, Paul, 65
Smith, Page, 55-56, 118, 132
Shaw, George Bernard, 120
Sheldon, Chas. M., 172
Simplex machine, 178
Sims, Newell, 132
Smith, Courtland, 161
Socialists, 119-120, 158
South Dakota, 4
Springfield, Ohio, Limestone Street, 4
Standard Oil Company, 148, 151
Stark's, 4,
Staunton, Virginia *Argus,* 44
Stein, Gertrude, 184
Stephens, E. W., 89

Taft, William H., 88
Taft, W. H. (of Missouri), 98
Tammany Hall, 114
Tarbell, Ida, 147
Tarkington, Booth, 88, 166
Taylor, Bayard, 166
Teapot Dome, 114
Tennessee, 161
Tilton, Theodore, 128
Times, Ansonia, 2
Twain, Mark, 2, 11-12, 19, 86, 107, 139, 165, 166, 169, 173, 176
Typesetting, 4, 7-15

U.S. District Court, 150-156
U.S. Government, 59; selling of votes, 114
U.S. Senate, 146, 149, 150-162

Volstead Act, 119

Washington *Post,* 28
Washington press, 20, 44, 64
Watson, Elmo S., 45, 162, 187
Watts, Alaric, 82

Wayne, Nebraska, *Herald,* 39
Webb, Sidney, 120
Weibe, Robert, 61
Webster, Noah, 123
Weisberger, Bernard, 118
Western Migration, 131
Western Newspaper Union, 23, 47, 57, 74; editorials, 120, Civil War, 124, 129,141,147, 148, 150-162
White House, 157
White, William Allen, 2, 104, 106-108, 166
Whitman, Walt, 166
Willey, Malcolm, 70
Williams, Walter, his ready-print company, 96
Wilson, Woodrow, 119, 216
Wisconsin, 18
Women's Christian Temperance Union, 183
Women's Home Companion, 138
Women's Rights, 119
World Press Congress, 99
World War II, 2, 147
Wright Brothers, 130

EUGENE C. HARTER was born in Brazil. His family moved to the United States when he was ten, living in Dayton and Springfield, Ohio. He graduated from Wittenberg College in 1949, later did his graduate studies at George Washington university and the Smithsonian Institute. He worked on newspapers in the midwest, later he purchased his own newspaper in Kentucky. In 1966 he became a career member of the U. S. Senior Foreign Service, serving in Arabia, Latin America and in Washington, D. C. In 1974 he published his first article on the history of American journalism, and followed with a story about America's attempt to run a publishing enterprise in war torn Beirut, Lebanon. In 1985 his first book was published by the University Press of Mississippi, *The Lost Colony of the Confederacy*, a story of the emigration of Southerners to Latin America. In 1988 Nordica Press published his portuguese language edition of the story, entitled *Colonia Perdida da Confederacão*. He is currently writing *The Confederados,* a story of American emigrants. He is married to Dorothy Harter, who worked with him in his newspapers, and edited this work. She is also a graduate of Wittenberg University and an experienced writer. Their children are Eugene III, Ann, David and Melissa.

Eugene C. Harter and Dorothy Harter